Managing Business with Electronic Commerce: Issues and Trends

Aryya Gangopadhyay
University of Maryland Baltimore County, USA

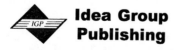
Idea Group Publishing

Information Science Publishing

Hershey • London • Melbourne • Singapore • Beijing

Acquisition Editor: Mehdi Khosrowpour
Managing Editor: Jan Travers
Development Editor: Michele Rossi
Copy Editor: Maria Boyer
Typesetter: LeAnn Whitcomb
Cover Design: Deb Andree
Printed at: Integrated Book Technology

Published in the United States of America by
    Idea Group Publishing
    1331 E. Chocolate Avenue
    Hershey PA 17033-1117
    Tel: 717-533-8845
    Fax: 717-533-8661
    E-mail: cust@idea-group.com
    Web site: http://www.idea-group.com

and in the United Kingdom by
    Idea Group Publishing
    3 Henrietta Street
    Covent Garden
    London WC2E 8LU
    Tel: 44 20 7240 0856
    Fax: 44 20 7379 3313
    Web site: http://www.eurospan.co.uk

JK

Library of Congress Cataloging-in-Publication Data

Managing business with electronic commerce : issues and trends / [edited by] Aryya Gangopadhyay.
    p. cm.
  Includes index.
   ISBN 1-930708-12-2 (paper)
   1. Electronic commerce--Management. I. Gangopadhyay, Aryya, 1962-

  HF5548.32 .M355 2001
  658.8'4--dc21   2001024744

British Cataloguing in Publication Data
A Cataloguing in Publication record for this book is available from the British Library.

NEW from Idea Group Publishing

- **Data Mining: A Heuristic Approach**
  Hussein Aly Abbass, Ruhul Amin Sarker and Charles S. Newton/1-930708-25-4
- **Managing Information Technology in Small Business: Challenges and Solutions**
  Stephen Burgess/1-930708-35-1
- **Managing Web Usage in the Workplace: A Social, Ethical and Legal Perspective**
  Murugan Anandarajan and Claire Simmers/1-930708-18-1
- **Challenges of Information Technology Education in the 21st Century**
  Eli Cohen/1-930708-34-3
- **Social Responsibility in the Information Age: Issues and Controversies**
  Gurpreet Dhillon/1-930708-11-4
- **Database Integrity: Challenges and Solutions**
  Jorge H. Doorn and Laura Rivero/ 1-930708-38-6
- **Managing Virtual Web Organizations in the 21st Century: Issues and Challenges**
  Ulrich Franke/1-930708-24-6
- **Managing Business with Electronic Commerce: Issues and Trends**
  Aryya Gangopadhyay/ 1-930708-12-2
- **Electronic Government: Design, Applications and Management**
  Åke Grönlund/1-930708-19-X
- **Knowledge Media in Healthcare: Opportunities and Challenges**
  Rolf Grutter/ 1-930708-13-0
- **Internet Management Issues: A Global Perspective**
  John D. Haynes/1-930708-21-1
- **Enterprise Resource Planning: Global Opportunities and Challenges**
  Liaquat Hossain, Jon David Patrick and M.A. Rashid/1-930708-36-X
- **The Design and Management of Effective Distance Learning Programs**
  Richard Discenza, Caroline Howard, and Karen Schenk/1-930708-20-3
- **Multirate Systems: Design and Applications**
  Gordana Jovanovic-Dolecek/1-930708-30-0
- **Managing IT/Community Partnerships in the 21st Century**
  Jonathan Lazar/1-930708-33-5
- **Multimedia Networking: Technology, Management and Applications**
  Syed Mahbubur Rahman/ 1-930708-14-9
- **Cases on Worldwide E-Commerce: Theory in Action**
  Mahesh Raisinghani/ 1-930708-27-0
- **Designing Instruction for Technology-Enhanced Learning**
  Patricia L. Rogers/ 1-930708-28-9
- **Heuristic and Optimization for Knowledge Discovery**
  Ruhul Amin Sarker, Hussein Aly Abbass and Charles Newton/1-930708-26-2
- **Distributed Multimedia Databases: Techniques and Applications**
  Timothy K. Shih/1-930708-29-7
- **Neural Networks in Business: Techniques and Applications**
  Kate Smith and Jatinder Gupta/ 1-930708-31-9
- **Information Technology and Collective Obligations: Topics and Debate**
  Robert Skovira/ 1-930708-37-8
- **Managing the Human Side of Information Technology: Challenges and Solutions**
  Edward Szewczak and Coral Snodgrass/1-930708-32-7
- **Cases on Global IT Applications and Management: Successes and Pitfalls**
  Felix B. Tan/1-930708-16-5
- **Enterprise Networking: Multilayer Switching and Applications**
  Vasilis Theoharakis and Dimitrios Serpanos/1-930708-17-3
- **Measuring the Value of Information Technology**
  Han T.M. van der Zee/ 1-930708-08-4
- **Business to Business Electronic Commerce: Challenges and Solutions**
  Merrill Warkentin/1-930708-09-2

Excellent additions to your library!

Receive the Idea Group Publishing catalog with descriptions of these books by calling, toll free 1/800-345-4332
or visit the IGP Online Bookstore at: http://www.idea-group.com!

Managing Business with Electronic Commerce: Issues and Trends

Table of Contents

Preface

Electronic commerce refers to any business activity that takes place using an electronic medium, frequently the Web. Electronic commerce has been widely cited as the fastest growing area in the computer industry. For example, Forester research has predicted that electronic commerce will be a $3.2 trillion industry by 2003. There are many reasons for the rapid adoption of electronic commerce across industry sectors, including increase in customer outreach, reduction of production cycle time and cost, ability to provide customized service and many others. Electronic commerce is being conducted for business transactions between business to business (B2B) as well as business to consumer (B2C). Business applications in electronic commerce include, but are not limited to, digital storefronts, electronic banking, digital financial markets, electronic auctions, supply chain management and electronic commerce services. Many challenges are being formed along with the opportunities created by electronic commerce. For example, large, established companies are facing increasing competition from fast and nimble startups because of low barriers of entry, customer demand is increasing for customizable interfaces and better content management, price competition is forcing companies to operate at lower profit margins, retaining customer loyalty is becoming difficult due to increased competition. Myriad of social and legal issues are also emerging due to the differences between electronic commerce and traditional commerce models. Approaches to solutions for these issues are coming from business innovations, technological solutions, and policy makers. Thus, electronic commerce is a new and rapidly growing area that is of interest to both practitioners and the academic community.

The overall mission of the book is to compile a collection of papers that represent some of the best thinking from researchers and practitioners who specialize in the various facets of electronic markets—namely computer technology, finance and banking, marketing, and logistics.

The book will be of interest to practitioners in the computer industry as well as other business sectors who have an interest in electronic commerce, researchers in business schools, information systems, policy sciences and computer science, and government agencies that are in the process of mplementing electronic commerce applications.

The book is divided into four sections, dealing with issues related to technology development, marketing, finance and business strategies.

The first chapter, written by Alem, Kowalczyk and Lee, reports on solutions for addressing the issues of negotiations with incomplete and imprecise information, dynamic coalition formation and negotiation ontologies. The authors introduce the concept of fuzzy negotiation in electronic commerce and describe a prototype system of intelligent agents to support fully autonomous multi-issue negotiations in the presence of limited common knowledge and imprecise information.

In the second chapter, Rittgen describes a methodology for modeling an enterprise called Multi-perspective Enterprise Modeling (MEMO). The methodology allows for the description of an enterprise on three levels: strategy, organization and information system, and from four angles: process, structure, resources and goals. All partial models for the views are integrated via a common object-oriented core. In this framework the author suggests a modeling language for the IS layer, the Event-driven Method Chain (EMC), a process-oriented language based on Event-driven Process Chains (EPCs), which is adapted to fit both the MEMO framework and the object-oriented paradigm. The methodology described in this chapter is suitable for the development of Web-based applications in an object-oriented programming language.

The third chapter, written by Strauch and Winter, tries to identify the "essence" of a Web-based information system and proposes a comprehensive conceptual model that captures the hierarchical document structure and hypertext semantics, as well as dynamic page generation from databases and various approaches to explicit and implicit navigation. The proposed model comprises several classes of information objects, various types of associations, activities for the design and quality checks. The authors illustrate the model using an existing Web-based information system.

In the fourth chapter, Joshi and Jiang describe a system to cluster search engine results based on a robust relational fuzzy clustering algorithm. They compare the use of the Vector Space-based and N-Gram-based dissimilarity measures to cluster the results from the search engines, such as *MetaCrawler* and *Google*. The chapter starts with a brief background on the clustering algorithm, followed by a description of the system and experimental results.

In Chapter Five, Subramanian and Yen examine Digital Asset Management (DAM) concepts, identify the desirable features and components of DAM, develop a taxonomy of the DAM systems, describe the e-commerce aspects of digital assets and discuss the various open research issues associated with Digital Asset Management.

In the Sixth Chapter, Altinkemer and Tomak adopt a four-layer description of the Internet economy. They analyze the pricing structures in each of the four layers of the Digital Economy, and analyze the relationship between different pricing strategies and customer service quality concept.

In Chapter Seven, Dasgupta and Chandrashekaran develop a framework for the delivery and tracking of rotating banner advertisements for e-commerce applications. They describe the pricing strategies for online banner advertisements, explain the reason for using rotating banner advertisements, and develop IS models for delivery and measurement of banner ads.

In Chapter Eight, Warkentin and Bajaj propose a new business model enabled by electronic commerce called the on-demand delivery services (ODDS) model. They sub-categorize the ODDS model into three submodels and analyze these models with structured interviews with key senior managers and survey of recent literature.

In Chapter Nine, Finnegan and Kilmartin study electronic payment systems. They describe five main categories of payment systems: credit card payment, electronic check, electronic cash, smart cards and micro-payments. The authors categorize the requirements of stakeholders into high, medium and low priorities, and compare electronic payment against these categorizes.

In Chapter Ten, Holowczak presents an overview of some of the current financial services and products in electronic commerce. He then discusses some important issues related to the application of electronic commerce and their strategic implications for financial services.

In Chapter Eleven, Ahmed shows how techniques used in valuing financial options can be used to evaluate projects or firms involving electronic commerce. He describes the real options theory in corporate finance with examples and illustrates how it can be applied to evaluate e-commerce projects under uncertainty.

Baumoel, Fugmann, Stiffel and Winter, in Chapter Twelve, develop the concept of e-commerce-ability and describe a methodology for measuring it for organizations. Their analysis consists of a four-dimensional framework for comparing the patterns of e-commerce role profiles and analyzing the success of e-commerce activities. The methodology can support management decisions regarding the medium and long-term strategies regarding e-commerce activities.

Burnett and Burn look at models for organizational development using the potential of virtual organization for established firms in Chapter Thirteen. The authors provide a definition of virtual organizations and models of virtuality, and propose six models of virtual organizations within a dynamic framework of change.

In Chapter Fourteen, Gupta and Sharma discusses the privacy issues in cyber shopping. They identify the privacy concerns, including spamming, surveillance and unauthorized access, personal information protection, intellectual property rights, and possible remedies and future trends.

In closing, I would like to thank all the authors for their excellent contributions to the book. I would also like to extend thanks to all the reviewers, without whom this book could not have, been completed. Many thanks to Michele Rossi, Jan Travers and Natasa Milanovic at Idea Group Publishing for continued support and help at all stages of this publication. Special thanks to Mehdi Khosrowpour for his help and guidance in preparing the book. Last but not the least, I would like to thank my wife Semanti and two sons Anirban and Abhiroop for making everything I do worthwhile.

Aryya Gangopadhyay
Baltimore, Maryland, USA
March 2001

Section I

Technology Development

Chapter I

Supporting Electronic Negotiation for Intelligent Trading

Leila Alem, Ryszard Kowalczyk and Maria R. Lee
CSIRO Mathematical and Information Sciences, Australia

Intelligent negotiation agents are software agents, which can negotiate the terms of transactions on behalf of purchasers and vendors on the Internet. Current solutions are mostly limited to single attribute negotiations, and are typically used to determine price. Moreover they typically assume information to be precisely defined and shared between the parties. Bargaining situations are, in most cases, characterized by conflicting interests among the agents that don't cater for common interests and possibility for collaboration to improve the outcomes of the parties. Another limitation of existing on-line negotiation agents is that their negotiation is usually taking place in a centralized marketplace where the agents meet and negotiate following a set of protocols that don't cater for more open and direct party-to-party negotiations. This chapter reports on solutions for addressing the issues of negotiations with incomplete and imprecise information, dynamic coalition formation and negotiation ontologies. The negotiation with incomplete and imprecise information uses fuzzy constraint-based reasoning and the principle of utility theory. The formation of coalition is based on negotiation over the distribution of the coalition value and the agent level of resources. The negotiation ontologies make use of shared ontologies as well as individual ontologies to avoid misunderstanding and make data exchange meaningful.

INTRODUCTION

E-commerce is growing at a staggering rate globally. Systems, which make e-commerce processes more efficient and competitive, will deliver huge benefits to these businesses and to their customers. Support for negotiations is becoming a widespread feature of electronic trading on the Internet. Recently a number of on-line negotiation agents have been developed such as AuctionBot (http://aution.eecs.umich.edu), eBay, E-Trade, FairMarket and Tete-a-Tete (http://e-commerce.media.mit.edu/tete-a-tete/). Such on-line negotiation agents make assumptions or do have limitations that are not always realistic in some real-world bargaining situations. Their negotiation is often limited to a price-only type of negotiation such as Kasbah (http://kasbah.media.mit.edu), AuctionBot. Their negotiation is also often based on precise information (Tete-a-Tete) and the sharing of private information (eBay, E-Trade, FairMarket). In addition, bargaining situations are in most cases limited to conflicting interests among the agents, they don't cater for common interests either. These mixed motive bargaining situations are quite common in real-world bargaining situations. Another limitation of the existing on-line negotiation agents is that their negotiation is usually taking place in a centralized marketplace where agents meet and negotiate following a set of protocols; they don't cater for direct party-to-party negotiations. The potential of on-line negotiation agents for truly assisting electronic trading can only be realized if such agents have means for direct party-to-party negotiation without the need for a central marketplace, means for multi-party/multi-issue negotiations, means to negotiate based on incomplete and imprecise information, means for dynamically forming coalitions in order to deal with mixed motive type of bargaining situation and finally means for adapting their negotiation strategy (Alem et al., 1999). This chapter reports on solutions for addressing the issues of negotiations with incomplete and imprecise information, dynamic coalition formation and inter-agent communication for direct party-to-party negotiation.

The negotiation with incomplete and imprecise information uses fuzzy constraint-based reasoning and the principle of utility theory (presented in the second section). The formation of coalition is based on a multi-agent approach in which each agent negotiates over the distribution of the coalition value and the agent level of resources (presented in the third section). The direct party-to-party negotiation makes use of shared ontologies as well as individual ontologies to avoid misunderstanding and to make data exchange meaningful (presented in the fourth section). The last section presents the results we have obtained as well as our conclusion.

FUZZY E-NEGOTIATION

Negotiation is a form of decision making where a number of parties jointly explore possible agreements in order to find a consensus that satisfies their private (and often conflicting) preferences, constraints and objectives (Raiffa, 1982; Rosenschein and Zlotkin, 1994; Frank, 1996). In the context of e-commerce, the objective of negotiation is to find an agreement on the terms of electronic transactions for goods and services exchanged between the parties. The negotiating parties usually have limited information about the preferences, constraints and objectives of each other. They exchange information in the form of offers in order to find the most satisfactory agreement for all participants. Negotiation typically involves a number of issues (e.g., price, quantity, delivery time, etc.) that may change during the negotiation process. For example new issues can be introduced by a party and some issues can be removed from negotiation. Therefore an offer can be a partial or complete solution currently preferred by a decision maker given the preferences, constraints, objectives and other offers. A consensus is a complete offer accepted by all negotiators as a mutual agreement. In addition to the presence of dynamic and incomplete information, most real-world negotiation problems can involve preferences, constraints and objectives that may be imprecisely defined (e.g., low price, budget about $50, more or less the same prices, high quality, short delivery time, etc.) and soft (i.e., they do not need always to be perfectly satisfied, e.g., one prefers to pay $100 but is still happy with paying a little bit more). An inherent presence of incomplete, imprecise and conflicting information, and complex trade-offs involved in negotiating multi-issue agreements between multiple parties are among the main challenges for providing automation support for the real-world negotiations and e-commerce negotiations in particular.

Our Proposed Approach

Fuzzy e-Negotiation Agents (FeNAs) is a prototype system of intelligent agents to support fully autonomous multi-issue negotiations in the presence of limited common knowledge and imprecise information. The FeNAs consider negotiation as an iterative decision-making process of evaluating the offers, relaxing the preferences and constraints, and making the counter-offers in order to find an agreement that satisfies constraints, preferences and objectives of the parties. The agents use the principles of utility theory and fuzzy constraint-based reasoning during negotiation, i.e., offer evaluation and counter-offer generation. They negotiate on multiple issues through the exchange of offers on the basis of the information available and negotiation strategies used by each party. The available information can be imprecise where constraints, preferences and priorities are defined as fuzzy constraints describing the level of satisfaction of an agent (and its user) with different potential solutions.

The overall objective of an agent is to find a solution that maximizes the agent's utility at the highest possible level of constraint satisfaction subject to its acceptabil-

Figure 1: Fuzzy constraints of two negotiating parties A and B

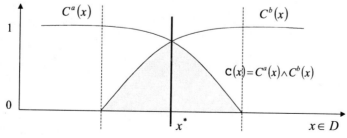

ity by other agents. Depending on the constraints, preferences and objectives of the parties, the FeNAs can support both distributive and integrative negotiations. During negotiation the agents follow a common protocol of negotiation and individual negotiation strategies. The protocol prescribes the common rules of negotiation (e.g., agents can accept or reject offers, send counter-offers or withdraw from negotiation; agents are expected to accept own offers; negotiation is successful if the final offer satisfies all parties, etc.). The private negotiation strategies specify how the individual agents evaluate and generate offers in order to reach a consensus according to their constraints and objectives. A number of negotiation strategies have been implemented in FeNAs, including the take-it-or-leave-it, no concession, fixed concession, simple concession strategies and their better deal versions.

In the FeNAs negotiation the set of fuzzy constraints of each party C^j prescribes a fuzzy set of its preferred solutions (individual areas of interest). The possible joint solutions of negotiation (common area of interest) are prescribed by an intersection of individual areas of interest. In this context the objective of the FeNAs negotiation is to find a solution within a common area of interest that maximizes constraint satisfaction of the parties. Figure 1 illustrates a simple example of a fuzzy constraint-based representation of the negotiation problem involving two parties a and b. $C^a(x)$ and $C^b(x)$ define individual areas of interest of the parties a and b, respectively. x* is a solution from an intersection of the individual areas of interest, i.e., the common area of interest, defined by a conjunctive combination $c(x) = C^a(x) \wedge C^b(x)$, with a maximal joint degree of constraint satisfaction.

It should be noted that the common area of interest, i.e., $c(x)$, is not known to the negotiating parties (agents) *a priori*. Therefore the main goal of the FeNAs is to move towards and to explore potential agreements within the common area of interest in order to find the most satisfactory agreement for the parties.

The FeNAs exchange their preferred solutions in the form of offers according to the individual negotiation strategies (e. g., trade-off and/or concession on a level

Figure 2: Fuzzy constraint-based negotiation

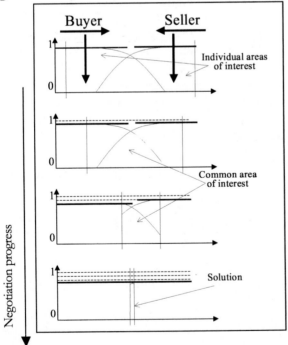

of constraint satisfaction). Typically each agent starts negotiation by offering the most preferred solution from its individual area of interest, i.e., a solution with the maximal satisfaction degree of the private constraints. If an offer is not acceptable by other agents, they make counter-offers in order to move them closer to an agreement. It can involve considering alternative solutions (trade-offs) at the same level of constraint satisfaction (if they exist), or making a concession, i.e., offering a solution with a lower degree of constraint satisfaction. The offers already exchanged between the agents constrain the individual areas of interests and the future decisions of the agents (e.g., a rational negotiator would not propose an offer with a lower satisfaction value than a satisfaction value of an offer already received from another party). Therefore, the individual areas of interests change (i.e., reduce) when the offers are exchanged during the negotiation process.

The principles of fuzzy constraint propagation based on the rules of inference in fuzzy logic (Zadeh, 1973, 1978; Dubois et al., 1994; Kowalczyk, 2000) are used in this process. Fuzzy constraint propagation supports searching for a solution by pruning the search space of potential solutions. It also allows the agents to track the changes in their individual areas of interest, i.e., the currently available values and levels of satisfaction of potential alternatives during the negotiation process (see Figure 3).

Discussion

Figure 3: A fuzzy negotiation agent for seller with constraint propagation

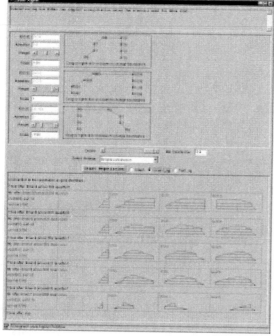

Negotiation has traditionally been a subject of study in Game theory (Rosenschein and Zlotkin, 1994), economics (Frank, 1996; Keeney and Raiffa, 1976) and management science (Lewicki, Sanders and Minton, 1997) research. It has also been an active area of research in Artificial Intelligence (AI) and in particular in distributed AI (DAI) and multi-agent systems (MAS) (e.g., Guttman, Moukas and Maes, 1998; Lander and Lesser, 1993; Parsons and Jennings, 1996; Sandholm and Lesser, 1997; Sycara, 1992). The increased potential of AI technology in supporting and automating negotiation has been recognized in a wide range of real-world problems, including group conflict resolution (Nunamaker et al., 1991; Sycara, 1992), business negotiations (Foroughi, 1995), resource allocation and scheduling (Sycare et al., 1991) and commerce (Beam and Segev, 1997; Guttman, Moukas and Maes, 1998). The developed approaches have also been the basis for most e-commerce negotiation agent systems.

Many existing negotiation agent systems support distributive negotiations based on auctions or other forms of competitive bidding where the terms of transaction typically involve a single issue (e.g., price) and/or the agents compete because of their mutually exclusive objectives (e.g., Kasbah and AuctionBot). Some systems that can support multi-issue integrative negotiations (e.g., Tete-a-Tete) may lead to win-win agreements if the agents have mutually non-exclusive objectives, usually provide a varying level of automation support and/or assume a high degree of information sharing (common knowledge) between the agents. They may share common knowledge explicitly (e.g., information about private constraints, preferences and utilities may be disclosed by fully cooperative agents) or implicitly (e.g., agents may have available or assume some information about probability distribution of utilities of other agents). The assumption of common knowledge that allows one to handle some aspects of uncertainty associated with incomplete information (e.g., mixed strategies in game theory) may be difficult to satisfy in the competitive e-commerce environment. Moreover the existing systems typically assume that all information available to the agents is precisely defined. For example users are usually required to provide exact and precise information about their private preferences, constraints and objectives (e.g., price < $99, delivery time = 1 day, etc.). Therefore autonomous negotiation agents that can handle both incomplete and imprecise information may be needed in the real-world negotiation settings.

COALITION FORMATION

Coalition formation is an important method for cooperation for on-line agents. Coalition among such agents may be mutually beneficial even if the agents are selfish and try to maximize their own payoff. A stated by Nwana et al., (1998) coalition formation will be a key issue in electronic commerce. On-line agents that will form a coalition can gain by using the greater market power that coalition provides. In e-commerce, where self-interested agents pursue their own goals, cooperation and coalition formation cannot be taken for granted. It must be pursued and achieved via argumentation and negotiation.

Our Proposed Approach

We have adopted the multi-agent approach to this problem where we typically create one or more agent, each with its own agenda and preferences and have the agents electronically negotiate with each other within a predefined set of rules. We are mostly interested in the question of which procedure the agents should use to coordinate their actions, cooperate and form a coalition. Constrains such as communication cost and limited computational time are taken into account. This

Figure 4: Negotiation engine

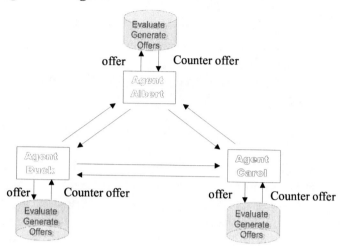

approach, while still primitive, offers the most hope for coalition formation in e-commerce as it is not constrained by Game Theory assumptions and does not limit itself to cooperative bargaining contexts as it handles mixed-motive bargaining context in which the agents compete as well as cooperate among each other.

The formation of a coalition among three agents is described as three agents (Albert, Buck, Carol) negotiating competitively in order to decide between which two agents coalition will form, and to agree on a division between the coalition members of the coalition value/utility.

Each agent makes use of a separate negotiation engine to generate and evaluate offers. The negotiation engines have been designed and developed based on the FeNAs presented in the previous section. Every offer an agent receives is sent to its negotiation engine for evaluation. The engine responds by sending a counter offer, an accept offer or a reject offer. Offer evaluations make use of agent preference values (level of gain and level of activity).

At the end of coalition formation negotiation, one of the following coalition structures is agreed upon:

[(Albert, Payoff A), (Buck, Payoff B)] ; Payoff A + Payoff B = Utility(Albert,Buck)

[(Albert, Payoff A'), (Carol, Payoff C')]; Payoff A'+ Payoff C' = Utility (Albert,Carol)

[(Buck, Payoff B'), (Carol, Payoff C)];Payoff B'+Payoff C = Utility(Buck, Carol)

The agent's payoff is the agent's personal gain (e.g., the agent portion of the coalition utility) minus the cost incurred in conducting the trading activities (negotiations etc.):

Payoff = Gain-Cost

The cost of an agent is a linear function of his/her activity level Cost = b AL. An agent sets its activity level depending on his/her circumstances/ preferences:

- AL = 1, in this case the agent has the computational resources and wants to conduct the trading activities on behalf of the coalition members.

- AL = 0, in this case the agent wants to share the computational workload of conducting the trading activities.
- AL = -1, in this case the agent has limited computational resources and does not want to conduct the trading activities; he/she prefers to leave it to the agent representing the coalition.

β is a constant used to balance cost and gain, $\beta = 500$. By setting β to 500, an agent not representing the coalition will gain \$500 when an agent representing the coalition will lose \$500. Such agent will accept such a loss provided he/she can get a greater portion of the coalition utility. A coalition will form once the agent agrees on two issues:

- Who is getting what: in other words which portion of the coalition utility each agent is getting?
- Who is doing what: in other words who will represent the coalition and will conduct the trading activities on behalf of the coalition members?

At anytime during the coalition negotiations, each agent has three possible actions: it can accept the offer it received from the agent it was negotiating with; it can make a counter offer to this same agent; or it can ask a third agent to better the offer received by the agent it was initially negotiating with.

Each agent makes use of the coalition formation algorithm presented below:

```
Begin
    A –> (B, Payoff B)
    Begin Loop
    If B 'accept'
      End Game [(A, UAB-Payoff B), (B, Payoff B)], (C,0)
    If B 'reject'
      A begins negotiations with C
    If B –> (A, (B, Payoff B) )              {better offer}
      Payoff B' = closes offer ~ Payoff B    {B already neg. with C}
      A –> (B, Payoff B')

    If B–> (A, Payoff A)                                  {counter offer}
      If A 'reject'
       A begins negotiation with C
      If A can 'accept'
        A –>(C, (A, Payoff A))        {ask C to do better}
        C –> (A, Payoff A')
        If Payoff A' > Payoff A
         End Game [(A, Payoff A), (B, UAB-Payoff A)], (B,0)
        If Payoff A' <= Payoff A)
         End Game [(A, Payoff A),, (B, UAB - Payoff A) ], (C,0)
      Else A –> (B, Payoff B')            {counter offer}
    Repeat Loop
```

This algorithm has been used in the experimental Intelligent Trading Agency for the user car trading test-bed (ITA) for three buyers trying competitively to negotiate between which two a coalition will form in order to get a better deal with the car dealer. We have tested this algorithm on a number of scenarios (each with different agent preferences and different negotiation strategies). Figure 5 shows results obtained with one of the scenarios.

Discussion

Coalition formation has been widely studied, among rational agents (Sandholm and Lesser, 1995; Rosenschein and Zlotkin, 1994), and among self-interested agents (Sandholm and Lesser, 1998).

Game theory most commonly employed by coalition formation researchers usually answers the question of what coalition will form, and what reasons and processes will lead the agents to form a particular coalition. The focus is on understanding why agents form a particular coalition among all possible ones. Game theory is concerned with how games will be played from both a descriptive and a normative point of view. Game solutions consist of strategies in equilibrium (Nash, Perfect, Dominant). Although existing theory is rich in insights and provides useful benchmarks, it cannot tell us how to program on-line agents for most bargaining contexts of interests. Relevant game-theoric solution techniques almost invariably make assumptions (e.g., of shared prior probability estimates, common knowledge of agent's preferences and perfect rationality) that do not apply to real bargaining contexts. The following more specific limitations/criticisms are raised by Linhart and Radner:

- *Common knowledge and rationality assumptions*: equilibrium are derived by assuming that players are optimizing against one another. This means that players' beliefs are common knowledge; this could not be assumed in e-trading scenarios.
- *Not predictive*: game-theorists are not able to predict the outcome of bargaining processes; their focus is more on being able to explain a range of observed behaviour.
- *Non-robustness*: results of negotiation depend crucially on the procedure of offers and counter-offers, and at what stage discounting takes place. In a real-world situation of negotiation, these features are not a given piece of data, but rather evolve endogenously. Results dependent on them may be too specific to be of any use.

Furthermore game theory has focussed almost exclusively on outcomes that under perfect rationality constitute equilibria of the game, playing scant attention to processes off the equilibrium path and the many vagaries of non-rational behaviour (Dworman, Kimbrough and Laing 1996). Consequently previous game theory has little to offer by way of instruction for programming for the on-line agent to negotiate effectively in complex real-world contexts.

Work in AI by Rosenschein and Zlotkin (1994) has aimed at circumventing this problem by seeking to design mechanisms (protocols) under which on-line agents

Figure 5: Results obtained with one of the scenarios

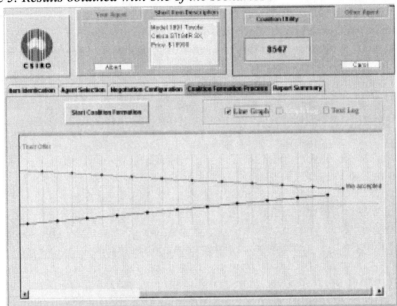

may negotiate using pre-defined strategies, known *a priori* to be appropriate. Work by Shehory and Kraus (1999) adjusts the game theory concepts to autonomous agents and presents different coalition formation procedures. The procedures presented concentrate on widely cooperative problems such as the postmen problem. While both works are certainly of useful value, their range of potential applicability does not cover all the requirements for electronic commerce.

ONTOLOGY-BASED NEGOTIATION

Electronic negotiations, where multiple parties are involved, need to exchange information for negotiation decision making. One of the big issues is how agents communicate. In order for this communication to be useful, the heterogenous information systems must agree on the meaning of their exchanged data such as colour, length, currency and time.

In order to solve these problems, Web-based information systems must be able to ensure semantic interoperability (Chandrasekaran, Josephson and Benjamins 1999; Ritter, 1998). Context information is an important component of the information systems. The context of a piece of data is defined to be the metadata relating to its meaning, properties (such as its source, quality and precision) and organizational knowledge. The explicit representation of such context information enables meaningful and effective data interchange and conversion. The explicit knowledge reduces errors and frees applications from being concerned with conversions. It also makes it possible to understand the impact of semantic changes to the data among different heterogeneous information systems.

Figure 6: Agent-based semantic-value architecture

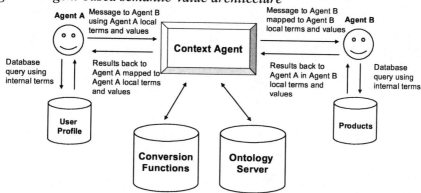

Our Proposed Approach

Agent technologies are having increasingly profound influences on the process of e-market information because they let systems of Web-based competitive self-interested agents do the negotiating, buying and selling (Ma, 1999). Our proposed system requires the development of agent technology, which can act on sellers' or buyer's behalf and interact with trading systems. A detailed description of the system appears in Lee (2000). Figure 6 shows the agent-based semantic-value architecture.

We model the exchange of data values as follows: the buyer-agent sends a query to the context-agent, requesting some semantic values from the seller-agent and providing target context for the result (message to Agent B using Agent A local terms and values as shown in Figure 6). The context-agent then sends this query to the seller-agent (message to Agent B mapped to Agent B local terms and values) and receives the resulting values (results back to Agent A in Agent B local terms and values). The context-agent then converts these values to the given target context and sends the results to the buyer-agent (results back to Agent A mapped to Agent A local terms and values).

It is important to provide a fast and inexpensive standardized communication infrastructure to support the automated negotiation systems (Sandholm and Lesser, 1995). We introduce a protocol ontology server by integrating a general common ontology (Lee, Kwang and Kowok, 2000) with a specific user-defined ontology. The general common ontology explicitly represents generic concepts that are used by agents. The specific user-defined ontology provides flexibility to the user to define their own concepts that they might want to use. Figure 7 shows the ontology server protocol.

In order for the data interchange to be meaningful during e-negotiation, two semantic values must be compared with respect to a context. This context is called the target context of comparison. The value of the comparison is defined by converting both semantic values to the target context and by comparing the associated simple values of the results.

The role of context-agent is to compare the context of the resulting semantic values with the target context. In particular, the context-agent must verify that the properties of the target context are a subset of the properties of each semantic value's context, so that conversion strategies will be used properly. In performing this comparison, the context-agent may need to access the

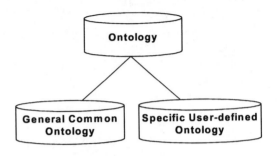

Figure 7: The ontology server protocol

terminology mapping in the ontology server. For example, if the buyer-agent is looking for "price" whereas the seller-agent defines as "value," then the ontology server is for finding the synonym.

If the buyer-agent does not explicitly specify a target context, then the context-agent can use the seller-agent data profile to determine the target context of the exchange. If the buyer-agent does not provide semantic values, then the context-agent converts the seller-agent's value to the target context, passing the simple value to the buyer-agent. Figure 8 shows the protocol using the context agent.

For example, suppose a buyer-agent wishes to retrieve all the car-trading having a latest trade price of more than $15,000 US and wishes to view their values in Australian dollars. The target-context defines the rule for the view that "currency" is "Australian dollars." The conversion strategy is to convert all the trade prices to latest trade price in US dollars in the temporary view. The rule > $15,000 US therefore selects all the latest trade prices greater than $15,000 and then convert those data to Australian dollars.

Discussion

Conventional information systems are designed for the exchange of simple values. However, this form of information exchange does not extend to real-world situations where the meaning of exchanged values can change. Semantic values, not simple values, can more closely fulfil the requirements for information exchange. A semantic value is associated with a simple value with its context that a context is to be set and each element of the set is associated to a property of a semantic value (Sciore, Siegel and Rosenthal, 1994). However, existing systems are not equipped to exchange information as semantic values, as they cannot evaluate properties,

Figure 8: Protocol using context-dependent semantic value

determine semantic comparability, select target contexts and resolve conflicts (Sciore, Siegel and Rosenthal, 1994).

Some of the previous work in semantic interoperability has been developed for static systems and used SQL-based data manipulation language (Sciore, Siegel and Rosenthal, 1994). Thanks to the technology rapidly improving, we can use XML to encode information and services with meaningful structure and semantics that computers can easily understand (Smith and Poutler, 1999). Expressing semantics in syntax rather than in first-order logic or other formal languages leads to a simpler evaluation function. This also provides us with more dynamic, expressive and extensible environment.

The proposed system also provides a context-dependent and model-independent approach for the exchange of data among heterogeneous information systems.

CONCLUSIONS

The proposed solutions allow agents to autonomously negotiate, form coalition and communicate in the presence of incomplete, imprecise and conflicting information. The agents are rational and self-interested in the sense that they are concerned with achieving the best outcomes for themselves. They are not interested in social welfare or outcomes of other agents (as long as they can agree on a solution). The rationality of the agents is bounded by the availability of the information and computational resources. It means that the agents try to achieve as good outcome as possible in both negotiating a deal and forming a coalition. In other words they do not have always the information and computational resources to obtain the theoretically optimal outcome (according to the game theoretical results).

The three solutions presented have been used and tested on the experimental Intelligent Trading Agency for the user car-trading test-bed (http://www.cmis.csiro.au/aai/projects). The FeNAs have also been tested with different negotiation scenarios for document translation services (Kowalczyk and Bui, 1999; Kowalczyk, 2000).

The results of the initial experiments with the fuzzy e-negotiation work indicate that the FeNAs system can handle a variety of e-negotiation problems with incomplete common knowledge and imprecise/soft constraints. In particular they can provide automation support for multi-issue integrative negotiation as experimented with scenarios for car-trading and document translation negotiation.

The results of the initial experiments with the coalition formation work indicates that simple artificial agents formulate effective strategies for negotiating the formation of coalition in mixed motive and multilateral negotiations contexts and therefore seems appropriate for developing practical applications in electronic commerce.

The results of the initial experiments with the ontology-based negotiation work indicates that the use of a uniform language for negotiation can free on-line negotiation agents from concerns about units and conversions and can assist communication among heterogeneous agents.

Although these initial results are encouraging, more comprehensive testing in the real-world e-commerce environment is necessary and a number of research issues need further investigation. For example analysis of optimality and convergence of the negotiation process, adaptability and learning of the negotiation strategies, dynamic multi-party negotiation, coalition negotiation using coevolving agents whose strategies are encoded as genetic programs, and negotiation with incomplete and imprecise offers (i.e., linguistic negotiation) are the subject of our current research. The research described in this chapter aims at advancing our effort in developing and deploying effective on-line negotiation agents in a real-world bargaining setting.

ACKNOWLEDGEMENT

We would like to thank Ms. Linda Whitford, Librarian of CSIRO Mathematical and Information Science, for generating the Book Index.

END NOTE

The work reported here was presented at the International Conference on Advances in Infrastructure for Electronic Business, Science and Education on the Internet, SSGRR'00 (Alem, Kowalczyk and Lee, 2000).

REFERENCES

Alem, L., Kowalczyk, R., Lee, M., Ni, Y., Van, B., Wong, W. and Zhang, D. (1999). Next generation of negotiation agents for electronic commerce trading: A CMIS research agenda perspective. *Proceeding of CollECTer'99*, December.

Alem, L., Kowalczyk, R. and Lee, M. (2000). Recent advances in e-negotiation agents. In *Proceedings of International Conference on Advances in Infrastructure for Electronic Business, Science and Education on the Internet (SSGRR'00)*, Italy, August.

Beam, C. and Segev, A. (1997). Automated negotiations: A survey of the state of the art. *CMIT Working Paper 97-WP-1022*. May. Retrieved on the World Wide Web at: http://haas.berkeley.edu/~citm/wp-1022.pdf.

Chandrasekaran, B., Josephson, J. and Benjamins, V. (1999). What are ontologies, and why do we need them. *IEEE Intelligent Systems*, January/February, 22-26.

Dubois, D., Fargier, H. and Prade, H. (1994). Propagation and satisfaction of flexible constraints. In Yager, R. and Zadeh, L. (Eds.), *Fuzzy Sets, Neural Networks and Soft Computing*, 166-187.

Dworman, G., Kimbrough, S. and Laing, J.(1996). Bargaining by artificial agent in two coalition games: A study in genetic programming for electronic commerce. The Wharton School, University of Pennsylvania, *OPIM Working paper*, April.

Foroughi, A. (1995). A survey of the use of computer support for negotiation. *Journal of Applied Business Research*, Spring, 121-134.

Frank, R. H. (1996). *Microeconomics and Behaviour*. 3rd ed. McGraw-Hill.

Guttman, R., Moukas, A. and Maes, P. (1998). Agent-mediated electronic commerce: A survey. *Knowledge Engineering Review*, June.

ITA. Available on the World Wide Web at: http://www.cmis.csiro.au/aai/projects.

Kasbah. Available on the World Wide Web at: http://kasbah.media.mit.edu.

Keeney, R. and Raiffa, H. (1976). *Decisions with Multiple Objectives: Preferences and Value Trade-Offs*. John Wiley and Sons.

Kowalczyk, R. and Bui, V. (1999). Towards intelligent trading agents. *The International Conference on Intelligent Systems and Active DSS*, in Turku/Åbo, Finland.

Kowalczyk, R. (2000). On negotiation as a distributed fuzzy constraint satisfaction problem. *World Automation Congress WAC'2000*, ISSCI, USA.

Lander, S. and Lesser, V. (1993). Understanding the role of negotiation in distributed search among heterogenous agents. *Proceedings of the 13th International Joint Conference on Artificial Intelligence*. Chambery, France, August, 438-444.

Lewicki, R., Saunders, D. and Minton, J. (1997). *Essentials of Negotiation*. Irwin.

Lee, M., Kwang, M. and Kwok, P. (2000). Concept acqusition modelling for e-commerce ontology. *International Conference in Information Resources Management Association (IRMA 2000)*, 450-453.

Lee, M. (2000). Context-dependent semantic values for e-negotiation. *Proceedings for the Second International Workshop on Advanced Issues of e-Commerce and Web-Based Information Systems (WECWIS 2000)*, 41-47.

Ma, M. (1999). Agents in e-commerce. *Communications of the ACM*, March, 42(3), 79-80.

Maes, P., Guttman, R. and Moukas, G., (1999). Agents that buy and sell. *Communications of the ACM*, March, 42(3), 81-84.

Maes, P., Guttman, R. and Moukas, A. (1999). Agents that buy and sell: Transforming commerce as we know it. *Communications of the ACM*, March, 42(3).

Nunamaker, J.F. Jr., Dennis, A. R., Valacich, J. S. and Vogel, D. R. (1991). Information technology for negotiating groups: Generating options for mutual gain. *Management Science*, October.

Nwana, H., Rosenschein, J., Sandholm, T., Sierra, C., Maes, P. and Guttmann, R. (1998). Agent-mediated electronic commerce: Issues, challenges and some viewpoints. *2rd International Conference on Autonomous Agents*, Minneapolis, May.

Parsons, S. and Jennings, N. R. (1996). Negotiation through argumentation-A preliminary report. *Proceedings of the 2nd International Conference on Multi-Agent Systems*, ICMAS'96, Japan, 267-274.

Raiffa, H. (1982). *The Art and Science of Negotiation*. Cambridge, MA: Harvard University Press.

Ritter, J. (1998). Facilitating interoperability and electronic commerce. *NIST ATP Workshop*. Available on the World Wide Web at: http://www.atp.nist.gov/elec-com/interop/ritter.htm.

Rosenschein, J. and Zlotkin, G. (1994). *Rules of Encounter: Designing Conventions for Automated Negotiation Among Computers*. MIT Press.

Sandholm, T. and Lesser, V. (1998). Issues in automated negotiation and electronic commerce: Extending the contract net framework. In *Reading in Agents*, Morgan Kaufmann Publishers, 66-73.

Sandholm, T. and Lesser, V. (1995). Issues of automated negotiation and electronic commerce: Extending the contract net framework. *Proceedings of the 1st International Conference on Multiagent Systems (ICMAS'95)*, San Francisco.

Sandholm, T. and Lesser, V. (1997). Coalition among computationally bounded agents. *Artificial Intelligence*, 94, 99-137.

Sciore, E., Siegel, M. and Rosenthal, A. (1994). Using semantic values to facilitate interoperability among heterogenous information systems. *ACM Transactions on Database Systems*, 19(2), 254-290.

Shehory, O. and Kraus, S. (1995). Feasible formation of stable coalitions among autonomous agents in general environments. *Computational Intelligence Journal*.

Shehory, O. and Kraus, S. (1999). Coalition formation among autonomous agents: Strategies and complexity. *Department of Mathematics and Computer Science*, Bar Ilan University, Preliminary report.

Smith, H. and Poulter, K. (1999). Share the ontology in XML-based trading architectures. *Communications of the ACM*, March, 42(3), 1.

Sycara, K. (1992). The persuader. In Shapiro, D. (Ed.). *The Encyclopedia of Artificial Intelligence*. John Wiley Sons.

Sycara, K., Roth, S., Sadeh, N. and Fox, M. (1991). Distributed constraint heuristic search. *IEEE Transactions on System, Man, and Cybernetics*, 21, 1446-1461.

Tete-a-Tete. Available on the World Wide Web at: http://e-commerce.media.mit.edu/tete-a-tete/.

Zadeh, L. A. (1973). Outline of a new approach to the analysis of complex systems and decision processes. *IEEE Transactions on Man. Cybernetics*, 3, 28-44.

Zadeh, L. A. (1978). Fuzzy sets as a basis for a theory of possibility. *Fuzzy Sets and Systems*, 1, 3-28.

Chapter II

E-Commerce Software: From Analysis to Design

Peter Rittgen
University Koblenz-Landau, Germany

Early information systems were mainly built around secondary, administrative processes of the value chain (e.g., accounting). But since the Internet came into use, more and more primary processes have become accessible to automation: customer acquisition, ordering, billing and, in the case of intangible goods such as software, even delivery. To facilitate this complex task, we suggest that the relevant parts of the enterprise be modeled according to the MEMO (Multi-perspective Enterprise MOdeling) method. It allows for the description of an enterprise on three levels-strategy, organization and information system-and from four angles-process, structure, resources and goals. All partial models for the views are integrated via a common object-oriented core. In this framework we suggest a modeling language for the IS layer, the Event-driven Method Chain (EMC), a process-oriented language based on Event-driven Process Chains (EPCs), which we adapt to fit both the MEMO framework and the object-oriented paradigm, thus making it suitable for the development of Web-based applications in an object-oriented programming language. To illustrate this we use the example of a software trading company.

INTRODUCTION

Early information systems were mainly built around secondary, administrative processes of the value chain (e.g., accounting). But since the Internet came into use, more and more primary processes have become accessible to automation: customer acquisition, ordering, billing and, in the case of intangible goods such as software, even delivery. Hence an increasing part of an enterprise has to be modeled and a substantial part thereof is implemented. To create such an information system and to adapt it constantly to a changing environment requires a much more efficient software development process than the one suggested by the traditional methods, namely the separation into the phases analysis, design and implementation where each phase is usually performed by a different team, each relying on the documents produced in the previous phase (possibly with backtracking). In these approaches, the coupling between the phases is weak: changes to an analysis model typically require a substantial reorganization of the design models, which in turn slows down software development considerably. The ARchitecture of Integrated information Systems (ARIS) (Scheer, 1992) is one such traditional method with a focus on analysis. It received substantial attention both from researchers and practitioners thanks to its close relation to the SAP suite of business applications.

Several reasons exist why such methods are not suitable for the development of Web-based applications (leading to corresponding requirements):

1.   The increasing number of automated business processes requires the integration of these processes with the relevant data. But the parts (views) of conventional models are only loosely coupled (e.g., the data and process models of ARIS). A suitable method for developing Web-based applications should integrate partial models, especially the process and the data/object model (model integration).

2.   Existing methods do not cater for the needs of object orientation. But the predominant use of object-oriented programming languages in developing Web-based software demands the compatibility of the modeling method with object-oriented concepts.

3.   Traditional software development is usually quite slow. But electronic markets require a quick adaptation of Web applications to changing needs.

4.   The development of design models typically consists of reinventing the analysis models in a different (more formal) language. A smooth transition from analysis to design, by merely refining the existing analysis models, is preferable (phase integration).

To solve these problems, we make use of the MEMO framework, which represents a multi-perspective approach to enterprise modeling where all views are strongly connected via a common object-oriented core. Within this framework, the integration of processes and their relevant data is achieved by an analytical, object-oriented process definition language called EMC. Apart from model integration, EMCs also facilitate the transition from analysis to design by providing a suitable level of abstraction/formalization, thus speeding up the software development process.

Hence, EMCs provide a way of an integrated analysis of the major aspects of an information system: its structure, its processes and the required resources. Because the underlying paradigm is object oriented, it enables a seamless transition to object-oriented design and implementation necessary for the development of Web-based applications. This is further supported by the unambiguous process semantics of EMCs. In addition, we assume that users already familiar with EPCs will experience few problems in handling EMCs because they resemble each other closely. The process-driven identification of objects helps modelers with less expertise in object-oriented design to create a complete object model, a task that is both highly abstract and challenging even for software engineers. Put together, these features facilitate an efficient development of Web-based applications.

The following sections will explore the details of such an approach: we start with an example scenario of a software trading company planning to go "on-line." This example motivates the necessity of an integrated modeling of business processes and information across the various phases of software engineering. It also serves as a framework of reference for the sections to follow. We introduce the basis for information modeling in a company: MEMO and EPCs showing how integration is achieved in this setting (in particular that of processes and related documents). Then we show interpretations of EPCs found in literature, and we argue why the EPCs are chosen despite their marginal usefulness as a starting point for software development and how they can be improved for this task: they are more easily understood and more readily accepted by most business people than typical process models from computer science (such as Petri nets, for example), which is an important plus in developing software for business. Trying to make Petri nets understandable is a much more difficult task than making EPCs (in the form of EMCs) suitable for software development. To achieve the latter we introduce the Event-driven Method Chain. The principal differences between EPCs and EMCs are explained. This includes the precise meaning of each construct given in terms of Petri nets and the integration of documents (i.e., objects) into EMC process models. The chapter concludes with an empirical assessment of the usefulness of the EMC (as compared to the EPC) regarding the clarity of the description of the modeled business process (or more precise: the lack of ambiguity).

AN EXAMPLE SETTING

To illustrate the problem of developing a Web-based application, we consider the example of a young mail-order company trading software products. Up to now, they were organized in a more or less conventional way: customers ordered via phone, fax or surface mail. Orders were processed manually and then entered into a database. The products were stocked in physical form as CD-ROMs. Stock management was done with the help of a stand-alone system. Delivery was effected by conventional posting, payment by cheque, credit card or money order.

Now, this company plans to operate over the Internet. Apart from offering new services (such as ordering via the World Wide Web and downloading of the ordered product), this also requires substantial reorganization: e.g., the isolated information systems for ordering and stocking have to be integrated to allow the potential customer a combined search for price and availability of a product. The head of IT is therefore asked to draw up a sketch of the principal architecture of the new system (see Figure 1). It consists of a central database containing information about customers, orders, items and so on. All applications, internal and external, operate on this database. Internal applications are the ones used only by the staff of the company, such as order and customer management, delivery, etc. The external applications can also be accessed by the (potential) customers. They are made accessible to the world by an applet server feeding the user's browser.

The next sections will show how such an information system can be analyzed and designed rapidly with the help of the EMC language, which integrates the different views of a system, as well as their migration from analysis to design models, because it adheres to MEMO as outlined in the following section. We also give a short background on the business process language, EPC, which forms the basis for EMC.

MULTI-PERSPECTIVE ENTERPRISE MODELING AND EPC

In the early phase of analysis, the modeler of any application is typically confronted with a yet largely unstructured problem domain. This applies to Web-based applications in particular, which involve a complete reorganization of a substantial part of the company: processes to be performed over the Web have to be designed newly; related internal processes have to be adapted accordingly. These changes affect not only the information system itself but also the organization as a whole, resulting in a significant strategical impact of the corresponding decisions. Hence a modeling methodology should distinguish three levels of an enterprise: strategy, organization and information system (see Figure 2). But even if we restrict attention to one of the levels, too much complexity remains to be handled by one model only. Therefore each level is further subdivided into the following four foci:

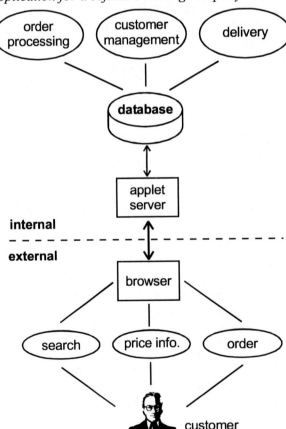

Figure 1: Example architecture of a Web application for a software trading company

- process: dynamic representation of the system
- structure: static description of the domain objects and their relations
- resources: means required to execute a process
- goals: results to be achieved and their relations

The resulting 12 partial models span the 4´3 matrix of the views of MEMO (Frank, 1997). Figure 2 gives iconized examples for the 12 views. The three-letter acronyms for each view consist of the first initial of the column header, the first initial of the row title and an M for Model. For example, the strategy process model (SPM) consists of a value chain á la Porter (1985) where the primary processes (procurement, production, distribution, marketing) form the basic chain (arrow-shaped boxes) with the subsidiary (supporting) activities attached to them (the flags). On the organizational and IS levels, an EPC-like language for modeling process is used. The OSM is represented in the form of an organizational chart and the ISM is an object class model. The remaining views in the matrix have not been covered yet.

Here we focus on developing an integrated modeling language for the IS level (abstracting from the goal view for the time being). We call this language EMC. It covers IPM (IS Process Model), IRM (IS Resource Model) and the integrative part of ISM (IS Structure Model). The details of the structure are thereupon specified with the help of MEMO-OML (MEMO Object Modeling Language) described in Frank (1998). Here MEMO-OML is explained only insofar as it is necessary to understand the integration of all three views.

Figure 2: Perspectives on an enterprise (MEMO)

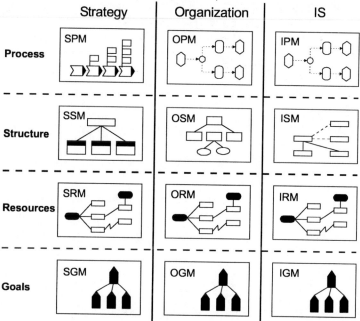

We start from the assumption that the processes of a problem domain are rather easier to identify than the objects because the latter represent a more abstract notion. Hence we put the process focus in the center of the EMC language and suggest that an initial EMC is drawn before the corresponding object model. In fact, the EMC even helps in the construction of the object model. The basic dynamic element of an EMC is the method (or service) which is linked to the objects involved in providing this service. The objects themselves and their relations are defined in MEMO-OML. We establish the resource focus by attaching the resources to the method which requires them.

The process modeling language EMC is based on the EPCs of ARIS. Although this language exhibits major shortcomings as demonstrated in the next section, we do not reject it outright because it has proved its ease of use in practice: it is the preferred choice of consultants and large IT departments, and it is a must for companies introducing SAP. Hence a process language based on EPCs has a better chance of being accepted by the practitioner than some completely new artefact. Still, the shortcomings have to be overcome to make EPCs fit into the MEMO framework (thus achieving model integration), to align them to the object-oriented paradigm and to ensure an unambiguous interpretation of the analysis models by the designers thus achieving phase integration (see points 1-4 in the introduction). The result is the EMC language described later.

Since the EPCs were introduced in Scheer (1992), there have been many opinions on how a correct EPC should look. Proposals ranged from syntactical issues (which nodes can be linked to each other) to semantics (what is the exact meaning of a connector?). On the syntactical level some rules have been established that are now generally accepted, for example Keller and Teufel (1997): An EPC consists of strictly alternating sequences of events and functions (i.e., processes) that are linked by logical connectors (AND, OR, XOR). There are opening connectors (splits) and closing connectors (joins). Among the syntactical restrictions are:

K1: There are no isolated nodes.

K3/4: Functions/events have exactly one incoming/outgoing edge (except start/end events).

K6: Connectors are either splits (1 input, many outputs) or joins (many inputs, 1 output).

K8/9: An event is always followed by a function and vice versa (module connectors).

Sometimes it is also requested that an event should not be followed by an XOR split because events cannot make decisions. Figure 3 gives an example of what an EPC looks like.

SEMANTIC MODELS OF EPC

There is considerably less unanimity on the subject of semantics. Here we sketch only two of the existing approaches: The first was suggested by Chen and

Scheer (1994). That is why we call it the original semantics although it covers only a subset of all EPCs. A more elaborate model was given later by Langner, Schneider and Wehler (1997). But it still requires the transformation of an arbitrary EPC into a well-formed one. Therefore we introduce a new semantics, the so-called modEPC semantics, which is applicable to any EPC. To facilitate the design of correct EPCs, we also slightly modify the syntax concerning the problematic OR join.

The Original Semantics

The first formal approach to a semantics of EPCs was suggested by Chen and Scheer (1994). The semantics is based on Petri nets, more precisely place/transition nets, which obviously closely resemble EPCs: the functions correspond to transitions; events can be represented by places. The XOR split and join are described by the modules in Figure 4.

The left module is the XOR split where on arrival of a token, only one transition can fire, removing the token necessary for the other transition to fire. Hence only one path can be activated at a time. The right module represents the XOR join which only fires if not more than one place is marked. Should both places hold tokens, the connector blocks (deadlock), thus indicating a possibly wrongful design of the EPC. This is achieved by the inhibitor edges (the ones with the small circles at the end) which inhibit firing in the presence of a token.

Analogously Petri-net modules for the AND connectors can be specified (see Figure 5).

Figure 3: Example EPC

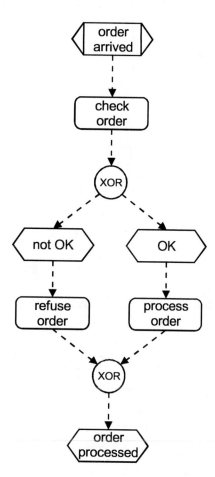

Figure 4: Petri nets for XOR split and join

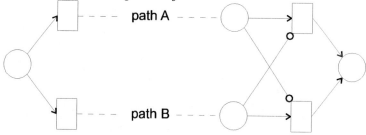

If we try to do the same for the OR connectors, we discover that here the semantics of the join cannot be determined on itself. The EPC on the left side of Figure 6, for example, has a unique interpretation because the join brings together again exactly

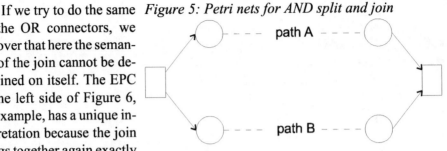

Figure 5: Petri nets for AND split and join

the paths separated by the split. So the join simply waits for the completion of all paths activated by the split.

But what is the meaning of the EPC on the right? According to the semantics of Chen and Scheer (1994), it has no meaning at all because the OR join has no corresponding split. Due to Langner, Schneider and Wehler (1997), explained below, the OR join is interpreted as an AND, i.e., it waits for both paths. But perhaps the modeler intended the join to be triggered by the first completed path. So there are at least three possible interpretations, a situation most probably provoking mistakes in later stages of software development. For this reason we suggest an unambiguous semantics and modify the syntax accordingly. But before that we sketch the OR semantics of Chen and Scheer (1994) and Langner, Schneider and Wehler (1997).

In Chen and Scheer (1994), there are different tokens for the branches of an OR e.g. token "a" for path A and token "b" for path B. The split informs the join of the tokens to be expected. In Figure 7 the split is to activate both paths and hence the first transition puts both a and b tokens on both successor places. The first two travel along their respective paths, the other two tell the join to wait for the travelling token from both path A and path B.

Figure 6: OR join with and without corresponding split

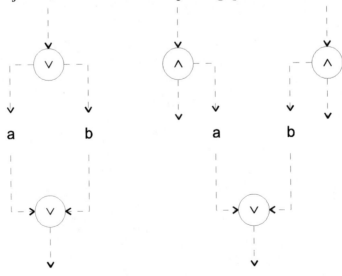

Figure 7: Petri net for the OR connectors according to Chen and Scheer (1994)

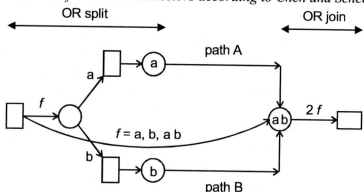

But unfortunately this approach limits the amount of interpretable EPCs severely. It forces the modeler to specify splits and joins correspondingly. This is clearly undesirable for the early phase of analysis where the ideas of the modeler are not yet well structured.

A Semantics for Well-Formed EPCs

A less restrictive semantics is given in Langner, Schneider and Wehler (1997). It makes use of boolean Petri nets with tokens 0 (false or inactive) and 1 (true or active). The OR problem is solved by the simple trick of sending tokens along all paths: a 1 to activate it and a 0 to deactivate it. Now the OR join can wait for the arrival of tokens from all incoming paths and if at least one 1 token is present, it activates its successor. The boolean transition is called branch/fork for the OR split and merge/join for the OR join. The opening and closing XOR transitions are branch and merge respectively. In the case of the AND, they are referred to as fork and join. The firing rules are given by the standard truth tables of propositional calculus with the following exceptions: the entries "0 1" and "1 0" of the AND are not applicable, and neither is the combination "1 1" of XOR. The corresponding joins block this input instead of passing on a 0 to the successor.

Strictly speaking this semantics only applies to well-formed EPCs. An EPC is well-formed if all generated tokens are extinguished eventually, no dead paths exist and no connector blocks. This is the case if all branches of a split come together in one corresponding join without jumps into or from the branches. Well-formedness is checked by a static and a dynamic analysis only after the transformation of the EPC into a boolean net. This process involves the restructuring of not-well-formed nets to meet the criteria. The result is always a well-formed net, but one that in general has not the same meaning as the EPC from which we started. Whether these fundamental changes are admissible can only be judged by the people from the responsible department. But they are usually not in a position to handle the complex transformations into well-formed nets. Hence problems of this kind can only be solved by a team of IT specialists and users, but such a process is rather costly. From an economic point of view, we should therefore avoid making EPCs well-formed.

IMPROVING EPC

When modeling business processes in ARIS, we identify core processes of the company and represent them as EPCs. An EPC consists of a strictly alternating sequence of events ("invoice arrived") and functions (or processes) such as "enter invoice" (hence its name). In addition, alternative or concurrent processes can be specified with the help of connectors (XOR, OR, AND). The model either captures existing processes or specifies planned ones, and it can be employed to reengineer inefficient business processes.

Concerning semantics, there is little unanimity. It is given only roughly (in a verbal form) in the original publication (Scheer, 1992). Later there have also been attempts to give EPCs a formal semantics (e.g. Chen and Scheer, 1994; Rump, 1997; Langner, Schneider and Wehler, 1997). But all approaches differ considerably, i.e., they attribute different meanings to the same EPC in many cases. Many of these discrepancies stem from diverging interpretations of the logical connectors, in particular of the (X)OR join. Additional problems are caused by an unclear concept of a start event, by the (non-)existence of a corresponding split and by the strict alternation of events and functions. The following sections will treat these issues in the order: start events, corresponding splits, OR join, XOR join and alternation of events and functions.

Start Events

Keller and Teufel (1997) define a start event as any event without an incoming edge. But there are such events which do not trigger the whole EPC. These so-called external events only require the EPC to wait for something happening outside the process. A start event, however, invokes a new execution of the EPC template. To identify an event as a start event in this sense, it is drawn with two additional vertical lines as suggested in Figure 3.

Corresponding Splits

The semantics of a join often depends on whether or not it has a corresponding split but his split cannot be derived automatically from the structure of the EPC. We have to rely on the modeler to identify it. The modeling tool can only provide him with a list of alternatives (all splits on backwards paths from the join). A pair of split and join are labelled with corresponding flags (see Figure 8). If the corresponding split is of the same type as the join we call it a matching split.

OR join

Assuming the OR join has input paths a and b (like in Figure 6, on the right), the following ambiguities may arise: if it has a matching split the semantics is usually taken to be "wait for the completion of all paths activated by the matching split." If there is no matching split, there are three symmetrical interpretations (i.e., interpretations not distinguishing between a and b) of an OR join (see Figure 6, on the right):

- Wait for the completion of all *activated* paths (called wait-for-all). This is the default semantics because it coincides with that of a matched OR.
- Wait only for the path that is completed first and ignore the second (called first-come).
- Trigger the outgoing path c on each completion of a or b (called every-time).

The semantical shortcomings mentioned above can be remedied by extending the syntax of the connectors. We suggest allowing the modeler to add a comment flag to a connector. This flag can uniquely identify corresponding connectors (see Figure 8), and it may serve to clarify the intended meaning of an unmatched join (see Figure 9). Alternatively, the meaning can also be encoded in the connector symbol itself: a standard OR symbol to denote wait-for-all, a funnel-like trapezoid for first-come and an inverse trapezoid for every-time.

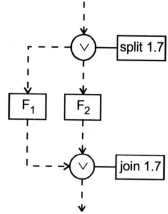

Figure 8: Matching split and join

XOR Join

Similar considerations hold for the XOR join. If it is matched by a split, its semantics is straightforward: it blocks if both paths are activated and it is triggered by the completion of a single activated path. But what happens in the unmatched case? Imagine the OR connector of Figure 6, right, as an XOR join. All feasible interpretations that do not involve blocking (first-come, every-time, wait-for-all) are already covered by the OR and contradict the exclusivity of the XOR: a token from one path may only be accepted if it is sure that no second token will arrive via the other path. But we cannot decide this if the tokens do not come from the same source (at least not statically). Hence we forbid the use of XOR in the unmatched case.

Figure 9: Making the OR join unambiguous

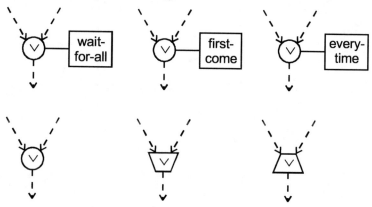

Alternation of Events and Functions

Beyond their semantical shortcomings, EPCs also exhibit some deficiencies originating in the syntactical domain. Empirical studies like Speck (1998) have shown that particularly middle and upper management people consider the strict alternation between events and functions as too restrictive. They find it hard to identify the necessary events on an abstract level of process description.

We suggest dropping this syntactical requirement as dummy events might always be added later if this proves to be necessary. On a conceptual level, there are good reasons to be able to omit events as Figure 10 shows: if "enter invoice" and "effect payment" are performed as one unit (i.e., uninterruptedly)

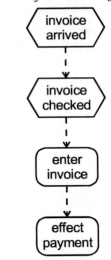

Figure 10: A non-alternating sequence of events and functions

there is no need for an event to trigger the second activity. A similar reasoning leads us to allow two (ore more) consecutive events (see also Figure 10).

If we change the syntax of EPCs accordingly, we arrive at the so-called modified EPCs (or modEPCs). We specify the semantics of modEPCs inductively in terms of Petri nets, more precisely of place/transition nets. Events and functions correspond to places and transitions respectively. The semantics of connectors is given separately for splits and joins. For convenience we assume that all splits have two outputs and all joins have two inputs. Defining the semantics of the splitting connectors is a straightforward matter: the AND puts tokens on both paths, the XOR on only one (see Figure 11).

Likewise the OR split activates the left path (left transition) or the right path (right transition) or both (centre transition). The corresponding Petri net is shown in Figure 12.

The semantics of the joining connectors is given in Figures 13-17. The AND join synchronizes the two paths (see Figure 13). The transition only fires when both paths have been completed. Observe that the AND blocks if only one path has been activated.

As already pointed out, the XOR join requires that the modeler identifies an explicit corresponding split. This might be supported by a modeling tool supplying a list of possible candidates. This split is represented in Figure 14 by the dashed

Figure 11: AND split (left) and XOR split (right)

Figure 12: OR split

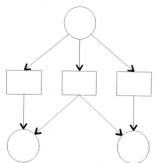

Figure 13: AND join

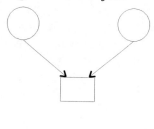

Figure 15: OR join (every-time)

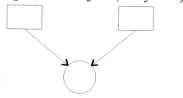

Figure 14: XOR join

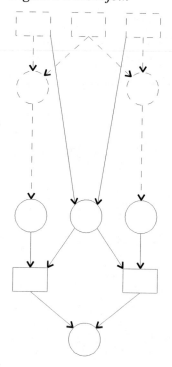

Figure 16: OR join (first-come)

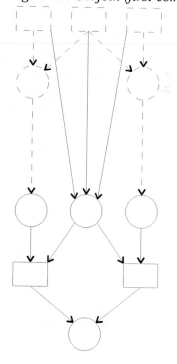

places and transitions. Left as it stands, it denotes an OR split. Omitting the centre transition (and its outgoing arcs) yields an XOR split. Doing the same with the left and right transitions instead leaves an AND split. Notice that the latter implies that the join always blocks.

Figure 17: OR join (wait-for-all and matched OR)

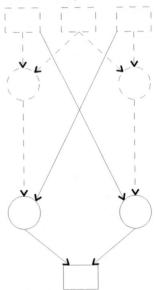

Figures 15-17 treat the different interpretations of the OR join. The simplest net is that for the every-time mode (see Figure 15). It just passes on every token it receives. So if both incoming paths have been triggered, the process following the join is executed twice.

For the first-come join, we need a corresponding split that puts a token on the center place to ensure that the join cannot fire twice (see Figure 16). Alternatively the token might be put there during start-up.

The wait-for-all join needs a corresponding split, too, because only a common source of tokens for both inputs can "tell" the join whether to wait for a second token or not. If not it is immediately put there by the split (see Figure 17). The same semantics is used for a matching OR split.

THE EVENT-DRIVEN METHOD CHAIN

After having effected all the modifications suggested in the previous section, the resulting modEPCs can be used as a process model for application development because a unique and formal interpretation can now be given for any EPC, e.g., in the form of a Petri net. Hence modEPCs can be understood unambiguously by the protagonists of the design phase. This leads to less mistakes in the design model and less backtracking from design to analysis, thus fulfilling the requirements of faster software development and phase integration.

Figure 18: General syntax of an EMC

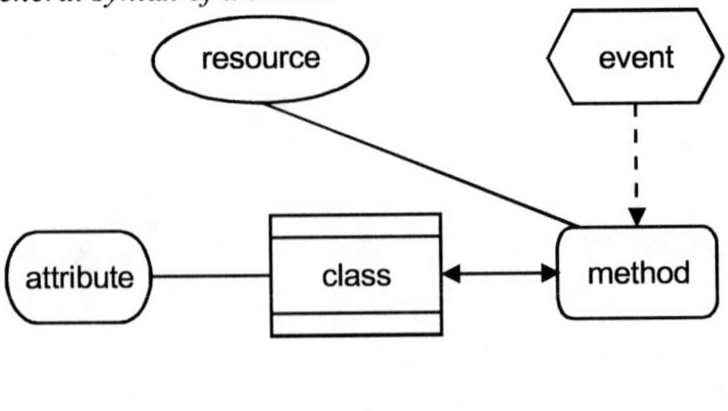

If we put together modEPCs (process focus), classes with their attributes (structural focus) and the resources (resource focus), we arrive at the EMC. Its syntax is shown in Figure 18.

The function of a modEPC is now performed by some object and hence called the service (or method) provided by this object. Apart from this, the process part of an EMC, consisting of events, methods, connectors and control flow arcs (dashed arrows), follows exactly the syntax of modEPCs. The object classes involved in providing the service are linked via a double-headed, solid arrow. A class can have attached to it a list of attributes. Classes are also called the internal resources required by a service because they form an integral part of the information system. An external resource is denoted by an oval. It is connected via a solid line to the method requiring it.

Now, classifying objects into classes sharing common attributes and methods is an important object-oriented feature. Together with the characteristics provided by the MEMO-OML (Frank, 1998), our approach fulfils all requirements of object-orientation. But how does EMC work in our example setting?

Figure 19 shows a part of the EMC for the order processing within the Web application outlined earlier. We assume that the process is fully automated, i.e., it requires no external resources. Upon the arrival of an order, it has to be entered into the system. This service is provided by the class order, but it involves also the class customer because the respective customer has to be recorded in the order. Note: the fact that the service enter order is provided by order and not by customer is not represented in the EMC. Although it would have been possible to distinguish between providing and otherwise involved classes by employing different arrows, we decided against this option because during

Figure 19: A part of the EMC for the example Web application

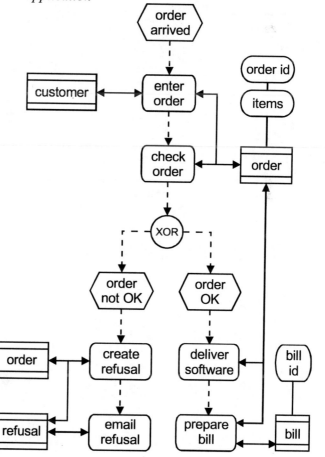

process analysis, the modeler is primarily concerned with conceptual issues such as "who has to do with a service?" and not with the exact role a class plays in performing the service. But the latter information, more precisely the assignment of services to classes, is vital for the following design phase and hence should be expressed in the object model (see Figure 20), i.e., while we are still in the analysis phase. According to the EMC, the attributes of order are order id (e.g., a number) and items (a list of ordered items and quantities). These attributes also constitute the skeleton of the respective class definition in the object model (see Figure 20).

After entering the order, it is checked for validity. The outcome of this check is represented by the occurrence of either the event "order OK" or the event "order not OK." The XOR split denotes that these events are mutually exclusive. In the case of an invalid order, a refusal of the order is generated and sent via e-mail. The items of a valid order, i.e., the software packages ordered by the customer, are delivered (e.g., via ftp) and the bill is prepared. After this, further processing may occur. Note that no attributes are specified for the class refusal. The reason might be that the modeler could not think of appropriate attributes and hence left this to the later stage of developing the object model.

On the basis of this EMC, an initial object model can be specified without further thinking: it simply consists of all classes and their respective attributes as found in the EMC. After this, the following steps yield a complete object model:

Figure 20: Object model (structural focus) for the example (in MEMO-OML)

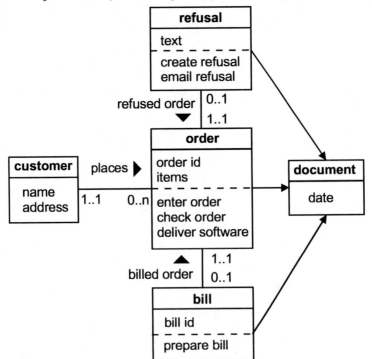

1. *Assigning services to objects*: From the classes involved in a service, the one providing it has to be selected. There the service is recorded.
2. *Finding missing attributes*: Each class is thoroughly examined to check whether attributes have been forgotten, e.g., because they are not necessary in the context of the current EMC. This step is best performed after all EMCs for the application lie before us.
3. *Identifying potentials for generalization*: Classes sharing common attributes or services are potential candidates for generalization inheriting these attributes from a common super-class.
4. *Establishing associations between classes*: If more than one class is involved in providing a service, there is usually an association between the involved classes.

Starting with the initial object model for the EMC of Figure 19, we assign the services to classes as indicated in Figure 20. The EMC gave no attributes for refusal. Looking at actual orders, bills and refusals stored in our file cabinet, we find that a refusal contains some explanatory text and that all letters carry a date. We update the classes accordingly (Step 2), and we generalize them to the super-class document with attribute date (Step 3). In the last step, we discover that customer and order are involved in enter order, which leads us to establish an association place between them, where a customer can place arbitrarily many orders (0..n) but an order is placed by exactly one customer (1..1). The black triangle indicates the reading direction: customer places order. In a similar way, bill and refusal are connected to order.

Please observe that the redundancy of having some of the information present in both EMC and object model (e.g., classes, attributes and services) helps to check inter-model consistency and thus serves model integration.

EVALUATION OF EMC

We conducted a student experiment in the course of an MIS class on process modeling. The objective of this experiment was to compare the quality of information systems built with the help of conventional EPCs and EPCs with the modified syntax. The class consisted of 20 students divided into two groups A and B. A group had five teams of two students. The experiment proceeded in three phases of 90 minutes each:

Phase 1: Each team had the task to model a core process of a hotel such as reservation, check-in, check-out and purchase. Group A used conventional EPCs, Group B the modified syntax. A verbal specification of the respective process was given: "To process an invoice it has to be checked, entered, paid and perhaps claimed. The check involves the ordered quantities, quality and the like. Payment is only effected after a positive check" etc. The specification was incomplete and imprecise to resemble a 'real' one. It left enough room for interpretation and gave only a partial order on the events and functions. Consequently, no two EPCs delivered were the same.

Phase 2: Each team "implemented" its own model. As a target language Petri nets were chosen to avoid the intricacies of programming languages. The formality of Petri nets was sufficient to achieve the goal of this phase: to remove any ambiguity present in the EPC and to make explicit the information present in both the model and the modeler's head.

Phase 3: Each team implemented a model of another team, a model of a process different from the one it designed in Phase 1 to avoid an influence of the own ideas on the interpretation of the other team's model. Again the result is a Petri net. The goal of this phase is to make explicit only the information present in the model.

From this follows that the difference between the two Petri nets for a model consists of the information added by the respective implementation team and not present in the model. The inverse measure, the congruence of the two nets, therefore represents the percentage of information contributed by the model: the higher the congruence, the clearer the model. To measure the congruence we proceeded as follows:

First we determined the node congruence by counting the coinciding nodes in both models, i.e., nodes labeled with the same event or function, and relating this to the total number of nodes in both nets. Then we computed the edge congruence for the subset of coinciding nodes in the same way. The overall congruence is the product of the node and edge congruencies.

- node congruence = 2 ´ coinciding nodes/node total
- edge congruence = 2 ´ coinciding edges/edge total
- congruence = node congruence ´ edge congruence

For example, if we have two Petri nets, one with 50 and the other with 60 nodes, and the nets share 33 nodes, we get a node congruence of 2 ´ 33 (the shared nodes are present in both nets) divided by 110, i.e., 60%. If we further assume that 75% of the edges between the 33 shared nodes agree, the overall congruence is 45%. Figure 21 shows the overall congruence of the two nets for each EPC model of the experiment.

Figure 21: Net congruences for conventional and modified EPCs

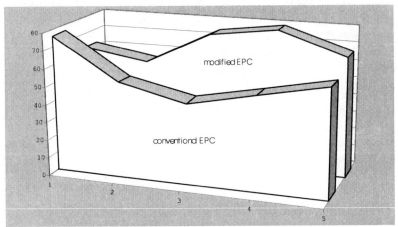

The results indicate that in general a higher congruence can be achieved on the basis of the modified EPCs. The only exception was delivered by Team 1 of Group A. Although using the conventional, more ambiguous EPC, they achieved a congruence of 76.2%, a value well above the average and the second best score of all teams. When looking into the reasons for this exceptional result, we found that the corresponding team drew a very simple EPC consisting of only 37 nodes (the others were between 100 and 200).

All in all the experiment allows the (cautious) conclusion that the suggested modifications lead to fewer misinterpretations of the model thus improving the agreement between model and implementation. Hence they facilitate a smooth transition from the analysis phase to later phases, speeding up the automation of business processes. We are currently planning a field study to verify these results in a practical setting of larger dimensions.

CONCLUSION AND FUTURE TRENDS

EMCs provide a way of integrated analysis of the major aspects of an information system: its structure, its processes and the required resources. Because the underlying paradigm is object-oriented, it enables a seamless transition to object-oriented design and implementation necessary for the development of Web-based applications. This is further supported by the unambiguous process semantics of EMCs. In addition, we assume that users already familiar with EPCs will experience few problems in handling EMCs because they resemble each other closely. The process-driven identification of objects helps modelers with less expertise in object-oriented design to create a complete object model, a task that is both highly abstract and challenging even for 'OO gurus.' Put together, these features facilitate an efficient development of Web-based applications.

But nevertheless, substantial work remains to be done especially concerning the still blank spots in the MEMO matrix. First of all, we need a language to describe goals to be achieved by the information system, the organization and the company as a whole. More important still, the achievement of the IS goals must be reflected in the respective IS models, i.e., the defined goals should somehow guide the development of these models in a goal-achieving direction.

Some preliminary work regarding the strategy and organization levels has been done already, in particular meta-models for value chains (SPM) and organizational charts (OSM). However, the inter-level integration remains to be specified. Syntactical integration only requires some kind of common terminology. It can be established by creating a small meta-meta model in the terms of which the meta-models for all languages are defined. Semantical integration, on the other hand, is harder to achieve. A possible approach is the object-oriented reconstruction of all models in MEMO-OML.

REFERENCES

Chen, R. and Scheer, A. W. (1994). *Modelierung von Prozessketten mittels Petri-Netz-Theorie (Modeling of Process Chains with the Help of Petri Net Theory)*. IWi-Hefte, 107. Saarbrücken, Germany: University of Saarbrücken, Institute of IS Research.

Frank, U. (1997). *Enriching Object-Oriented Methods with Domain-Specific Knowledge: Outline of a Method for Enterprise Modeling*. Arbeitsberichte des Instituts für Wirtschaftsinformatik, 4. Koblenz, Germany: University Koblenz-Landau, Institute of Business Informatics.

Frank, U. (1998). *The Memo Object Modeling Language (MEMO-OML)*. Arbeitsberichte des Instituts für Wirtschaftsinformatik, 10. Koblenz, Germany: University Koblenz-Landau, Institute of Business Informatics.

Keller, G. and Teufel, T. (1997). *SAP R/3 prozessorientiert anwenden Iteratives Prozess Prototyping zur Bildung von Wertschöpfungsketten (The process-oriented use of SAP R/3–Iterative process prototyping for building value chains)*. Bonn, Germany: Addison-Wesley.

Langner, P., Schneider, C. and Wehler, J. (1997). Prozessmodelierung mit ereignis-gesteuerten prozessketten (EPKs) und Petri-Netzen (Process modeling with event-driven process chains (EPCs) and Petri nets). *Wirtschaftsinformatik, 39*, 479–489.

Porter, M. E. (1985). *Competitive Advantage: Creating and Sustaining Superior Performance*. New York: Simon & Schuster.

Rump, F. (1997). Erreichbarkeitsgraphbasierte analyse ereignisgesteuerter prozessketten (Analysis of event-driven process chains based on reachability graphs). *Technische Berichte*, April. Oldenburg, Germany: University Oldenburg, OFFIS Institute.

Scheer, A. W. (1992). *Architektur Integrierter Informationssysteme (Architecture of Integrated Information Systems)*. Berlin, Germany: Springer.

Speck, M. (1998). Akzeptanz und operationalität von EPK in der modelierungs-praxis–ein erfahrungsbericht aus einem reengineering-projekt (Acceptance and operational effectiveness of EPC in modeling practice–An experience report from a reengineering project). Talk presented at the meeting of the *Workgroup on Formalization of EPC*. Münster, Germany, March. Available on the World Wide Web: http://www-is.informatik.uni-oldenburg.de/~epk/treffen_170398/speck.ps. Accessed August 23, 200.

Chapter III

Towards a Methodology for the Development of Web-Based Systems: Models, Methods and Activities for the Conceptual Design of Large Web-Based Information Systems

Bernhard Strauch and Robert Winter
University of St. Gallen, Switzerland

E-commerce is changing the nature of business. To support 'buying and selling over digital media' for private and corporate Web users, companies need not only appropriate transaction systems, but also new information systems. While the systems development challenge for transaction systems is mostly restricted to separating access channel functionality from business transactions processing and developing systems support for new access channels, systems development needs for information systems are much more challenging since different media and different information source systems have to be integrated, novel forms navigation has to be supported and information objects become more complex and more volatile.

Based on a review of related work from hypertext design, Web site/intranet design and database-oriented CASE environments, this chapter tries to identify the "essence" of a Web-based information system and proposes an adequate conceptual model. The model is intended to capture not only hierarchical document structure and hypertext semantics, but also dynamic page generation from databases and various approaches to explicit and implicit navigation. It becomes evident that Web-based information systems can be regarded as supersets of traditional information systems, thereby requiring conceptual modeling to include various additional features. The proposed model comprises several classes of information objects, various types of associations, activities for the design and quality checks. For illustration purposes, the model is applied to an existing Web-based information system. Current Web-based information system development tools are analyzed with regard to the extent to which conceptual Web-based information system modeling is supported.

INTRODUCTION

E-commerce is changing the nature of business. To support 'buying and selling over digital media' (Kalakota & Robinson, 1999) for private and corporate Web users, companies need not only appropriate transaction systems, but also new information systems. The systems development challenge for transaction systems is mostly restricted to separating access channel functionality from business transactions processing and developing systems support for new access channels (e.g., PC via HTTP, mobile phone via WAP, POS terminal via TCP/IP). In contrast, systems development needs for information systems are much more challenging since different media and different information source systems have to be integrated, novel forms navigation has to be supported, and information objects become more complex and more volatile.

Early systems development was dominated by using authoring tools ('editors') to manually edit procedural program code. As a consequence, handwritten code mixing up data usage and functional aspects was difficult to maintain (Martin, 1992). Besides expensive quality control and communication problems among developers, the resulting code suffered from various implementation dependencies, thereby forcing developers to re-do large portions of the development process when technical details (e.g., file structures, access paths) change. A rather similar approach can be observed for early development of Web-based information systems (Rosenfeld & Morville, 1998). By using HTML authoring tools, complex code is created that not only mixes up appearance and contents, but also depends widely on implementation details. Moreover, the utilization of different authoring tools complicates communication between developers. As an example, the following problems usually occur with regard to navigation when different Web-based information systems have to be integrated:

- Navigation is interpreted and implemented in different ways depending on the authoring tool in use. Different tools use identical terms for different concepts or different terms for identical concepts.
- Navigation is not based on user requirements for optimal access to information objects or associations between information objects (e.g., Morville & Rosenfeld, 1999; Richmond, 1999). Instead, implementation details like various frame implementations dominate design.
- As a consequence, similar navigational concepts are implemented (and specified) in different ways so that explicit integration efforts are necessary to identify common structures and implement them consistently.

In order to enable efficient communication between developers and to provide a stable foundation for adopting new technologies, conceptual modeling of Web-

Figure 1: Classes of systems

	Focus on Processing of Business Transactions	Focus on Informational Processes
Traditional Technologies (Host; Client/Server via proprietary protocols)	Traditional Transaction Systems	Traditional Information Systems
Internet Technology (Client/Server via HTTP)	Web-Based Transaction Systems	Web-Based Information Systems

based information systems is essential. We understand Web-based information systems as server components of distributed applications which use the HTTP protocol to exchange data between servers and clients ('browsers'). By this definition, the principal problem of Web-based information system development becomes apparent: although conceptual modeling should be independent of all technical and application-dependent details, even the relevant class of application components is defined by technical attributes (HTTP protocol, server functionality) instead of conceptual differences (see Figure 1).

Traditional Information Systems vs. Web-Based Information Systems

From a business perspective, Web-based systems can be classified as follows (Kaiser, 2000):

- **Business platform:** For e-conomy business models like electronic auctions or process portals, certain Web-based systems become the backbone of their operations.
- **Sales and purchase channel:** For traditional business models like mail-order resellers, banks, insurance companies or producing industries, certain Web-based systems are used to support an additional sales and/or purchasing channel (e-commerce), while other channels and basic operations are supported by traditional systems.
- **Self-service:** In any business, certain Web-based systems can be deployed internally to decentralize selected support processes (e.g., procurement, management of personnel data).
- **Information management:** In any business, certain Web-based systems support the creation, integration, analysis and distribution of information, particularly for supporting management processes.

While the first three classes focus on the processing of business transactions, the last class characterizes Web-based information systems. To what extent do Web-based information systems conceptually differ from traditional information systems? While traditional information systems focus on querying, reporting and analyzing structured data related to business transactions, Web-based information systems go beyond this functionality by integrating different media for knowledge representation and by hypertext functionality, thereby supporting not only the creation, integration, analysis and distribution of structured information related to business transactions, but also the storage and transfer of knowledge. While Web-based transaction systems do not conceptually differ from respective traditional systems, Web-based information systems allow for more advanced forms of information management than traditional information systems can (Kaiser, 2000). As a consequence, not only organizational, functional and data views of business processes have to be specified during conceptual design of Web-based information systems. Moreover, complex knowledge components and their associations must be specified in order to enable flexible access and efficient navigation.

As an example, the data view of traditional information systems development and Web-based information systems development is compared: A traditional data model comprises:

- types of structured information objects (e.g., order, customer, product);
- certain types of relationships between information object types (e.g., generalization dependencies, references = existential dependencies);
- consistency constraints valid for all instances of a certain information object type; and
- eventually attributes of information object types.
  All modeling is done on a type level.

Of course, all of these element types can be found in the data model of a Web-based information system. But a Web-based information system representing complex knowledge may also comprise the following additional element types:

- one-of-a-kind information objects (i.e., single object instances not belonging to any object type, e.g., a mission statement);
- unstructured information objects (e.g., documents); and
- additional types of associations between information objects (e.g., "part-of" relationships used for structuring a knowledge domain and "association" relationships used for navigation within a knowledge domain).

Related Work and Overview

While early work on the development of Web-based information systems concentrates on navigational, text-related issues (e.g. Diaz, Isakowitz, Maiorana & Gilabert, 1997), recent work also covers interface design and overall site design (e.g. Lyardet, Mercerat & Miaton, 1999; Lynch & Horton, 1999). In the following, navigational and text-related work as well as work on hypermedia design is discussed first. After that, more holistic approaches to the conceptual design of Web-based information systems are discussed.

Conceptual Modeling of Hypertext/Hypermedia Systems

Based on hypertext design (e.g., Isakowitz, Stohr & Balasubramanian, 1995), the design of Web-based information systems has been addressed since the mid-90ies, e.g., the HYDESIGN model (Marmann & Schlageter, 1992) proposes classes of (hypermedia) objects comprising 'atomic nodes,' 'SBL nodes,' and links between those nodes. Atomic nodes inherit general class properties and represent 'content.' SBL (Structure Behavior Locality) nodes represent additional information: Structure defines how nodes and links can be connected, behavior defines the dynamics of nodes and links, and locality defines a 'local' environment, i.e., a sub-module of the hypermedia network. By this approach, important conceptual constructs like navigation paths or aggregate objects (=sub-networks) are introduced into hypermedia design. When hypermedia design approaches (e.g. De Bra & Houben, 1992; Diaz et al., 1997; Isakowitz et al., 1995; Marmann & Schlageter, 1992) are used for conceptual modeling of Web-based information systems, however, important aspects like common standards of Web navigation, interface design, conceptually different classes of links and overall site design are not taken into account. Since many problems addressed by hypermedia design like 'disorientation' or 'cognitive overhead' are also prevailing in large Web-based information systems, however, the basic approach of a hierarchical, recursive model of node classes and link classes is useful for Web-based information system design. But in addition to static links between particular documents, common standards of Web navigation imply dynamic links (Chen, 1997).

HDM (Hypertext Design Model), a conceptual model for hypermedia applications, separates information modeling, navigational modeling and presentation modeling. Information objects are connected by semantic links, while the internal structures of information objects are represented by structural links between components (Garzotto, Paolini & Schwabe, 1993).

From both approaches, important features of information modeling and site design can be adapted, while navigational issues, unstructured information objects and 'one-of-a-kind' information objects need to be complemented.

Holistic Approaches to Web Site and Intranet Design

ARANEUS (Atzeni, Mecca & Merialdo, 2000) separates database design and hypertext design, but neglects navigational issues in favor of information modeling. Although information objects are represented as networks of components, the central role of database design in ARANEUS imposes numerous restrictions for unstructured information objects and navigational design.

W3DT (initially called SHDT) was proposed as an early approach (and tool) for conceptual Web-based information system design (Bichler & Nusser, 1996; W3DT-Team, 1997). In W3DT, the development process comprises seven steps, guiding the designer from requirements analysis to implementation of the Web-based information system. For the first phase (requirements analysis), a collection of methods to determine user requirements is provided. The design phase is divided into information structuring, navigational design, organizational design and interface design. Information structuring and navigational design is understood as an iterative mental process where a large knowledge domain has to be organized and structured into information objects, which are then linked and evaluated. Organizational design assigns information on maintenance and organizational integration to the information objects. When the design phase is completed, the information objects are implemented by HTML pages and gateway scripts, and the access structures of the model are implemented by links within the WWW site.

The W3DT research group has shown that it is possible to capture the navigational structure of real-world Web-based information systems. In W3DT's meta-model, a Web-based information system is composed of pages, links and layouts. While layout is not further specified, two different types of links and four different types of pages are differentiated. This simple classification, however, is not sufficient to capture the diversity of current HTML pages. Moreover, it is not differentiated between page templates and page contents.

A more holistic and advanced approach has been developed by Kaiser (2000). Although intended as a methodology for the conceptual design of intranets, his results are also applicable to the conceptual design of Web-based information systems. Being the most important part of the methodology, the specification of a Web-based information system comprises not only the modeling of the information structure (represented by an entity-relationship schema), but also the modeling of navigational aspects (represented by a W3DT schema).

Summing up, most features of conceptual design of Web-based information objects have already been proposed in hypertext design, intranet design or database design. A holistic approach that covers all systems aspects and information object classes, however, is lacking.

Overview

Following this introduction, we try to identify the 'essence' (McMenamin & Palmer, 1984), i.e., the implementation independent specification, of a complex Web-based information system. In the third section, an appropriate conceptual model is proposed that captures not only hierarchical document structure and hypertext semantics, but also allows for an implementation by dynamical page generation from databases and using various approaches to explicit and implicit navigation. For illustration purposes, the model is then applied to an existing Web-based information system, and current Web-based information system development tools are analyzed with regard to the extent to which conceptual Web-based information system modeling is supported. The chapter closes with some conclusions.

THE 'ESSENCE' OF A WEB-BASED INFORMATION SYSTEM

The benefits of conceptual modeling result from creating stability: often contents change, but the general page structure remains unchanged. At other occasions, templates change, but contents remain stable. For conceptual modeling of Web-based information systems, therefore, content should be separated from navigational structure, navigational structure should be separated from layout (i.e., general page structure) and layout should be separated from content.

But if all implementation-related specifications are to be neglected, what is then the essence of a Web-based information system? As for traditional applications, organizational, functional and data aspects of business transactions have to be specified. In addition, representation and access aspects of complex information areas have to be specified by means of:

- (structured and non-structured) information objects,
- 'part-of' (i.e., hierarchical) relationships between information objects, and
- 'associative' (i.e., non-hierarchical) relationships between information objects.

Information objects may be one-of-a-kind instances that do not match any type definition, or may belong to some class of information objects. They may be administrated internally (i.e., within the same organizational context as the Web-based information system) or externally. They may be implemented by operating system files, file records, tuples of relational tables or mail accounts.

Hierarchical relationships may be implemented by file system structure, HTML navigation or by applets. Non-hierarchical relationships may be implemented by hyperlinks, mailtos or downloads.

Information objects may be complex, i.e., may comprise several components. As a consequence, we have to represent:

- components of information objects (e.g., character strings, pictures, textual tables), and
- hierarchical relationships between information objects and their components.

Information object components are usually implemented by operating system files or tuples of relational tables. Hierarchical component links may be implemented by physical inclusion, as reference using frame or border techniques, or using style sheets.

Why Should Information Objects and Their Components be Differentiated?

The easiest conceptual interpretation of a Web-based information system is a multi-stage 'assembly' of elementary information objects. We propose, however, to differentiate information objects from their components, thereby introducing an additional representation level.

Information object contents change often. Since conceptual models should provide some basic amount of stability, it is necessary to differentiate a stable and a volatile part in the 'assembly' structure of a Web-based information system. Information objects denote the borderline between the volatile and the stable portion of the network: while their contents change often (which has to be reflected in updating components and/or updating hierarchical component structure), their conceptual representation is stable so that the 'upstream' portion of the Web-based information system remains unchanged.

For example, status, employee assignments, schedule, available documents and other attribute-like properties of a project vary quite often, while its organizational embedding and its links to other projects remain quite stable. As a consequence, project documents should be regarded as information object components, while the project itself should be regarded as an information object.

In systems implementation, the differentiation of information objects from their components is reflected, making the former accessible by hyperlinks, while the latter cannot be separately accessed.

Information object components are the building blocks of every Web-based information system. Information objects can be identified as the simplest information component aggregates that guarantee some degree of stability. Navigation areas are those portions of a Web-based information system which are so tightly coupled that some degree of navigation traffic is to be expected. Web-based information systems are those portions of the World Wide Web whose contents can be updated in some organizational context. The resulting conceptual structure of the World Wide Web can be interpreted as a five-level hierarchy illustrated by Figure 2. The Web-based information system level, the navigation area level and the component level may comprise several sub-levels to reflect organizational responsibilities (Web-based information system level), relationships between information objects (navigation area level), and information object structure (component level).

How Can Relevant Information Objects, Components and Their Relationships be Identified?

This chapter focuses on methods to represent the essence of a Web-based information system. Of course, in order to represent information objects, components and relationships, it is necessary to identify respective real-world objects first. The Object Type Method, a semi-formal approach to identify conceptual structures that is well grounded in linguistic theory, has been summarized in Ortner and Söllner (1989). Following this approach, identifying conceptual structures is achieved by reconstructing terms that professionals use by means of a set of basic construction operators (e.g., inclusion, association, aggregation). For details regarding the Object Type Method, we refer to Ortner and Söllner (1989) and the literature referenced in their paper.

Figure 2: Conceptual WWW hierarchy (Strauch & Winter, 2001)

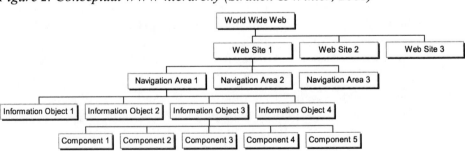

CONCEPTUAL MODEL

Based on the discussion of related work in the first section and the identification of conceptual components of a Web-based information system in the second section, we propose a conceptual model that is intended to cover all relevant components and their relationships, to imply some important quality rules and to be a suitable foundation for an appropriate activity model which is presented in the fourth section.

META-MODEL

The meta-model illustrated in Figure 3 (UML class diagram (UML, 2000)) represents all components of the conceptual model and their relationships. Basically, our meta-model comprises information objects (with several subtypes), components of information objects (with several subtypes) and relationships between information objects (with several subtypes) or between information objects and their components. The components of the conceptual model and an appropriate graphical notation are presented in the following subsections.

Components of Information Objects

Structured Classifiable Components

This class of components represents information that can be regarded as an instance of some generalized class of information with certain attributes. For example, data about a person's publications are structured because every publica-

Figure 3: Meta-model

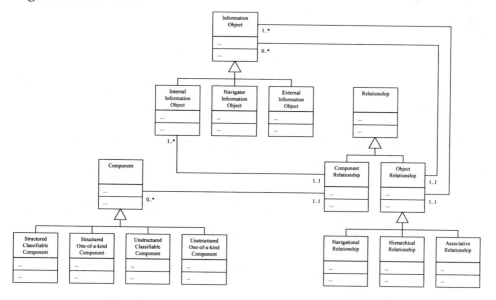

tion has certain attributes (title, year of publication, etc.) and are classifiable because each data is an instance of a common class 'publication.' For structured classifiable components, structure and contents can be separated.

Unstructured Classifiable Components

This class of components represents information that can be regarded as an instance of some generalized class of information, but has no common attributes within that class. For example, job descriptions may not follow some formal structure, but are nevertheless classifiable because each job description is an instance of a common class 'job description.' For unstructured classifiable components, structure cannot be separated from contents.

Structured, One-of-a-Kind Components

This class of components represents information that does not belong to some generalized class of information, but comprises certain attributes. For example, a form is a structured, one-of-a-kind component because every form has certain attributes (layout, boilerplate texts, field names, etc.), but cannot be assigned to some common meaningful class. For structured, one-of-a-kind components, structure and contents can be separated.

Unstructured, One-of-a-Kind Components

This class of components represents information that neither belongs to some generalized class of information nor has certain attributes. For example, a mission statement is an unstructured, one-of-a-kind component because only one such text exists within a Web-based information system, and no general statement structure is available. For unstructured, one-of-a-kind components, structure cannot be separated from contents.

Information Objects

(Internal) Informational Objects

Information objects are the simplest information component aggregates that guarantee some degree of stability. For example, employee homepages are information objects because they are composed from personnel data (name, date of birth, etc.), images, links to organizational units, etc. that frequently change, but do not change as an aggregate as long as the employee is part of the organization.

Navigators

Navigators are application components that allow users to efficiently navigate within some portion of the Web-based information system. In contrast to ordinary information objects, navigators represent informational structure instead of the information itself. However, navigators are composed of several components so that they represent a subclass of information objects.

External Information Objects

External information objects are not part of a Web-based information system, but can be accessed from that Web-based information system, e.g., by hyperlinks. In contrast to (internal) information objects, the structure of external information objects is unknown. At most, some basic, structural information can be generated from the URL extension (HTML, IDC; HTX, ASP, NSF, CGI, etc.).

Relationships

Hierarchical Relationships

Hierarchical relationships represent 'part-of' links between internal information objects. Navigators usually are based on hierarchical relationships. For example, department information and open position information can be linked by a hierarchical relationship.

Associative Relationships

Associative relationships represent associations between information objects that are not related hierarchically or by navigators. For example, open position information and project information can be linked by an associative relationship.

Navigational Relationships

Navigational relationships represent associations between (internal and external) information objects and navigators. In contrast to hierarchical and associative relationships that are used to represent information semantics, navigational relationships represent the application interface and are used to support the browsing process (Morville & Rosenfeld, 1999). For example, department information can be linked to subordinate unit information as well as superior unit information by navigational relationships.

Component Relationships

Component relationships represent the structure of internal information objects. In contrast to hierarchical and associative relationships, component relationships do not imply any hypertext functionality.

Notation

We denote the element of the conceptual model as shown on the following page.

Components of information objects   *Information objects*

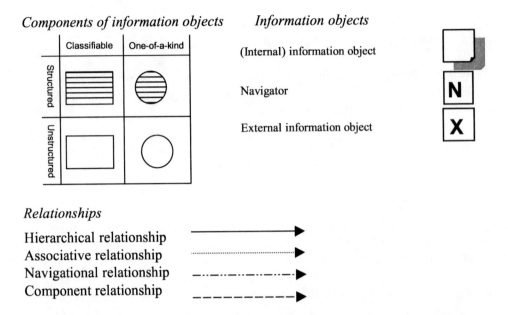

Relationships

Hierarchical relationship

Associative relationship

Navigational relationship

Component relationship

Figure 4 illustrates the application of the proposed model to an existing Web-based information system of a university workgroup. The levels are related to hierarchical relationships within the information objects of the Web-based information system.

Figure 4: Conceptual schema of a Web-based information system (Strauch & Winter, 2001)

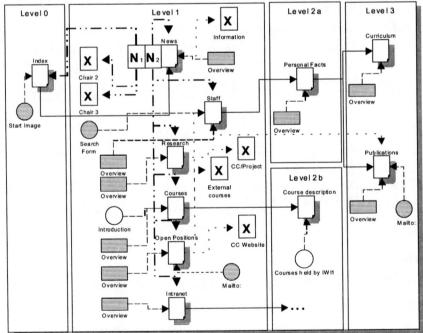

Quality

The proposed conceptual model implies the following quality controls:

Within the Web-based information system:

- All hierarchical relationships must link an internal information object to one or more internal information objects.
- All associative relationships must link an internal information object to one or more internal or external information objects.
- All navigational relationships must link a navigator to one or more internal or external information objects.
- All component relationships must link an internal information object to one or more components.

Within the World Wide Web

- All URLs referenced by associative or navigational relationships must exist.

ACTIVITIES FOR THE CONCEPTUAL DESIGN

For conceptual modeling of a Web-based information system, model elements, graphic notation and quality controls have to be complemented by some basic methodology, i.e., at least by basic activities for the design and a recommendation of a certain sequence of design phases. Based on our experience with Web-based information system design and the discussion of essential Web-based information system elements, we propose the activity sequence described in this section.

Identification of Information Objects

Whether an information representation is an information object or should be regarded as a component of an information object should be decided by analyzing its update behavior: if frequent updates can be expected not only for its contents, but also for its relationships, it should be represented as a component. If updates will mostly be restricted to contents, it may be represented as an information object.

(Re-)Construction of Hierarchical Structure

In contrast to associative relationships, hierarchical relationships create a consistent directed graph of information objects. Based on the hierarchy, levels of the conceptual Web-based information system schema can be identified (see Figure 6). All hierarchical relationships link an information object on level n to one or more information objects on level n+1. Since hierarchical relationships help to structure the knowledge domain to be modeled (i.e., re-constructed), conceptual modeling should start with building hierarchical relationships.

Figure 5: Identification of information objects (Strauch & Winter, 2001)

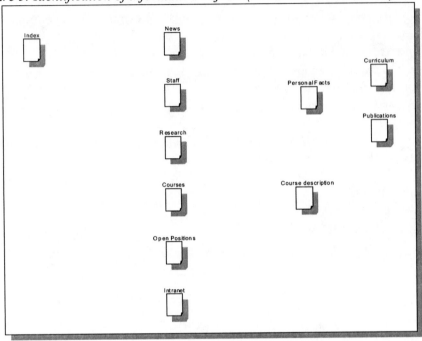

Figure 6: (Re-)Construction of hierarchical structure (Strauch & Winter, 2001)

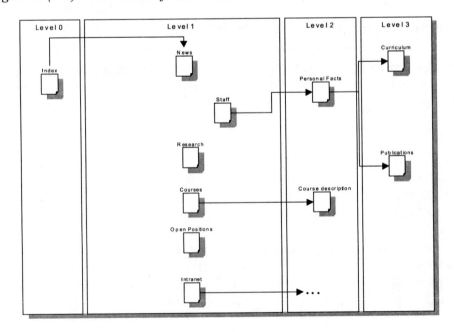

Figure 7: (Re-)Construction of associative structure (Strauch & Winter, 2001)

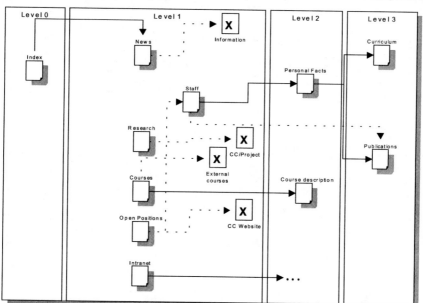

(Re-)Construction of Associative Structure

All semantic links that do not represent "part-of" relationships are represented by associative relationships in the next step. Associative relationships are bound to certain levels of the schema. External information objects are always linked to internal information objects by associative relationships. They should be modeled on the same schema level as the internal information objects they are linked to.

Design of Navigators

Although usually being based on hierarchical or associative relationships, navigators and navigational relationships represented a separate semantic concept. While the navigator itself represents application interface properties, navigational relationships represent its behavior. Using navigators, application users can easily navigate in a knowledge domain without having to follow hierarchical or associative relationships.

One or more navigators can be directly linked to an information object. If more than one navigator is linked to an information object, an index number is introduced. A navigator is linked to that information object whose browsing shall initially create the navigation menu. A navigator is 'inherited' by a set of other information objects on the respective schema level and on the next schema level. By separating schema levels according to information object sets related to navigators, elements of complex Web-based information system schemas can be arranged.

Figure 8: Design of navigators (Strauch & Winter, 2001)

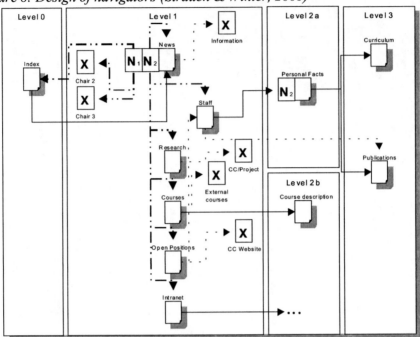

Representation of Components

Component relationships and information object components can be represented either in the schema (see Figure 4) or, for large schemas or complex information objects, in a sub-schema for the respective information object. Since relationships (including navigational relationships) are defined between information objects only, modifications of component structure do not affect the overall schema. Components could be reused by more than one information object.

TOOL SUPPORT

In this section, the state-of-the-art of tool support for the development of Web-based information systems is analyzed. There are two classes of tools available: on the one hand, WWW authoring tools could be used to design not only small sets of Web pages, but also complex Web-based information systems. On the other hand, traditional CASE toolsets could be used to design Web-based information systems as a special implementation of traditional, client/server information systems.

WWW Authoring Tools

In our opinion, the most advanced tools in this regard are Microsoft's Frontpage 2000, Microsoft's Visual Interdev and Macromedia's Dreamweaver. Most other tools are just HTML coding tools and provide no support for conceptual modeling at all.

Microsoft FrontPage 2000

Frontpage 2000 provides two types of information objects which are internal information objects and external information objects. Internal information objects are directly corresponding to HTML files stored on the Web server. Component structure cannot be modeled. Navigators, however, are automatically generated. But these structures depend on Frontpage's navigational model and properties that have to be coded (no conceptual representation). For each Web-based information system, the designer has to decide globally whether borders should appear or not.

Hierarchical relationships between information objects can be modeled as 'navigational model' in Frontpage 2000 (see Figure 9). Associative relationships, however, as well as navigational relationships in our definition and component relationships are unknown. When updating hierarchical relationships, deletions of entire sub-trees (including the respective information objects) may occur when a single relationship is deleted.

Summing up, just a few basic concepts of conceptual Web-based information systems design are currently supported by Frontpage 2000. It is necessary to extensively re-code Web-based information systems generated by Frontpage 2000 to allow for features like associative links, component reuse, non-standard navigators, etc. Obviously, respective Web-based information systems are not really based on a stable conceptual schema so that technical innovation will require significant development efforts.

Figure 9: Web-based information system schema in Frontpage 2000 (Strauch & Winter, 2001)

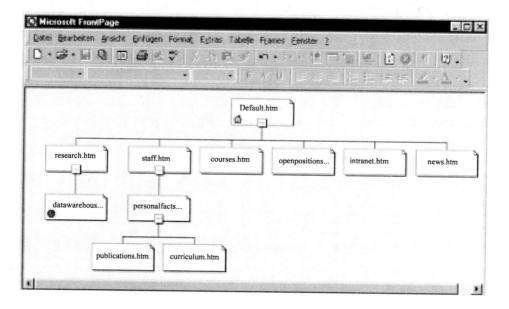

Microsoft Visual Interdev 6.0

Visual Interdev is intended for professional developers. It provides the same kind of navigational model as Frontpage 2000 and has the same limitations. Therefore, the same conclusions can be drawn.

Macromedia Dreamweaver 3.0

In Dreamweaver's conceptual model, two classes of information objects exist. On the one hand, there are information objects which represent a physical HTML file on the Web server. On the other hand, there are information objects like external links, mailto tags and images. To some extent, these two classes correspond to information objects (files) and components (links, images) in our model (see Figure 10). However, the latter group of objects is not differentiated so that meaningful quality checks or activities for the design cannot be applied.

Between information objects, hierarchical relationships as well as associative relationships can be modeled. However, Dreamweaver does not provide a different notation for these two classes of relationships. Although associative links can be modeled, Web-based information systems can only be displayed as expandable trees (based on hierarchical relationships) and not as networks that also include associative relationships.

Dreamweaver does not support the design of navigators (and navigational relationships). The generator directly creates HTML hyperlinks from associative relationships.

Other Web Design Tools

Adobe PageMill 2.0 for Windows is basically an HTML editor with WYSIWIG capabilities, i.e., there are no real modeling features. However, the product over-

Figure 10: Web-based information system schema in Dreamweaver 3.0 (Strauch & Winter, 2001)

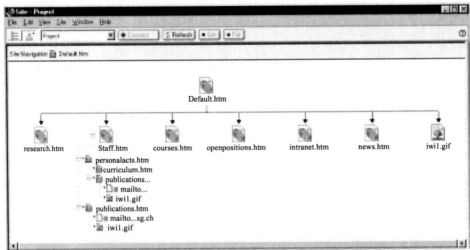

view of SiteMill for Macintosh (ADOBE SYSTEMS Inc., 1997) claims that the tool has some modeling features like a 'site view' and an 'external reference view.'

Aimtech's Jamba is a generator for Web pages that includes multimedia objects implemented by Java code. Applets can be generated without any knowledge of the Java syntax by using a graphical interface for the assembly of multimedia objects to pages. Generated applications are stored in three different files:

- The project file (extension .jmb) comprises all information provided by the developer.
- The HTML file (extension .html) comprises all applets and can be processed by Internet browsers.
- The text file (extension .jtf) comprises information on interactive multimedia objects and is accessed by the HTML file.

During page development, an object viewer can be used to simulate Web pages without having to use a browser. As building blocks for multimedia pages, a large number of buttons, graphics, menus, text fields and links are provided. Jamba can be regarded as a comfortable Web page editor with Java generation capabilities and a large number of reusable components. It is, however, restricted to the development of single pages (not complete sites) without extended procedural features and without support for requirements specification, analysis or design.

CASE Toolsets

As an example for advanced, state-of-the-art CASE toolsets, Oracle's Designer is regarded. To implement a conceptual design, Designer offers a Web site generator in addition to client/server generators for Oracle's 4GLs, for Visual Basic, for C++ and others. Based on a long tradition of database design, structured analysis and more recently integrated process modeling, CASE toolsets like Designer offer an adaptable application development repository, advanced graphical design tools, simulation capabilities, workgroup support, a scalable environment, powerful generators, open interfaces to other development tools, lots of reports and quality checking tools, lots of utilities, etc. Various systems views can be (more or less) concurrently developed by deploying different design tools, and the information systems lifecycle can be completely covered by using requirements specification tools, systems design tools, implementation tools, and maintenance/reverse engineering tools. In Figure 12, the data view (in contrast to the display view) of a module subtree in systems design is illustrated. Data links and component structure are represented in that schema, while navigational links (that are widely based on data links) are represented in the display view of that module subtree.

In most cases, advanced CASE toolsets are built around a relational database. As a consequence, the concept is more or less restricted to structured information objects: while form-and-menu-based information systems of any complexity can be developed very efficiently, non-trivial navigational structures, documents/images and one-of-a-kind information objects cannot be covered effectively.

Figure 11: Module data view of information system schema in Designer

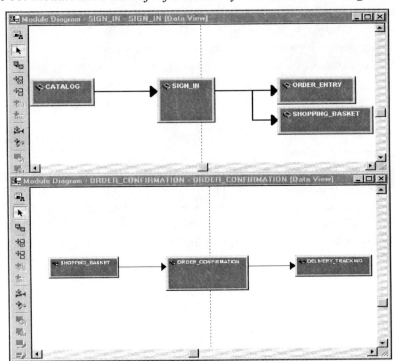

CONCLUSIONS

Based on a short discussion of related work and an analysis of the essence of a Web-based information system, a conceptual model has been proposed that combines advantageous conceptual modeling features of several approaches to hypermedia design, intranet design and Web site design. Application to a real-life example shows that useful quality checks can be specified, complex navigational constructs and information object structures can be designed, and schema elements can be usefully arranged based on the proposed model. An analysis of both WWW authoring tools and CASE toolsets, however, shows that neither tool type is currently able to support such a rich conceptual model. While WWW authoring tools are generally better in designing the special features of Web sites (e.g., navigation), CASE toolsets are better in supporting large schemas, providing workgroup support and supporting several views and phases of systems development.

In order to prevent current Web-based information system development to create the legacy systems of the future, it is necessary to base implemented systems on a stable conceptual foundation. To provide a dependable specification for Web design software vendors, approaches to conceptual modeling from scientists and practitioners have to be integrated, thereby taking into account findings from hypertext design as well as experience from CASE practice. Hopefully, specific discussion of Web-based information system modeling issues will help such specifications to emerge.

REFERENCES

ADOBE SYSTEMS Inc. (1997). *Adobe PageMill Details-SiteMill for Macintosh*. Available on the World Wide Web at: http://www.adobe.com/ prodindex/ pagemill/siteben.html. Accessed November 27, 1997.

Atzeni, P., Mecca, G. and Merialdo, P. (2000). *Design and Maintenance of Data-Intensive Web Sites*. Available on the World Wide Web at: http://www.dia.uniroma3.it/Araneus/publications/rt25-97.zip. Accessed August 11, 2000.

Bichler, M. and Nusser, S. (1996). SHDT-The strucured way of developing WWW sites. In Dias Coelho, J. (Ed.), *Proceedings of the 4th European Conference on Information Systems*, 1093-1101.

Chen, C. (1997). Structuring and visualising the WWW by generalized similarity analysis. In N.A., *Proceedings of the 8th ACM Conference on Hypertext HYPERTEXT'97*, 177-186.

De Bra, P. and Houben, G. J. (1992). An extensible data model for hyperdocuments. In N.A., *Proceedings of the ACM Conference on Hypertext ECHT'92*, 222-231.

Diaz, A., Iskowitz, T., Maiorana, V. and Gilabert, G. (1997). *RMC: A Tool To Design WWW Applications*. Available on the World Wide Web at: http://www.stern.nyu.edu/~tisakowi/ papers/www-95/rmcase/187.html. Accessed November 27, 1997.

Garzotto, F., Paolini, P. and Schwabe, D. (1993). HDM-A model-based approach to hypertext application design. *Transactions on Information Systems*, 11, 1-26.

Isakowitz, T., Stohr, E. A. and Balasubramanian, P. (1995). RMM: A methodology for structured hypertext design. *Communications of the ACM*, 38, 34-44.

Kaiser, T. (2000). Methode zur konzeption von intranets. (Method for the conceptual design of intranets). *Doctoral Dissertation*, University of St.Gallen, Switzerland.

Kalakota, R. and Robinson, M. (1999). *E-Business: Roadmap for Success*. Boston: Addison-Wesley.

Lyardet, F. D., Mercerat, B. and Miaton, L. (1999). *Putting Hypermedia Patterns to Work: A Case Study*. Available on the World Wide Web at: http://pelican.info.unlp.edu.ar/ht992/patternsAtWork.html. Accessed May 10, 1999.

Lynch, P. J. and Horton, S. (1999). *Web Style Guide: Basic Design Principles for Creating Web Sites*. Available on the World Wide Web at: http://info.med.yale.edu/caim/manual/contents.html. Accessed May 10, 1999.

Marmann, M. and Schlageter, G. (1992). Towards a better support for hypermedia structuring: The hydesign model. In N.A., *Proceedings of the ACM Conference on Hypertext ECHT'92*, 232-241.

Martin, J. (1992). *Application Development Without Programmers*. Englewood Cliffs, NJ: Prentice-Hall.

McMenamin, S. M. and Palmer, J. F. (1984). *Essential Systems Analysis*. New York: Yourdon Inc.

Morville, P. and Rosenfeld, L. (1999). *Designing Navigation Systems*. Available on the World Wide Web at: http://Webreview.com/wr/pub/98/02/20/arch/index.html. Accessed April 28, 1999.

Ortner, E. and Söllner, B. (1989). Semantische datenmodellierung nach der objekttypenmethode (Conceptual data modeling using the object type method). *Informatik-Spektrum*, 12, 31-48.

Richmond, A. (1999). *Navigation Architecture of The WDVL*. Available on the World Wide Web at: http://www.stars.com/WebRef/Navigation/WDVL.html. Accessed April 28, 1999.

Rosenfeld, L. and Morville, P. (1998). *Information Architecture for the World Wide Web–Designing Large-Scale Web Sites*. Sebastopol: O'Reilly & Associates.

Strauch, B. and Winter, R. (2001). Conceptual Web site modeling. In Rossi, M. and Siau, K. (Eds.). *Information Modelling in the New Millennium*. Hershey, PA: Idea Group Publishing.

UML. (2000). *OMG Unified Modeling Language Specification*. Available on the World Wide Web at: http://www.omg.org/technology/documents/formal/unified_modeling_language.htm. Accessed January 22, 2001.

W3DT-Team. (1997). *W3DT-WWW Design Technique*. Available on the World Wide Web at: http://wwwi.wu-wien.ac.at/w3dt/. Accessed November 26, 1997.

Chapter IV

Retriever: Improving Web Search Engine Results Using Clustering

Anupam Joshi
University of Maryland Baltimore County, USA

Zhihua Jiang
American Management Systems, Inc., USA

Web search engines have become increasingly ineffective as the number of documents on the Web have proliferated. Typical queries retrieve hundreds of documents, most of which have no relation with what the user was looking for. The chapter describes a system named Retriever that uses a recently proposed robust fuzzy algorithm **RFCMdd** to cluster the results of a query from a search engine into groups. These groups and their associated keywords are presented to the user, who can then look into the URLs for the group(s) that s/he finds interesting. This application requires clustering in the presence of a significant amount of noise, which our system can handle efficiently. N-Gram and Vector Space methods are used to create the dissimilarity matrix for clustering. We discuss the performance of our system by comparing it with other state-of-the-art peers, such as Husky search, and present the results from analyzing the effectiveness of the N-Gram and Vector Space methods during the generation of dissimilarity matrices.

INTRODUCTION

Today, the WWW represents one of the largest, distributed, heterogeneous, semi-structured repositories of multimedia content. It is the de-facto medium for electronic commerce. Most e-tailer sites have a large amount of information, and presenting the appropriate information to the user is an important task. Other sites, which primarily deal with information provision (such as news organizations), deal with even larger volumes of information. The state-of-the-practice today is to use existing search engines to provide search functionality to the user. However, typical queries elicit hundreds, sometimes even thousands, of URLs from search engines, forcing the user to wade through them in order to find the URL(s) she needs. The same, at a reduced scale, happens when these engines are used to provide search capabilities at e-tailer sites. In large part, this limitation of search technology can be attributed to the following:

- *Polysemy: the words involved in the search have multiple meanings.* For example, a user searching for windows may be interested in either the operating system or the physical artifact.
- *Phrases: a phrase may be different from words in it.* For example, the meaning of the phrase "partition magic" (a disk partition management tool) is quite different from the meaning of the individual words "partition" and "magic."
- *Term dependency: words in the terms are not totally independent of each other.* For example, a user may look for details about a product made by a particular company and type in Sun's Enterprise Computer Series. Obviously, each word in this term is dependent on each other.

Notice that these problems are independent of how good the algorithms that associate keywords with the contents of a page are.

One possible solution to this problem is to realize that the responses from search engines to a particular query can be broadly grouped into meaningful categories. If the user is shown these groups, possibly with some keyword type descriptions, they can select one (or more) that fit their perceived interests. Note that this is different from the site-oriented grouping that some search engines present, typically in the form of a similar page from this site link, since the aim here is to group together pages that potentially originate from completely different servers. There has been some prior work along these lines, such as that by Croft (1978), and more recent work by Cutting et al. (1992). However, this work is in the context of general text collections.

The recent work of Zamir and Etzioni (1998) proposes the notion of clustering Web search engine results. To the best of our knowledge, this is the only other work besides our own that seeks to cluster search engine results on the fly. They have proposed an algorithm called Suffix Tree Clustering (STC) to group together snippets from Web pages. Snippets are typically the first few lines of (raw) HTML from the document. Essentially, this algorithm uses techniques from literature that allow the construction of suffix trees in time linear in the number of snippets assuming that the number of words in each snippet can be bounded by a constant. Each node in this tree captures a phrase (some suffix of the snippet string), and has associated with it those snippets that contain it. These nodes are viewed as base clusters since they group documents having a phrase in common. Each cluster is assigned a score based on the number of URLs in the cluster as well as the size of the phrase that they have in common. In order to account for the fact that Web pages in the same group may have more than a phrase in common, they then create a graph that has as its vertices the clusters identified by the suffix tree. They define a binary similarity measure between the clusters that is set to 1 if at least half of the documents in each cluster are common to both. Vertices representing similar clusters are connected by an edge. They then run a connected component finding algorithm, and each connected component is identified as a grouping of documents that are similar.

The rationale behind clustering snippets rather than the Web documents themselves is essentially speed. Clearly, clustering the (much) shorter snippets takes much less time than clustering full pages, and makes it possible to create clusters on the fly in response to a user's search request.

Given that clusters are formed out of snippets, the efficacy of the phrase commonality criterion used by STC is not clear. While commonality of phrases may be a valid criterion in grouping large document collections, it is not clear if it is quite as appropriate for grouping snippets. Once common words (e.g., HTTP-related terms, which are treated as stop words) are eliminated from a snippet, what remains are essentially the heading of the page and the first sentence or two. Thus a phrase-based approach will likely do no better than a word-commonality-based approach, and may even be detrimental. Further, the use of binary similarity definition between the initial clusters leads to arbitrary decisions on whether two clusters should be merged. For example, using 0.5 as the threshold would imply that clusters with 0.49 similarity would not be merged, whereas those with 0.51 similarity would. The aim of clustering the results would be better served by defining a soft similarity measure that takes continuous values in the 0 to 1 range. Fuzzy clustering thus seems to be appropriate in this context. Moreover, clustering snippets involves dealing with a significant amount of noise. One reason for the noise is that the responses from the search engines themselves are noisy-many of the URLs returned have little or no connection with the original query, nor are they a part of any coherent "group" of URLs. The other reason is the use of snippets-often the first few sentences of a document will fail to capture its essence. Thus the clustering technique used must be robust, i.e., able to handle significant noise and outliers.

In this chapter, we describe a system to cluster search engine results based on a robust relational fuzzy clustering algorithm that we have recently developed. We compare the use of the Vector Space-based and N-Gram-based dissimilarity measure to cluster the results from the search engines, such as MetaCrawler and Google. We start by providing a brief background on the clustering algorithm. We then describe our system, and discuss results from our experiments. These include a study of the efficiency on the Vector Space and the N-Gram methods, as well as a comparison with Husky Search (Huskysearch Web Site).

BACKGROUND

The Robust Fuzzy c-Medoids Algorithm (RFCMdd)

In related work, Krishnapuram et al. (2000) have recently proposed an algorithm for fuzzy relational clustering based on the idea of identifying k-medoids. This algorithm is called Robust Fuzzy c-Medoids (RFCMdd). The worst case complexity of RFCMdd is $O(n^2)$, but in practice it can be made linear and is an order of magnitude faster than the well-known RFCM algorithm (Bezdek et al., 1991). Since we use a fuzzy algorithm, we are able to handle partial membership situations common in this task-in other words when the same URL may belong to two different groups but to different "degrees." Moreover, RFCMdd is highly robust and thus able to handle noise much better than traditional clustering approaches. Note that the data we cluster here (snippets) are highly noisy to begin with in terms of representing the actual documents. In addition, noise is also introduced in our distance generation measures. We now briefly describe RFCMdd as follows (Krishnapuram et al., 2001).

Let $\mathbf{X} = \{\mathbf{x}_i \mid i = 1,..,n\}$ be a set of n objects. Let $r(\mathbf{x}_i, \mathbf{x}_j)$ denote the dissimilarity between object $\mathbf{x}_i$, and object $\mathbf{x}_j$. Let $\mathbf{V} = \{\mathbf{v}_1, \mathbf{v}_2, \ldots, \mathbf{v}_c\}$, $\mathbf{v}_i \in \mathbf{X}$ represent a subset of $\mathbf{X}$ with cardinality c, i.e., $\mathbf{V}$ is a c-subset of $\mathbf{X}$. Let $\mathbf{X}_c$ represent the set of all c-subsets $\mathbf{V}$ of $\mathbf{X}$. Each V represents a particular choice of prototypes for the c clusters in which we seek to partition the data. The Robust Fuzzy Medoids Algorithm (RFCMdd) minimizes the objective function:

$$J_m(\mathbf{V}; X) = \sum_{i=1}^{n} \sum_{i=1}^{c} u_{ij}{}^m \, r(\mathbf{x_j}, \mathbf{v_i}) \qquad (1)$$

where the minimization is performed overall $\mathbf{V}$ in $\mathbf{X}_c$. In (1), u_{ij} represents the fuzzy membership of $\mathbf{x}_j$ in cluster i. The membership u_{ij} can be defined heuristically in many different ways. We use the Fuzzy c-Means membership model given by:

$$u_{ij} = \frac{\left(\dfrac{1}{r(x_j, v_i)}\right)^{1/(m-1)}}{\sum_{k=1}^{c} \left(\dfrac{1}{r(x_j, v_i)}\right)^{1/(m-1)}} \qquad (2)$$

where $m \in [1, 00)$ is the "fuzzifier." This generates a fuzzy partition of the data set X in the sense that the sum of the memberships of an object x_j across all classes is equal to 1. Since u_{ij} is a function of the dissimilarities $r(x_j, v_k)$, it can be eliminated from (1), and this is the reason J_m is shown as a function of $\mathbf{V}$ alone. Substituting the expression for u_{ij} in (2) into (1), we obtain:

$$J_m(v_i X) = \sum_{i=1}^{n} \left(\sum_{i=1}^{c} (r(x_j, v_i))^{1/(1-m)} \right) = \sum_{j=1}^{n} h_j \qquad (3)$$

where

$$h_j = (\sum_{i=1}^{c} (r(x_j, v_i)^{1-m}))^{1-m} \qquad (4)$$

is $1/c$ times the harmonic mean of the dissimilarities $\{r(x_j, v_i)) : i=1,..,c\}$ when $c=2$. The objective function for the Robust Fuzzy c-Medoids (RFCMdd) algorithm is obtained by modifying (3) as follows:

$$J^T_m(V; X) = \sum_{k=1}^{s} h_{k:} \qquad (5)$$

However, the objective function in (5) cannot be minimized via the alternating optimization technique, because the necessary conditions cannot be derived by differentiating it with respect to the medoids. (Note that the solution space is discrete.) Thus, strictly speaking, an exhaustive search over X_c needs to be used. However, following Fu's (1982) heuristic algorithm for a crisp version of (1), we describe a fuzzy algorithm that minimizes (5).

In (5) $h_{k:n}$ represents the k-th item when h_j, j=1,..,n, are arranged in ascending order, and s<n. The value of s is chosen depending on how many objects we would like to disregard in the clustering process. This allows the clustering algorithm to ignore outlier objects while minimizing the objective function. For example, when s = n/2, 50% of the objects are not considered in the clustering process, and the objective function is minimized when we pick c medoids in such a way that the sum of the harmonic-mean dissimilarities of 50% of the objects is as small as possible.

The quadratic complexity of the algorithm arises because when looking to update the medoid of a cluster, we consider all n objects as candidates. In practice, the new medoid is likely to be one that currently has a high membership in the cluster. Thus by restricting the search to say k objects with the highest membership in the cluster, the process can be made linear, i.e., O(kn), where k is a low integer. In that case, the complexity will be determined by the sorting operation required to find the smallest s (or equivalently the largest n-s) of the h_js. This is a good result, considering that robust algorithms are typically very expensive.

Notice that the algorithms as described assume that the number of clusters is known *a priori*, which is not the case here. This is a well-known problem in clustering. We use a heuristic to automatically determine the number of clusters by initializing it to some large number, much larger than the expected (final) number of clusters. A SAHN type process is then used to hierarchically reduce the number of clusters. As we ascend up the hierarchy, we have to progressively increase the dissimilarity over which clusters will be merged. We note the change in this distance at each step, and assume the level at which the greatest change occurred has the right number of clusters.

Diagram 1: The Robust Fuzzy c Medoids Algorithm (RCMdd)

Fix the number of clusters c, and the fuzzifier m;
Randomly pick initial set of medoids; $V = \{v_1, v_1, ...,v_c\}$ from X_{ci}
iter = 0;
Repeat

        Compute harmonic dissimilarities h_j for *j=1*,..., n using (4);
        Sort h_j, *j*=1,..., n to create h_{jm};
        Keep the objects corresponding to the first δ h_{jm};
        Compute memberships for δ objects;
        for j=1 to δ do
                for i=1 to c do
                        Compute u_{ijm} by using (2);
                endfor
        endfor
        Store the current medoids; $v^{old} - v$;
        Compute the new medoids;
        for i=1 to c do
        q = argmin $\sum_{j=1}^{\alpha} u^m_{ijm} r(x_{km},x_{jm})$
          1< *k*< *n*

        $v_i = x_{qi}$
        endfor
        iter = *iter* +1;
Until (V^{old} = V or *iter* = MAX _ITER).

SYSTEM DESIGN

Introduction

    In this section, we present the design of our Web clustering application called Retriever. Basically, our system is designed as a client-proxy-server system, and its architecture is illustrated in Figure 1. The proxy server is a Perl-based system that connects to regular search engines, such as MetaCrawler (www.metacrawler.com) and Google (www.google.com). The search term(s) entered by the user are passed onto the proxy via a CGI program. The proxy server then forwards the search term(s) to a specific search engine after transforming the query to a request in a format appropriate for that engine. The results that are returned by the search engine, including the Web links and their brief description (snippets), are trapped by the proxy. They are displayed to the user and are also saved to a file. The proxy then processes these results, applying the Vector Space or N-Gram method to create the (dis)similarity matrix. It then calls the RFCMdd algorithm to generate clusters of snippets. Each cluster is associated with a set of keywords, which is assumed to represent a concept. Next, the search engine proxy extracts the five most frequently occurring keywords as the representation of each cluster.

    We will explain the process of query forwarding and describe the grouping results to the user in later sections.

Query Term Delivery

We use three different search engines as our URL sources, namely, MetaCrawler, Google and Husky Search. We have also in the past used Lycos as a source. Note that Husky Search is not really a search engine, but a system to cluster search engine results similar to ours. The reason that we use Husky Search is that we aim to compare our system with it, as discussed in a later section 4. For the comparison to be fair, both systems must cluster the same set of Web links and snippets.

We point out that different search engines have individual query formats, and their returned results are presented in different forms as well. For example, MetaCrawler does not accept a GET-based query request, which we may see from the address box of any Web browser, such as Netscape. Instead, we have to send several header lines together with the query request. This information may involve the contents of "Referer" and "Cookie" headers.

After receiving query request, MetaCrawler will return its results page by page. In order to retrieve the whole set of the query results, our search engine proxy will submit the HTTP request repeatedly until either the end of result or the maximal number of Web links is reached. On the contrary, Google is quite simple and does not require compiling multiple headers during request. However, it also returns results page by page, so similar procedures should be called to retrieve the whole collection of query results. Husky Search does not need either multiple headers or repeat page requests, but sends the results as another URL. Thus, we have to send another HTTP request to gather the actual query results.

In our experiment, extra effort is made to eliminate duplicate Web links in the query responses. We also introduce a special Java program to erase the HTML tags in the snippets and present only the title, URL, and snippets of the returned results. We do not include the set of HTML tags in the stop word list, because of two reasons. One is that we notice that search engines, like Google and Husky Search, may add some tags to highlight the query terms in the results. More importantly, we may treat different tags differently. For instance, we may erase specific tags, such as "&" and " " because we believe that they are irrelevant to the meaning of this page. For others, both the tag and its corresponding close (e.g., <font> and </font) might need to be eliminated.

Illustration of Clustering Results

In response to a query, the system first returns a page quite similar to the page returned from any common search engine. It contains a brief list of titles, URLs and their descriptions. If users can easily locate the links they want from among the first few paragraphs, they may simply click the link to the destination. Otherwise, they may click the button on the upper right corner, labeled "Clusters," to see the grouped results. After the button is clicked, another Web browser window will pop up to show the results in frames (Figure 2). Users may browse each cluster to pick out topics that they are interested in by following the link in the left frame. This causes the corresponding group of URLs to be displayed in the right frame

Figure 1: System architecture

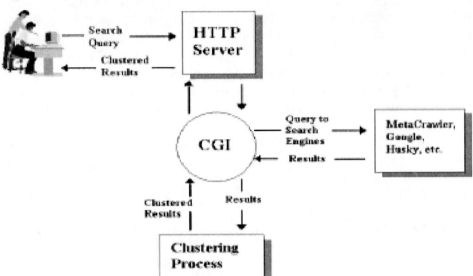

(Figure 3). In addition, a miscellaneous group is included for each query result page. It could be empty, but if not, it will collect all URLs in clusters that contain less than 5% of total URLs returned from search. On the other hand, if the number of URLs returned is below some amount, say 20, the cluster algorithm will not be initiated, because we believe that with this small number of URLs, users could identify their interests easier and faster rather than waiting for the clustering results. Moreover, clusters formed from this small total may not be very meaningful.

Two different methods for the calculation of distance matrix are included in our system. The first one associated with "VectorSpace Search" button utilizes the TF/IDF method to generate the distance matrix. The second one, invoked by the "N-Gram Search" button, utilizes the N-Gram-based measure to compute the dissimilarity matrix. Unlike the Vector Space measure, the N-Gram measure will not erase stop words and will not do word stemming either.

We also have a perl program which will periodically check the directory where all search results reside and clean the directories which contain the query results and exist more than 12 hours. This helps "garbage collect" free disk space. In practice, this method is quite powerful, because it does not compete for CPU time when users are waiting for search results and also it runs in background so it will not affect the running of other functions.

Figure 2: Group Index Page

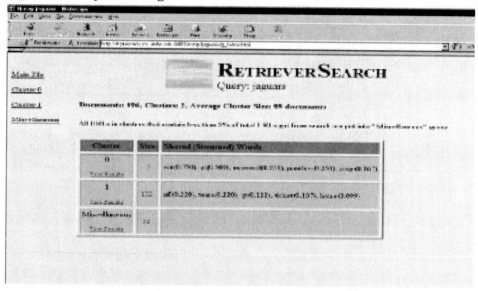

Figure 3: Cluster Example Page

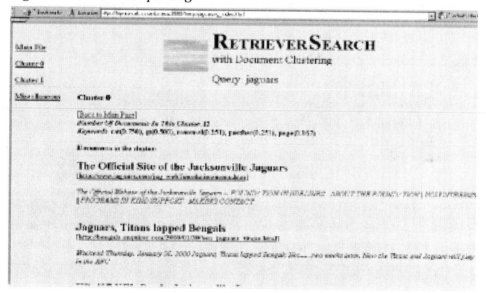

EXPERIMENTAL RESULTS

Introduction

This section presents several experimental results from-our comparative analysis of N-Gram vs. Vector Space techniques for dissimilarity generation, and a comparison of these to Husky Search (Zamir & Etzioni, 1998), which is based on Suffix Tree Clustering (STC). We first evaluate the importance of the value of n in the N-Gram-based method in the second section. Next, we compare the efficiency of the N-Gram-based method vs the Vector Space-based method for distance matrix generation in the third section. We then illustrate the comparison of our system with Husky Search in the fourth section. Next, we study the effect of noise elimination, achieved via in-process trimming, upon the RFCMdd algorithm in the fifth section. Finally, we will provide a summary of some users' feedback we obtained from the preliminary survey of our site. We note that we do not require any personal identifying information for participation in the test. Thus, all results come without any individual information associated with a specific feedback answer form.

It should be pointed out that the cluster numbers are simply arbitrary labels assigned by the clustering algorithm each time it is run. Thus when we show the cluster numbers across different methods (for example, N-Gram vs. Vector Space) in the same row of the table, Cluster 1 of the Vector Space-based test is not the same as cluster 1 of the N-Gram-based one and so on. The significance of these tables is in showing the distribution of URLs within the clusters generated by the same algorithm. In addition, we have used at least 10 to 15 examples for experiment of each section, but for the purpose of saving space here, we only show three of them as a brief illustration of the experimental results. More detailed results can be found in Jiang, (2000).

The Influence of the Value of n in the N-Gram-Based RFCMdd Algorithm

In this section, we evaluate the effect of the value of n in the N-Gram-based RFCMdd algorithm in order to discover the best value of n for the RFCMdd algorithm. Moon river, mobile robots and salsa are used as examples. Table 1 shows the different number of clusters generated given different value of n, and Table 2 illustrates the number of URLs in each cluster and URL distributions. We notice that in the query, "mobile robots," when n=3, N-Gram RFCMdd creates nine clusters, its largest number of clusters. This is nearly half the number of clusters generated by Vector Space-based RFCMdd. However, when n=2, the least number of clusters are generated. The reason is that when the length of gram is too small, say n=1 or n=2, it is difficult to tell apart two different snippets due to the fact that the probability of the same gram appearing in different snippets becomes larger.

We also did the similar comparison on queries of salsa and moon river. The results do not show dramatic change of the number of clusters given the different length of grams, as in the experiment of mobile robots. But we observe that when n=5 and n=6, the number of clusters will stay similar and the major distribution of URLs in clusters will narrow down to one to three clusters. This observation is in consonance with prior work in IR, where five grams have been shown to be useful in document identification tasks.

Table 1: Number of clusters generated in each experiment as the N-Gram length is varied

moon river	2	3	4	5	6
number of URLs	100	100	100	100	100
number of clusters	2	3	3	2	2

Mobile robots	2	3	4	5	6
number of URLs	200	200	200	200	200
number of clusters	2	9	8	5	4

Salsa	2	3	4	5	6
number of URLs	200	200	200	200	200
number of clusters	4	4	3	3	4

Table 2: URL distribution and number of URLs in each cluster as the N-Gram length is varied

moon river	2		3		4		5		6	
	Absolute	percentage	Absolute	percentage	Absolute	percentage	Absolute	percentage	Absolute	percentage
C0	25	0.250	1	0.01	13	0.13	39	0.39	47	0.47
C1	75	0.750	43	0.430	86	0.860	61	0.610	53	0.53
C2			56	0.56	1	0.01				

mobile robots	2		3		4		5		6	
	Absolute	percentage	Absolute	percentage	Absolute	percentage	Absolute	percentage	Absolute	percentage
C0	105	0.525	9	0.045	7	0.035	28	0.14	42	0.210
C1	95	0.475	3	0.015	16	0.08	120	0.6	18	0.09
C2			48	0.240	47	0.235	45	0.225	131	0.655
C3			6	0.030	17	0.085	1	0.005	9	0.045
C4			4	0.020	15	0.075	6	0.03		
C5			3	0.015	68	0.340				
C6			122	0.610	27	0.135				
C7			4	0.020	3	0.015				
C8			1	0.005						

salsa	2		3		4		5		6	
	Absolute	percentage	Absolute	percentage	Absolute	percentage	Absolute	percentage	Absolute	percentage
C0	73	0.365	2	0.01	7	0.035	25	0.125	40	0.2
C1	25	0.125	182	0.91	183	0.915	163	0.815	152	0.76
C2	28	0.140	15	0.075	10	0.05	12	0.06	1	0.005
C3	74	0.370	1	0.005					7	0.035

N-Gram vs. Vector Space

In this section, we compare the performance of the N-Gram and Vector Space methods for generating the dissimilarities between snippets. One possible evaluation metric is to compute the intra and inter distance among clusters that result from these dissimilarity measures. The intra cluster distance is the average distance between any two snippets within the same cluster. The inter cluster distance is the average distance between snippets in the two clusters. It is computed by averaging the distance of any pair of snippets in which one is from one cluster and the other is from the other cluster. Notice that shorter intra distance means that the members within the same cluster are more relevant to each other, while longer inter distance interprets that the members of different groups become more irrelevant to one another.

We use moon river, star war and salsa as examples of comparison. Tables 3, 4 and 5 present the summary of comparative results of intra and inter distance on these examples. Each table includes the total number of clusters generated by each method, the number of clusters after ignoring clusters which only contain one snippet (this is for intra distance calculation only), the average intra distance, the average inter distance and the difference between the two. Notice that for N-Gram method, we employed two coefficient measures, namely, Dice Coefficient and Overlap Coefficient, which are denoted by formulas 6 and 7. **A** is the number of n-grams in one string, **B** is the number of n-grams in the other and **C** is the number in common. Moreover, for each measure, we computed dissimilarity both with and without stop word elimination prior to computing the n-grams. These are labeled as **SWE** and **WSWE**, respectively. Therefore, for every example using N-Gram method, we have four results. Considering the space, we use shortened names on title of columns; for instance, NGOverlapSWE stands for the result from N-Gram method by using Overlap coefficient with Stop Word Elimination, NGOverlapWSWE, means that the result was generated by N-Gram-based method using Overlap coefficient measure but without stop word elimination. The Dice Coefficient is:

$$\text{Coef}_{\text{Dice}} = 1 - \frac{2 * C}{4 - R} \qquad (6)$$

while the Overlap coefficient is:

$$\text{Coef}_{\text{Overlap}} = 1 - \frac{C}{\min(A,B)} \qquad (7)$$

In general, we note that the difference between intra and inter distance of clusters by four applied N-Gram-based methods is much more significant than the one by Vector Space method. Specifically, in the examples of moon river and salsa, we observe that NGOverlapWSWE gives the largest difference between intra distance and inter distance, which are 0.266 and 0.162, and NGOverlapSWE gives the largest difference in the example of star war, which is 0.491, while Vector Space-based method only provides 0.035, 0.086 and 0.061, respectively, for the examples of moon river, salsa and star war. We also observe that normally, N-Gram based RFCMdd regardless of the variant used, usually creates fewer clusters than Vector Space-based method. In addition, the URLs are distributed more narrowly across clusters in the result of the N-Gram-based RFCMdd than Vector Space-based one.

On the other hand, we point out that in the N-Gram method, there is not much difference between the intra and inter distance generated with stop word elimination (SWE) and without stop word elimination (WSWE). Sometimes N-Gram method with stop word elimination gives greater difference between intra and inter distance, such as in the examples, human resource and CDMA 2000 (Jiang, 2000), while sometimes the N-Gram method without stop word elimination (WSWE) gives greater difference, such as in the examples, moon river and salsa. This conclusion is also reflected in Ekmekcioglu's research (Ekmekcioglu et al., 1996) which claims that stop words and stemming are superior for a word-based system but are not significant for an N-Gram-based system.

In summary, N-Gram-based RFCMdd always generates a fewer number of more focused clusters than the Vector Space-based RFCMdd. In most queries, N-Gram-based RFCMdd provides greater difference between intra and inter distance than Vector Space-based RFCMdd. Therefore, it is obvious that N-Gram-based (dis)similarity measure is more suitable to this application than Vector Space-based measure.

RFCMdd vs Husky Search

We use an implementation of Etzioni et al.'s system (Huskysearch Web site), which is called Husky Search and is based on Suffix Tree Clustering (STC) as a comparison with our Retriever system, which is based on RFCMdd algorithm.

We present the summary result of comparison in Table 6. The keyword list generated from STC and from N-Gram-based RFCMdd is presented in Tables 7 to 9. The URL distribution of three examples is shown in Table 10.

Table 3: Summary of inter and intra distance for moon river

moon river	VectorSpace	NGOverlapSWE	NGDiceSWE	NGOverlapWSWE	NGDiceWSWE
Num of URLs	92	92	92	92	92
Total Clu	21	4	5	20	17
After Adjusted	16	2	3	2	6
Average Intra	0.962	0.805	0.872	0.710	0.827
Average Inter	0.997	0.997	0.998	0.976	0.982
Difference	0.035	0.192	0.126	0.266	0.155

Table 4: Summary of inter and intra distance for salsa

salsa	VectorSpace	NGOverlapSWE	NGDiceSWE	NGOverlapWSWE	NGDiceWSWE
Num of URLs	97	97	97	97	97
Total Clu	21	3	6	7	5
After Adjusted	7	3	4	6	3
Average Intra	0.914	0.859	0.886	0.823	0.865
Average Inter	1.000	0.961	0.986	0.985	0.989
Difference	0.086	0.102	0.100	0.162	0.124

Table 5: Summary of inter and intra distance for star war

Star war	VectorSpace	NGOverlapSWE	NGDiceSWE	NGOverlapWSWE	NGDiceWSWE
Num of URLs	89	89	89	89	89
Total Clu	18	17	20	18	9
After Adjusted	17	3	7	3	3
Average Intra	0.934	0.475	0.817	0.633	0.823
Average Inter	0.995	0.966	0.973	0.974	0.984
Difference	0.061	0.491	0.156	0.341	0.161

For Zamir and Etzioni's STC algorithm, we present the keywords/phrase with the associated strength as reported by their algorithm in the tables. For the N-Gram-based RFCMdd algorithm, we present the keywords most often associated with the cluster, as well as its normalized frequency of occurrence. For purposes of displaying these tables within page confines, we have sometimes presented only a part of a phrase or a long word, and indicated that by placing a *.

We observe that N-Gram-based search leads to a fewer number of more focused clusters. When the set of snippets is large, such as in the example human resource (illustrated in Jiang 2000), the major distribution of URLs in clusters will narrow down to one to three clusters by N-Gram-based search, while neither Vector Space search nor Husky Search could provide such distribution. In addition, N-Gram-based method could cluster pages with languages other than English, which neither Vector Space methods nor Husky Search can.

Vector Space search requires about the same amount of time as Husky Search to return results; however, N-Gram search takes much longer time. This is because computing N-Grams and comparing them needs much more space and computation time. Thus there is a clear trade-off between the better results that the N-Gram-based approach provides versus the time it takes to compute the results. The precision of the lists of keywords in both Retriever search and Husky Search is similar. The user feedback (Jiang, 2000) suggests that neither engines' keyword list is the clear winner-sometimes one could better help users identify the right group of URLs, sometimes the other.

Therefore, we could say that Retriever search is at least as good as Husky Search, and can lead to better clusters if the user is willing to wait longer.

Noise Elimination

The RFCMdd algorithm mentioned earlier uses "in-process " trimming-i.e., trims the outliers while it updates the medoids. The parameter it controls the percentage of data points (URLs in this case) that are thrown out as noise. Figure 4, 5 and 6 show the results of three query examples, i.e., moon river, mobile robots, and shuttle. Tables from 11 to 13 present the same results in a clearer tabular form.

Table 6: Number of URLs clustered by the two methods for three queries

moon river	Ngram RFCMdd	STC
number of URLs	34	34
number of clusters	3	3

mobile robots	Ngram RFCMdd	STC
number of URLs	28	28
number of clusters	1	4

Source code	Ngram RFCMdd	STC
number of URLs	426	426
number of clusters	2	15

Table 7: Clustering of moon river responses

STC	Key words/phrases				
C0	Classroom emc topicals (0.57)	Stand (0.57)	Sons (0.57)		
C1	City (1.0)	Hudson (0.50)	History (0.50)	Historic (0.50)	York (0.50)
C2	Music (1.0)	Theatre (0.5)	Branson (0.5)	Featured (0.5)	

N-Gram	Key words/phrases				
C0	paradis (0.376)	life (0.376)	photograph (0.376)	Gphy (0.251)	Grunion (0.251)
C1	son (1.0)	wheel (0.858)	evolut (0.715)	stephan (0.572)	famou (0.429)
C2	your (1.5)	Fairchild (1.0)	fish (1.0)	kirkwood (1.0)	Moonthousand (1.0)

Table 8: Clustering of mobile robots responses

STC	Key words/phrases				
C0	Mobile Robotics (0.38)	robotics (0.77)	autonomous (0.38)	Learning (0.31)	Robot (0.61)
C1	mobile robots (1.0)				
C2	Robots Pages (1.0)	Exclusion (0.40)	document (0.40)	people (0.40)	programs (0.40)	Automatically (0.40)
C3	Research (1.0)	Robotics (0.60)	robots (0.60)	vision (0.40)	sensors (0.40)

N-Gram	Key words/phrases				
C0	Interfac (0.297)	Grow (0.223)	Approachfrequent (0.186)	Depart (0.186)	Ccd (0.186)

From Figure 4, 5 and 6, we notice the number of ejected URLs will increase when the value of option "it" is increased-this is evident from the definition of the parameter. We also observe that the CPU time that was used to compute the grouping results decreases with the decreasing number of URLs available for clustering; in other words as the algorithm recognizes more points as noise and discards them, it speeds up as well.

SUMMARY OF SURVEY

We conducted user studies for this system by organizing trials among a small group of students in our school who were conversant with search engines and the Internet, but had little knowledge of our research and the techniques underlying our prototype system. Each participant was asked to use the system over a period of time and fill out a feedback form on-line. Due to privacy concerns, we do not ask or save any personal identifying information associated with specific answers during this survey, so all the feedback is anonymous.

Table 9: Clustering of source code responses

STC	Key words/phrases					
C0	Subobject Code (0.11)	payroll unit code (0.07)	source documents (0.07)	Transaction Code (0.06)		
C1	section of the (0.14)	Faculty Members (0.13)	Advisory Committee on (0.10)	Committee on Faculty (0.09)		
C2	Program (1.0)					
C3	Document (1.0)					
C4	Data (1.0)	Funding (0.38)	Distribution (0.38)	Object (0.35)	Budget (0.35)	HEPPS (0.35)
C5	IMAP (1.0)					
C6	Note that the (0.32)	Note (1.0)	data (0.36)	funding (0.36)	record (0.36)	
C7	Morse code (0.56)	input (0.63)	special (0.44)			
C8	Command (0.55)	Subroutine (0.40)	initialization (0.35)	switch (0.35)	function (0.35)	
C9	added (0.79)	additional (0.54)	faculty (0.37)			
C10	Class (1.0)	Documents (0.35)	object (0.35)			
C11	type (1.0)	Funding (0.46)	object (0.46)	time (0.42)	budget (0.42)	data (0.35)
C12	implementation (0.67)	fair (0.44)	paper (0.44)	document (0.38)		
C13	code examples (0.44)	specific (0.69)	programmer (0.63)	directory (0.43)	Request (0.37)	
C14	current (1.0)	distribution (0.55)	department (0.48)	funding (0.44)	units (0.44)	Budget (0.44)

N-Gram	Key words/phrases				
C0	code (4.825)	sourc (3.039)	faculti (0.863)	fund (0.771)	Perl (0.474)
C1	Code (3.289)	Sourc (1.919)	Cours (0.458)	Perl (0.231)	Data (0.224)

Table 10: Number and percentage of URLs in each cluster

moon river	Ngram RFCMdd		STC	
/	Absolute	percentage	Absolute	percentage
C0	8	0.24	7	0.21
C1	7	0.21	4	0.12
C2	2	0.06	4	0.12
Misc	17	0.50	22	0.65

Mobile robots	Ngram RFCMdd		STC	
/	Absolute	percentage	Absolute	percentage
C0	27	0.96	13	0.46
C1			12	0.43
C2			5	0.19
C3			5	0.19
Misc	1	0.04	6	0.21

source code	Ngram RFCMdd		STC	
/	Absolute	percentage	Absolute	percentage
C0	131	0.31	189	0.44
C1	295	0.69	77	0.18
C2			44	0.10
C3			43	0.10
C4			42	0.10
C5			41	0.10
C6			22	0.05
C7			16	0.04
C8			20	0.05
C9			24	0.06
C10			31	0.07
C11			28	0.07
C12			18	0.04
C13			16	0.04
C14			27	0.06
Misc	0	0.00	131	0.31

Figure 4: Test of it's influence-moon river

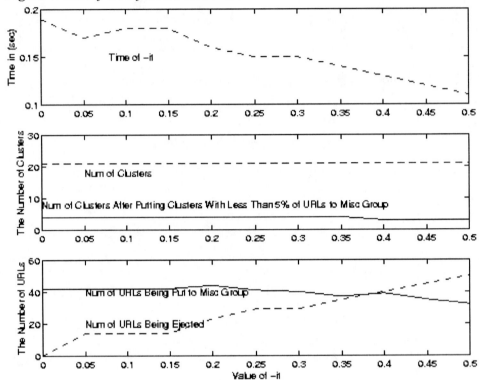

Figure 5: Test of it's influence-mobile robots

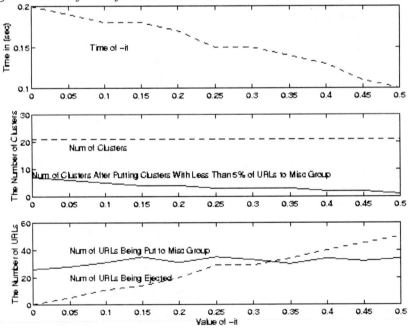

Figure 6: Test of it's influence-shuttle

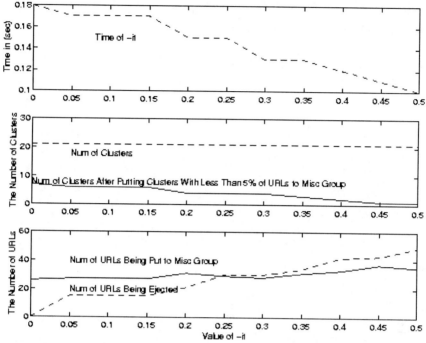

Total URLs: 100   Total Clusters: 21

After putting clusters with less than 5% of total URLs into Miscellaneous group ("X" means the snippets in this cluster have been moved to Miscellaneous group)

Table 11: Clustering results: moon river (it)

clu/-it val	0	0.05	0.1	0.15	0.2	0.25	0.3	0.35	0.4	0.45	0.5
C0	30	16	16	16	14	13	13	11	11	11	10
C1	X	X	X	X	X	X	X	X	X	X	X
C2	X	X	X	X	X	X	X	X	X	X	X
C3	X	X	X	X	X	X	X	X	X	X	X
C4	X	X	X	X	X	X	X	X	X	X	X
C5	X	X	X	X	X	X	X	X	X	X	X
C6	X	X	X	X	X	X	X	X	X	X	X
C7	X	X	X	X	X	X	X	X	X	X	X
C8	X	X	X	X	X	X	X	X	X	X	X
C9	X	X	X	X	X	X	X	X	X	X	X
C10	X	X	X	X	X	X	X	X	X	X	X
C11	7	7	7	7	7	7	7	6	X	X	X
C12	15	15	15	15	15	12	11	11	10	9	8
C13	X	X	X	X	X	X	X	X	X	X	X
C14	6	6	6	6	X	X	X	X	X	X	X
C15	X	X	X	X	X	X	X	X	X	X	X
C16	X	X	X	X	X	X	X	X	X	X	X
C17	X	X	X	X	X	X	X	X	X	X	X
C18	X	X	X	X	X	X	X	X	X	X	X
C19	X	X	X	X	X	X	X	X	X	X	X
C20	X	X	X	X	X	X	X	X	X	X	X
Ejected	0	14	14	14	23	29	29	35	40	45	50
Miscell	42	42	42	42	44	41	40	37	39	35	32
CPUTime	0.19	0.17	0.18	0.18	0.16	0.15	0.15	0.14	0.13	0.12	0.11

Total URLs: 100   Total Clusters: 21

After putting clusters with less than 5% of total URLs into Miscellaneous group
("X" means the snippets in this cluster have been moved to Miscellaneous group)

Table 12: Clustering results: mobile robots (it)

clu/-it val	0	0.05	0.1	0.15	0.2	0.25	0.3	0.35	0.4	0.45	0.5
C0	X	X	X	X	X	X	X	X	X	X	X
C1	X	X	X	X	X	X	X	X	X	X	X
C2	X	X	X	X	X	X	X	X	X	X	X
C3	X	X	X	X	X	X	X	X	X	X	X
C4	X	X	X	X	X	X	X	X	X	X	X
C5	X	X	X	X	X	X	X	X	X	X	X
C6	X	X	X	X	X	X	X	X	X	X	X
C7	X	X	X	X	X	X	X	X	X	X	X
C8	X	X	X	X	X	X	X	X	X	X	X
C9	X	X	X	X	X	X	X	X	X	X	X
C10	X	X	X	X	X	X	X	X	X	X	X
C11	X	X	X	X	X	X	X	X	X	X	X
C12	X	X	X	X	X	X	X	X	X	X	X
C13	X	X	X	X	X	X	X	X	X	X	X
C14	7	7	7	6	6	X	X	X	X	X	X
C15	7	7	7	7	7	7	7	6	X	X	X
C16	7	6	X	X	X	X	X	X	X	X	X
C17	X	X	X	X	X	X	X	X	X	X	X
C18	6	X	X	X	X	X	X	X	X	X	X
C19	32	32	29	29	27	23	23	22	20	17	16
C20	9	9	9	9	9	8	8	8	6	6	X
Ejected	0	5	11	14	20	29	29	34	40	45	50
Miscell	26	28	31	35	31	35	33	30	34	32	34
CPUTime	0.2	0.19	0.18	0.18	0.17	0.15	0.15	0.14	0.13	0.11	0.1

The survey contains four parts. The first one is called "Vector Space vs. Common search engine." Its purpose is to solicit a user's comments based on his/her experience of Vector Space search in our Retriever site and his/her experience of other common search engines, which do not group query results. It involves two groups of questions. One group inquires about the user's impression on using this site compared to other common search engines, from the perspective of the employed grouping function, the speed and the layout. The other queries the user's satisfaction on grouping results, such as the effectiveness of locating the desired URLs and the precision of keyword list associated with each group to see if it facilitates users to select the right group of URLs. The second part is similar to the first one, except that it is designed with the comparative questions between N-Gram search and Common search engines. The third page is to survey users' opinions comparing Vector Space-based search vs N-Gram-based search. This requires users to first utilize both methods on the same or similar queries before filling out the form. The last part of this survey is to compare the performance, speed, precision of the list of keywords of each cluster, and other issues related to Retriever search and Husky Search. Users were instructed to select "HuskySearch" as the source of URLs in Retriever, and also open another browser window direct to Husky Search

Total URLs: 97 Total Clusters: 21

After putting clusters with less than 5% of total URLs into Miscellaneous group ("X" means the snippets in this cluster have been moved to Miscellaneous group)

Table 13: Clustering Results: shuttle (it)

clu/-it val	0	0.05	0.1	0.15	0.2	0.25	0.3	0.35	0.4	0.45	0.5
C0	16	X	X	X	X	X	X	X	X	X	X
C1	5	5	5	5	5	5	5	5	5	X	X
C2	7	7	7	7	7	5	5	5	X	X	X
C3	X	X	X	X	X	X	X	X	X	X	X
C4	X	X	X	X	X	X	X	X	X	X	X
C5	5	5	5	5	X	X	X	X	X	X	X
C6	X	X	X	X	X	X	X	X	X	X	X
C7	X	X	X	X	X	X	X	X	X	X	X
C8	X	X	X	X	X	X	X	X	X	X	X
C9	X	X	X	X	X	X	X	X	X	X	X
C10	5	5	5	5	X	X	X	X	X	X	X
C11	X	X	X	X	X	X	X	X	X	X	X
C12	X	X	X	X	X	X	X	X	X	X	X
C13	X	X	X	X	X	X	X	X	X	X	X
C14	X	X	X	X	X	X	X	X	X	X	X
C15	X	X	X	X	X	X	X	X	X	X	X
C16	X	X	X	X	X	X	X	X	X	X	X
C17	X	X	X	X	X	X	X	X	X	X	X
C18	9	9	9	9	9	6	6	X	X	X	X
C19	24	24	24	24	24	23	23	22	17	17	13
C20	X	X	X	X	X	X	X	X	X	X	X
Ejected	0	15	15	15	21	30	30	34	42	43	49
Miscell	26	27	27	27	31	29	28	31	33	37	35
CPUTime	0.18	0.17	0.17	0.17	0.15	0.15	0.13	0.13	0.12	0.11	0.1

(zhadum.cs.washington.edu/). Then they type in the same query terms in both search sites and compare the results.

We point out that in the comparison between HuskySearch and Retriever, in order to get the same data set for clustering, we need to first send the query to Husky Search and retrieve their results without grouping. This takes about the same amount of time when users type in the same query in the Husky Search site and obtain the results from it. Users were made aware of this additional delay, and asked to ignore it in so far possible when comparing Retriever's speed with Husky Search.

The records of this survey show that most users prefer the grouping results introduced by our site, both Vector Space search and N-Gram search. Some users are satisfied with the fewer number of more focused clusters created by N-Gram search, while some of them are inclined to use Vector Space search, in that N-Gram search requires more time and space than Vector Space search when dealing with the generation of gram-based (dis)similarity matrices. In real life, this is understand-able because sometimes users may not intend to obtain the most precise grouping results. They would rather wait for a shorter time to get reasonable but not exact grouping results than wait for longer time, especially when the number of URLs retrieved is not large. However, when the data set becomes larger, more users seem to turn to N-Gram search.

In the comparison between N-Gram search and Husky Search, about 20% of users feel that N-Gram search is slower or slightly slower than Husky Search, but most of them agree that N-Gram search returns fewer number of clusters. As for the precision of lists of keywords associated with each cluster, there is no clear winner, with user opinion split half-half.

In the "other comments" section, most users recognize that in general, N-Gram search provides a fewer number of more focused clusters and it could handle pages with languages other than English, but it needs to shorten the computation time and improve the performance of the function to better create a keyword list of each cluster.

CONCLUSIONS

In this chapter, we have presented a system that seeks to improve the process for finding relevant URLs for the users. We show that such information personalization is important for e-commerce. In particular, the results returned from a search engine are clustered on the fly into groups, and these groups and their associated keywords are presented to the users. The user can then choose to examine URLs in one or more of these groups based on the keywords. We have used a new robust relational fuzzy clustering algorithm based on the idea of medoids that have been recently developed (RFCMdd). In addition, we introduce and compare the N-Gram method and the Vector Space method to generate the (dis)similarity distance matrix. Our preliminary results show that the algorithm gives good results on Web snippets. The N-Gram-based approach seems to perform better than the Vector Space-based approach, and as well as similar systems reported in literature. Moreover, our approach captures the overlapping clusters idea (a URL can belong to more than one group to different degrees) more elegantly and does not force the user to make an arbitrary "binary" choice of declaring two groups to be similar. In addition, our system is robust, i.e., not sensitive to noise and outliers which are the common occurrence in this domain. We realize of course that in order to achieve speed (clustering the results from the search engine as they come back), we are sacrificing accuracy by clustering only the snippets rather than the documents themselves.

ACKNOWLEDGMENTS

Partial support of this work by grants from National Science Foundation (IIS 9801711 and IIS 9875433 to Joshi) is gratefully acknowledged. We also thank Professor Raghu Krishnapuram from the Colorado School of Mines and his student Liyu Yi, with whom we collaborated in developing the clustering algorithm. The authors would also like to thank Karuna Joshi for proofreading the paper and reformatting it, from latex to MSWord.

REFERENCES

Bezdek, J. C., Hathaway, R. J. and Windham, M. P. (1991). *Numerical Comparison of the RFCM and AP Algorithms for Clustering Relational Data*, 24, 783-791.

Croft, W. B. (1978). Organizing and searching large files of documents. *PhD Thesis*, Cambridge University.

Cutting, D., Krager, D., Pedersen, J. and Tukey, J. (1992). Scatter/gather: A cluster-based approach to browsing large document collections. In *Proceedings of the 16th ACM SIGIR Conference*, 318-329.

Ekmekcioglu, F. C., Lynch, M. and Willett, P. (1996). Stemming and N-Gram matching for term conflation in Turkish texts. *Information Research News*, 7(1), 2-6.

Fu, K. S. (1982). *Syntactic Pattern Recognition and Applications*. San Diego, CA: Academic Press.

HuskySearch. Available on the World Wide Web at: http:/zhadum.cs.washington.edu.

Jiang, Z. (2000). Using robust clustering methods to group query responses from Web search engines. *Master's Thesis*, University of Maryland Baltimore County.

Krishnapuram, R., Joshi, A., Nasraoui, O. and Yi, L. (2001). Low complexity fuzzy relational clustering algorithms for Web mining. Accepted for publication in *IEEE Transactions on Fuzzy Systems*.

Zamir, O. and Etzioni, O. (1998). Web document clustering: A feasibility demonstration. In *Proceedings of the ACM SIGIR '98*.

Chapter V

Digital Asset Management: Concepts and Issues

Ramesh Subramanian and Minnie Yi-Miin Yen
University of Alaska Anchorage, USA

INTRODUCTION

Dramatic changes have occurred on the corporate front in the last few years, as more and more businesses have started to conduct commerce on the Internet. Web sites have become an integral part of an organization's operations, and are used to actively promote companies and their products, deliver services and information, manage transactions and facilitate communications. New business concepts and products are being developed on a daily basis. The accent is on speed, and changes occur quickly–daily, hourly or even minute to minute.

Two major facets of these changes are:

1. Large amounts of data are created and stored in digitized forms in organizations, and
2. New, "digital products" are created.

As more and more information is created in electronic form, organizations are being faced with a volume of digital data that has become cumbersome to manage and reuse (Sharples, 1999). The problems are particularly acute in "media organizations"–organizations that primarily deal with the creation, storage and manipulation of media products. Over the last few years, these organizations have struggled to reduce cycle time, maintain brand consistency and coordinate cross-media publishing as well as one-to-one marketing efforts.

The explosion in the number of digital assets that an organization may manage has been further compounded by the exponential growth of the Internet. According to a report by London-based Frost and Sullivan, with the ever-increasing growth of the World Wide Web, companies find the ever-increasing need to manage various Web data types. "The resulting flood of digital assets is creating tremendous opportunities for vendors who can quickly provide solutions. Users can save precious hours, even days, by having the images, audio, video or text they need right at their fingertips" (Sharples, 1999).

Gistics, a California-based research firm that has studied media asset management for several years, has found that corporations are squandering profits as they lose track of their media assets (which include digital assets) and end up duplicating efforts. According to a 1997 Gistics study, approximately 30% of all media assets are misplaced, and then reworked or duplicated.

The Frost and Sullivan study forecasts tremendous future growth in the U.S. digital media management market. "Before long, virtually all media created will have a digital form, presenting tremendous opportunities in the U.S. Digital Media" (Frost & Sullivan, 1998). The three market segments that will be affected represent the capture, storage and access, and distribution of digital media, respectively.

Given this scenario, it is not surprising that there is currently a tremendous interest within organizations in Digital Asset Management (DAM). This interest has in turn spawned more than 100 software products, including single-station image libraries, server-based media asset management and workflow systems, document management systems and Web-based content management systems. The systems cover a wide range, and cost anywhere from $50,000 low-end systems to some enterprise systems that cost in the millions (Sharples, 1999).

In this chapter, we examine Digital Asset Management concepts, detail the desirable features and components of DAM, the taxonomy of the DAM systems, the e-commerce aspects of digital assets and discuss the various open research issues associated with Digital Asset Management.

Definition

A digital asset is any asset that exists in a digitized form, and is of intrinsic or commercial value to an organization. Digital Asset Management can be defined as a set of processes that facilitate the search, retrieval and storage of digital assets from an archive. While DAM is a fairly simple problem, it has a lot of far-reaching implications from both the technology and e-commerce perspectives when we try to scale it to really large data sets.

Basic Features of DAM

The basic features of any DAM system include: storage, search and retrieval, and "thumb nail browsing" (Rosenblatt, 1998). Thumb nail browsing is the ability to browse a small representation of the contents such as an image thumb nail or a video clip in a low resolution format like Quicktime or RealVideo, or an audio clip. This provides the user with just enough ability to get a basic indication of what a particular file contains before uploading the high resolution version. A good DAM system will also include the ability to perform object check-in and check-out.

Other desirable features include:

- Integration of the DAM system with content creation applications on the desktop. Examples of such applications are QuarkXPress for publishing, audio and video editing, and Adobe Illustrator, etc.
- Enterprise features, i.e., features that are necessary for a digital media management system to be useful in a large-scale deployment at a large media company. The most important of these is really an industrial strength, scalable database.
- The ability of a DAM system to have a user interface that can function in a cross-platform environment. The Java language from Sun Microsystems and the development of XML technology are emerging as key technologies to enabling that.
- The ability to extend the functionality of the DAM system through programming interfaces.

DIGITAL ASSET MANAGEMENT SYSTEM ARCHITECTURE

Building a DAM system requires that digital assets of an organization be loaded into a database where they can be understood, searched, retrieved and updated when necessary. Once the assets are incorporated into a database, they can be integrated with other tools such as search, retrieval and update tools. Figure 1 uses a three-tiered architecture of the generic DAM system architecture to show the process flow during an asset creator's session and a client's query session.

In the asset creation flow, the **Asset Creator** creates an asset, which could be in any digital format, and provides the asset and its associated information to the Asset manager. The **Asset manager** converts the information associated with the asset into an XML metadata format, builds the appropriate data type definitions, and passes the information and the asset to the Metadata manager. The **Metadata manager** manages the organization of the **Metadata Store**, which is a database containing meta information on the assets. Appropriate links between the metadata and the actual assets are created and maintained here. The Metadata Store contains information about the digital assets, typically in an XML DTD format. The assets are passed by the Metadata manager to the File manager, which is responsible for the check-in and check-out of the assets into and out of the **Digital Asset Store**, which is a combination of file systems and databases.

In the query processing flow, the **Client** asks a query. The **Query processor** parses the query and sends the user information as well as the parsed query to the **Metadata manager**, which maintains the metadata for the assets. The metadata includes not only information about the asset but also information on who is allowed to access the asset. After this information is retrieved from the **Metadata store**, a message is sent back to the **Query processor** by the **Metadata manager**. The

Figure 1: Architecture for Digital Asset Management

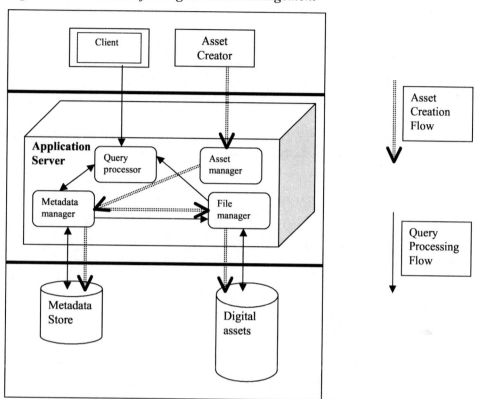

message passed may either be a refusal to access the asset, or an affirmation that the requested asset is being retrieved.

If the client has the appropriate authority to access the asset requested, then the **Metadata manager** passes the request as well as the appropriate metadata to the **File manager**, which then uses the metadata to access and return the asset to the client. Thus the metadata component acts as a store, search, retrieve and security tool, managed by the **Metadata manager**.

Thus, the first step in DAM architecture is developing a basic asset repository in the organization that provides value to its customers. Understanding how to solve the user and system problems for captioning, searching, workflow retrievals, etc. is critical to the long-term development and use of digital assets. In this chapter, we discuss several important additional architectural issues in building a DAM system.

An Open and Distributed Architecture

The key to any Digital Asset Management system is to create an open and distributed architecture. A well-designed DAM system first should provide the ability for people to take an asset, repository or archive and be able to customize it into their environment and extend it to their existing system and other new systems. The performance of a DAM system is then related to the ability to search and find an object, the ability to make sure that the correct object is found and the ability to get the object to the user efficiently no matter what platform it is on, what data format it is in and what interface and language the user uses. The first conference on DAM was held in the Annenberg School of Communication, University of Southern California (Annenburg DAM Conference, 1998). In that conference, several panelists discussed the architectural issues pertaining to the development of DAM systems. In this section, we adapt some of the ideas that were presented there and discuss the scaling, user interface, custom interface, file management and asset association, platform independence and transportability issues in building the DAM system architecture.

Scaling

As more things are put into digitized format, organizations may be required to manage a hundred thousand, half a million or million assets with terabyte- and gigabyte-sized media files. The growth rate of digital assets increases at least four to five times faster than most people anticipate. This has ramifications on how the architecture of a DAM system looks.

If we consider distributed models, there is a likelihood of several systems connecting all of the processes, extended spatially. This means that people can put process and functionality any place that they want where it makes sense. This allows people to actually put video servers, media servers, 2-D image servers, etc. closer to the point of deployment. It doesn't make sense necessarily to be transferring large (gigabyte) files from distant locations if such files can be represented in a set of media servers that are replicated in different physical (off-line) locations.

However, the distributed organization has some problems. We need the ability to connect various locations to a hierarchical storage management system (tertiary storage), which will allow for various digital assets to be accessed on-line, near-line and off-line storage, without getting into the detailed management of every individual request.

User Interface and Custom Interface

DAM systems should have very customizable, platform-independent interfaces. In addition, it should be kept in mind that the interface should be easy to use and understood by the end users. A software development that facilitates development of platform-independent interfaces is Sun Microsystems' Java™ language. Sun Microsystems has also developed a Digital Media Management (DMM) project that has a Java-based interface for its main client software that could deploy on most of platforms. In addition, Sun Microsystems has developed a Web client.

The DAM architecture should also incorporate features for rapid interface development. Features for the rapid development of custom interfaces is also a key issue. Whether the client is Web-based or an application installed on end-user systems, its development should be a very simple, straight forward process. This can be achieved by designing a back end architecture that supports all the functions required, such as features that enable the creation of specific look and feel graphics and adding workflow into the interface.

File Management and Asset Association

DAM systems require very sophisticated file management. One of the problems with conventional file management systems is that it is very difficult to locate objects. People typically rely on a very strict convention for inserting and retrieving data. If somebody does not follow the strict convention, data may never be located. Approaches for designing file management systems for DAM should include appropriate classification of the digital files. Appropriate classification allows identification, search and fast retrieval. For example, what does it mean to say that two assets are equivalent or similar, or to be able to create unique relationships within an organization using terminology that is specific to the organization?

The DAM system architecture should incorporate features that will enable designers and end-users to specify and manage the relationships among files. These relationships include versions, sequences, equivalent assets, etc. The DAM system architecture should also have the ability to track the evolution of assets over time throughout the database. Digital assets constantly involve check-in and check-out processes, and it is important for a user to be able to visually take a look at the work and be able to go back to any version of an asset that he/she might have in the system.

It is more than likely that a physical file may be related conceptually to more than one hierarchy. In order to represent that in the file system, we need to physically put the file into two different hierarchies, obviously having redundancy problems, update problems, etc. The asset management solution needs to incorporate the idea of creating arbitrary relationships that are user-defined associations. Key to the development of this is having a strong object model. The object model should understand how the user's digital files interact with the network, media service, video service, etc., so that can be represented in the asset management solution.

Platform Independent and Transportability

A distributed architecture is important to disperse the digital assets and associated processes to different locations. The key to this is making sure that there is database independence, platform independence and client independence, as most users may access the repository through very heterogeneous network systems.

An asset management solution really needs to have platform independence especially when it comes to the client. Most organizations currently deal with Macintosh and PC clients, and have the traditional problem of not being able to see thumbnail information across those two environments. So, the asset management solution should solve that problem.

The transportability of DAM system involves the ability to batch-transport files between locations, and automatically index and classify them. That, in turn, requires the ability to create thumbnail representations, proxies or any other type of representation, to avoid having to transfer large files across the network.

This architecture issue of DAM system can also be extended to include changing media formats and plug-ins. The digital asset archive should be extensible. Digital media formats change all the time. Therefore there is a need to make sure that the architecture will support users' needs as they change with new formats. One approach that some vendors use (e.g., Bulldog) is "plug-ins" i.e., allowing people to customize and register plug-ins into their system so that if they need to handle a specific type of asset not handled by the archive, they can do that with a plug-in structure. This gives flexibility to the users, as they need not be tied into somebody else's development schedule (to achieve custom solutions). The plug-in's responsibility is understanding and analyzing the media content as it goes into the database. This will enable people who are formulating queries to search and find the types of assets in the database that they need. Plug-ins should provide thumbnail generation, format conversions, understanding dimensions of images, the concept of understanding gaps or inaudible durations, etc.

Representation and Identification Issues of Digital Assets

Digital assets can be described in an unlimited number of ways. In this section, we first address the issues of digital asset representation and addressable units. We then discuss how to describe the addressable units with meta-data creation, as well as standardization issues.

Representation Issues and Addressable Unit

Understanding how to solve the user and system problems for captioning, searching, workflow retrievals, etc., are critical to the long-term development and use of digital assets. In the following, we expand the issues raised by the researcher of Picture Network International (PNI) in the three categories of digital asset representation issues: **Production Workflow, Creative Workflow** and the **Addressable Unit** (Romer, 1998).

Production workflow is the ability for meta-data to be added throughout the lifecycle of digital asset handling (captioning or cataloging), with appropriate knowledge management capabilities to establish standardization and consistency.

While a production workflow is often a backroom activity with more static properties, the creative workflow is far more dynamic. Production workflows often deal with known items. Creative workflows are more discovery-oriented, hence more volatile and browse intensive. This workflow is characterized by the need to do many interactive searches and temporarily store candidate assets until a final decision can be made. Since creative people rarely work in isolation, there is also a need to collaborate with others as part of the decision process.

A working example of the creative workflow process is PNI's tool "Lightbox." The Lightbox provides a capability to create named folders where images can be stored persistently. These folders may be shared with other system users also with notes attached. The creative workflow process needs seamless collaboration. The PNI Lightbox provides sharing functions that enable users with the ability to do that.

Assets placed in Lightboxes are also an indication of an asset's implicit value. When an asset is selected, whether it is used or just temporarily stored in the folder, it has gotten a stamp of visual approval by a system user. By retaining that information over time, it is possible to start determining relative value for items in a repository. In other words, users' selections create value, regardless of whether an asset has actually been used or not. Images selected, even once, out of a repository dramatically increase the likelihood that they will be chosen again. PNI has implemented Lightboxes with the capability to derive that value from within the system automatically. Both implicit and explicit choices for an asset are important meta-data that is retained.

Although the organization of digital assets has moved from office shelving to digital video files, the actual content of the videotape or digital video files remains opaque. Taking the contents of a movie as example, 'content' refers to the scenes, cuts, actors' appearances, dialog, costumes, etc.—the stuff that makes up the movie. In most content management or asset management systems, descriptions of video content refer to the entire video program. It is the smallest addressable unit. It is like searching for a particular scene of a movie using just the information contained on the videotape jacket. The same holds true for most database systems—the descriptive information or meta-data of a video program refers to or points to a BLOB (the entire digital video file). One of the first challenges is to go beyond the BLOB and locate specific moments within a video. One of the promises of digital asset management is random access and non-linear editing systems.

Digital, non-linear editing systems give random access to content via time code markers. The same type of functionality is needed for searching and browsing video stored on computer systems. During the production process a lot of knowledge is being generated about the video content. Yet, when cataloging, one typically refers only to the final product.

A good DAM system must allow the designer or user to leverage this valuable production knowledge to help search for what one is looking for, by defining appropriate addressable units within a particular digital asset such as a digital video movie. The ability to address finer and finer units of data would enable us, for instance, to search for all scenes in all movies where Humphrey Bogart appears, from digitized movie repository.

Identification Issues and Meta-Data Creation

How can a digital asset be identified? This basically involves putting keywords and property information on top of assets in the database. Currently, most people are typically reliant on the file name and a very sparse amount of meta-data that is associated with it.

Organizations are becoming increasingly aware that library science techniques need to be a very integral part of the process of identifying digital assets. Currently,

DAM vendors spend as much time deploying software at organizations as they do working with people to come up with a classification scheme. For example, if one is searching "Jaguar" as it relates to an automobile, it is important to avoid searching for wildlife-related assets.

DAM systems need to have a very sophisticated meta-data model that will store and classify property information, details, names and descriptions, and anything else that the user defines and can be put on top of his/her digital assets. One promising method for classifying digital assets is through the use of "controlled vocabulary." This technique addresses how the hierarchical keywords work, so that one can take a system, like the keyword structure from the Library of Congress, and apply it to assets inside one's database. The advantage of this is that the user can pose sophisticated queries through a database that cannot be done through a file system. For example, a query such as: "Show me all things that have this color of red in it" could be posed to such a system. This will enable a search for objects with specific optical features. DAM vendors such as Virage are doing this.

Searching digital asset repositories is a much larger area, and we address that separately in the next section, where we discuss alternate approaches to searching.

Once the addressable unit issue is solved, the next challenge is to figure out the best way to describe the addressable units since digital assets can be described in an unlimited number of ways. This brings the issue of standards. There has to be some governing body or standards committee that enforces how a particular asset is going to be described in digital asset management systems. An issue that arises from this is: is it possible to describe the content of a digital asset for all possible uses? Some industry experts think that is almost impossible. They contend that it is not possible to impose too much descriptive structure from the start, as it will be exceedingly difficult and time consuming (e.g., it will be very time consuming to exhaustively describe each frame of a movie.).

Searching for Digital Assets

Searching digital asset repositories is a much wider area to address. Therefore, we address it separately and discuss alternate approaches for searching. We categorize two approaches to searching digital repositories. "Content-based analysis" and "search extenders" are categorized as representative of the top-down approach, and approaches such as Picture Network International (PNI)'s image representation schemes with a "decision support" subsystem are categorized as representative of the bottom-up approach.

The "Top-Down" Approach

The top-down approach usually provides specialized searching routines that recognize the properties of the objects being searched. It is also referred to as "content-based analysis." Image understanding and pattern recognition are all technologies that automatically process images based upon certain inherent properties of the image itself. Some examples are the color, texture and shape recognition systems from Virage (http://www.virage.com) or IBM's QBIC application (Flickner et al., 1995; Faloutsos et al., 1994).

"Search extenders" facilitate content-based searching of digital files (e.g., content-based searching of textural images). Bulldog's Search Extender™ technology allows the search mechanism to recognize the properties of various file types and implement specialized searching routines. They allow users to do context searching, such as finding the name "Bulldog" very close to information about Sun Microsystems inside the database. (Note: The Bulldog Group is partnering with Sun Microsystems in the latter's Digital Media Management project.) This type of search extender technology is actually implemented for Bulldog/Sun Microsystems DMM project. Equivalent search extender technology exists for images, video and audio. This will enable one to license technologies that will find objects inside a database that sound like a gun shot, for instance. A good example is Muscle Fish, a Berkeley, California, software vendor dealing with sound, music and related software, which uses that type of sound recognition.

These technologies are very important to the cost reduction and error reduction for media management systems. The whole meta-data description process is extremely costly because humans have to intervene throughout the entire description process. Content analysis, when applied to still images, is able to find such artistic processes as "silhouettes," where there is a portion of an image that is of very high contrast. These are typically very dramatic images, and if a user is trying to find more images in a database like that, content analysis can support that kind of retrieval. However, there is yet some distance to go before media management systems will be able to effectively harness the power of content analysis technology.

The "Bottom-Up" Approach

Visual media, by their nature, are very complex entities and are highly contextual. Representing images for searching in any system is extremely important. A good example of a firm using the "bottom-up" approach is Picture Network International (PNI). PNI solves the problem of locating objects that people are looking for by designing image representation schemes that will match the goals of the search process used for retrieval. Its philosophy is that when planning a captioning strategy for an enterprise, it is important to design a caption or catalog entry that will match the goals of the search process used for retrieval. At PNI, the search sub-system was designed with "decision support" in mind. The questions that were asked when designing the search engine were, "How do creative people search for images?" "What kinds of incremental decisions do people make leading to final image selection?" "How can people who think visually translate their ideas into words for searching?"

"It is so common to find asset management systems that have overlooked this very fundamental aspect of system design. There is a great misconception that a general, all-purpose caption can be created for visual media that will satisfy all uses and categories of users. Some of that misconception is the fault of the database industry that has been creating systems for years with the premise that all answers are to be found in the database with existing meta-data definitions. For visual media, or any content whose perception results in subjective interpretation, the answer is generally found in the thought process of the user. So the important criteria for search sub-systems is clearly to model user selection behavior. How do we build a system to help you do that?" (Romer, 1998). Following along these lines, PNI has developed a meta-data model for media assets that takes into account how users search and make decisions about images.

They think the method adopted by many venders of creating controlled vocabularies and very strict rules about how users have to think when they are using the system to be "too brittle." Their view is that especially in creative processes, there is a need of systems that allow multiple viewpoints in order to support a variety of users. A Natural Language search tool that uses Natural Language description for the caption process is developed. The company has also developed a semantic network that is tuned for visual media. An example of a search using that technology is to enter the phrase "athletes making mistakes." The semantic network, by using all the nodes of association in the network, essentially understands that tennis players are some kind of athletes and understands that "hands to her head" has an association with something going wrong. It also understands that a bobble was a kind of a mistake in baseball. The system then retrieves a set of images. The word "athlete" doesn't appear and neither does the word "mistake" in the image captions. This demonstrates the ability to provide a single description for an image, and then have the ability to create searches with different words to find the image. While keyword systems may provide a sense of control for system implementation, users rarely can abide by the stiff procedures that are needed for access in that model.

TAXONOMY OF DAM SYSTEMS

Because the term "digital assets" is very broadly defined, it can include images, text, video, sound files, etc. The DAM market covers an enormous spectrum of industries, each with its own specialized set of needs. Within the overall DAM market, one can find products tailored for broadcast media, book and magazine publishing, catalog publishing, variable data printing, corporate marketing departments, prepress service bureaus, small graphic arts shops and large dynamic Web developers, among many other niches.

Needless to say, these lines can blur easily. Few products fit purely into a single niche, and most vendors are understandably eager to sell their products to as many people as possible. Therefore, it is common phenomena that the vendor releases enhanced or specialized versions of the same product to target more than one market segment.

We have categorized the DAM systems based on two criteria. The first criterion is based on how many people DAM systems need to serve, the price range and their complexity level. In this criterion, DAM can be divided into three categories (Rosenblatt, 1998):

1. The *Enterprise* category to give an organization the capabilities to be scalable and with industrial strength. It typically costs in the millions of dollars. The way it is typically deployed is by building a few specific business solutions initially to help justify the cost, and then extending it to incorporate more solutions at a later date.

2. The *Mid-range* category where the system is purpose-built for a specific asset management purpose. They typically cost in the one hundred to five hundred thousand dollar range.

3. The *Low-end* category for basic, low-end solutions that are useful for small installations. These systems cost typically cost around $50K. These are systems that have basic features, and they run on workgroup class servers.

The second criterion we use is based on several representative functionality of the DAM. We list the following functionality areas and a few example products equipped with them.

1. *The Image Cataloging Feature.* With the image cataloging feature, systems capture low-resolution thumbnails and descriptive meta-data to allow a user to quickly browse a collection of images for the full resolution media file retrieval. The products in this category include Canto Software's Cumulus and Extensis's Portfolio.

2. *The Object Repository Feature.* With the object repository feature, systems can capture not only thumbnails and meta-data, but also high-resolution media files. The example products of this category include Cinebase DMMS by Cinebase and Bulldog Software by the Bulldog Group.

3. *Content Management Back End for Web Sites Feature.* This provides service/editorial environment with content management for the Web. The content can be in different file formats, such as text, graphics, multimedia, XML and SGML documents. The example products include Vignette's Story Server and Texcel International's Information Manager.

4. *Intelligent Cataloguing and Indexing Feature.* This intelligent cataloguing and indexing feature, to have Web-based interface with intelligent navigation tools, allows the user to search and organize images, video, audio and text documents easier and more efficiently. The example products include Virage's Media Manager & Browser and Dalim Imaging's Galerie.

PROTECTION AND DISTRIBUTION ISSUES IN DAM

Protecting digital assets means the protection of works that are stored, managed, transmitted and distributed from being made available to the public, or from being publicly performed by any means including digital means over the network.

Digital Assets Protection

The rapid growth of multimedia manipulation tools and the wide availability of network access lead to the convenience of digital data processing, delivery and storage. Powerful digital facilities can produce a large amount of perfect digital asset copies in a short period of time. The advanced compression technology also contributes to makeing the digital content compacted into a small data stream to facilitate transmission. These advantages benefit content users definitely to raise concerns from content creators and content owners if the intellectual property right cannot be enforced successfully (Su, Wu and Kuo, 1999). The digital assets protection can be discussed from three different categories, legal, technical and non-technical means to ensure protection of digital assets.

Legal Methods: Patents, Copyrights and Trademarks

A patent is a grant of exclusive right that's given by the government to anybody who files an application for patent protection. It confers upon the applicant the right to exclude everyone else from making, using or selling that patented invention. The term of protection offered by a patent is somewhat shorter than copyright by a good deal. The term of protection for a patent is generally 20 years from filing throughout the world. Under the U.S. patent system, that protection is available for any invention. Anything that can be conceived of by man, and put into practice in a useful way that is new and novel, can be subject to patent protection. This includes any creation of man's mind, such as drugs, pharmaceuticals, computer software, inventions, processes, methods of manufacture, chemical compounds, electronic devices, etc.

A copyright differs from a patent. A copyright protects an original work of authorship. Original in this sense means created by someone, not copied from someone else. The term of protection for a copyright under U.S. law is "life of the author and 50 years for the case of a work made in the course of employment by an employee working for an employer." Under certain conditions, the protection period for the latter case could be 75 years from publication or 100 years from creation, whichever expires first. There is a proposal currently in the U.S. Congress to extend the term of copyright protection by an additional 20 years, to bring it up to the level that's guaranteed in the European Union.

A trademark is a right that attaches to a marking used to identify goods and commerce. It helps serve as a guarantee of the source of those goods for consumers, so you know where they come from and you may have expectation as to the quality associated with that mark. Trademarks may be registered with the USPTO; they may also be registered with State authorities. Many states have their own trademark registries. Trademark can also arise by the operation of common wall.

Copyright laws can be separated into the Anglo-American and the European copyright laws. The Anglo-American laws are followed by America, Great Britain and other British colonies. They adopt a pragmatic, market-oriented approach towards copyrights. According to this approach, copyrights are rights granted in return for the encouragement of the production of more works that will benefit all. On the other hand, under European laws, the copyright is seen as a basic fundamental human right. The economic incentives that it provides are secondary to insuring the protection of someone's personality. In European intellectual property law, copyright law is generally a part of the so-called "right of personality"-that a person has a work protected because it embodies a little bit of his/her soul, a little bit of the person. Because of that, it's entitled to a very high level of protection under the law. A key feature of that approach is trying to protect that personality issue interest, and most European copyright laws have detailed provisions on something called moral rights, which is the right of an author to always be identified as the author of the work and object to uses of that work that could bring dishonor or discredit upon that author's reputation.

The World Intellectual Property Organization (WIPO) is a specialized UN agency responsible for administering treaties pertaining to intellectual property protection. They cover the spectrum of patents, trademarks, copyrights, neighboring rights, rights in semiconductor chip products and some new additional rights in databases. In December 1996, WIPO convened a diplomatic conference at which two new treaties were developed. They are the WIPO Performances and Phonograms Treaty and the WIPO Copyright Treaty. These are intended to be new treaties that bring international copyright law up to speed, especially with new developments such as electronic commerce. One of the main aims of these treaties is to bridge the difference in the philosophy of European authors' rights law and the Anglo American copyright law. Countries provide for the essential levels of protection that they need. In the case of both these treaties in the world of electronic transactions, they require that anyone who signs these treaties provide to authors and other right holders the exclusive right to authorize or prohibit the distribution of their works by electronic means to the public. It's a right that's already guaranteed in American copyright law. It is the first time that a distribution right, the right to control the distribution of a work from producer to consumer, has been recognized in an international treaty on copyright. The previous principal international treaties--The Berne Convention for the protection of literary and artistic works and the Agreement in the World Trade Organization on the trade-related aspects of intellectual property--do not deal with distribution rights.

Technical Methods for Intellectual Property Protection

Encryption and watermarking are the two most important digital assets content protection techniques. Encryption protects the content from anyone without the proper decryption key while watermarking, on the other hand, further protects the content by embedding an imperceptible signal directly into the content for ownership declaration, play control or authentication (Su, Wu and Kuo, 1999).

There are two types of encryption existing: symmetric (secret-key) mechanism and asymmetric (public-key) mechanism. Symmetric mechanism uses the same security key to "lock" and scramble a digital file and to recover a bit-exact copy of the original content at the destination. Asymmetric encryption employs dual keys.

The sender encrypts the digital with the recipient's public key, and the recipient decrypts it with his or her private key (Cravotta, 1999). DES algorithm and its derivatives are the premier technologies for symmetric cryptosystem and the RSA algorithm is the primary one for public-key cryptosystem. The primary advantage of symmetrical encryption is its high-speed encoding and decoding. However, if something intercepts the bit stream and the unintended recipient figures out the key, the asset is vulnerable. For asymmetrical encryption, exchange of public keys requires no secure channel, and the recipient can ensure authentication of a valid sender. However, the key-generation, encryption and decryption algorithms, commonly based on prime-number techniques, require multiplication operations that are time-consuming and performance-intensive (Dipert, 2000).

Most of crypto-applications use hybrid schemes of both to achieve trade-off between performance and security. Asymmetric encryption establishes the initial authorization between host and display, as well as the periodic reauthorization. Faster symmetric compression handles the content transfer. Any performance-critical application needs to incorporate a similar approach. DTCP (Digital Transmission Copy Protection) comprehends support for both asymmetric and symmetric protocols. It supports symmetric protocols for their supposed lower value, single- and free-copy material (Dipert, 2000).

The primary application of digital watermarking is copyright protection. The imperceptible and indelible water-mark can establish the ownership, identify the source and the legitimacy of the digital asset, while preserving the quality of the host media. Basically, a watermark is similar to the old, traditional kind where one can hold up a piece of paper to the light at the right angle and see what paper manufacturers have put in there. A digital watermark is similar, except that one cannot look at an image and actually see the watermark. However, the watermark can be identified by specialized software. A digital watermark that is inscribed into a digital asset is meant to be read by anyone at no cost, wherever the digital asset goes. This is true also of a digital asset that is distributed in digital content or reproduced in any other media formats.

The fundamental goal of digital watermarking is to put an identity into an image (or digital asset). It is a code imbedded in the image that says to whom it belongs. Anybody using, for instance, an image that has been watermarked can find out whom that asset belongs to in 30 seconds. This facilitates the person using the asset to contact the owner or negotiate permissions for use. An example of a vendor currently providing digital watermarking is Digimarc.

Non-Technical Methods for Intellectual Property Protection

A very illustrative example of a non-technical approach to protecting intellectual property was given by the researcher of Griffin Records during a panel discussion at the First Digital Asset Management Conference Issue at the Annenberg School of Communications in 1998: "...We think the protection of intellectual property comes down to an economic equation. It's not one that is left to lawyers and technology, it has to do with our providing products at a value above and beyond that provided by those who would pirate our products" (Griffin, 1998).

The issue was pointed out "So long as we look at that equation, we think that there is a solution" (Griffin, 1998). The main point wasn't whether the pirate copy providers could legally do what they were doing, or technically do what they were doing, but they were stealing bandwidth from their Internet Service Provider or from their university. Therefore, there was clearly a fundamental economic question at stake: Can we economically give away enormous multi-media files and still pay for our bandwidth? The answer was "No." Pirates cannot do that and so merely identifying the pirates to their Internet Service Provider, quite aside from any question of the law or any question of the technology, was enough to get them to stop.

Digital Assets Distribution

In order to manage the asset owner and the user, the owner of a digital asset must be able to determine the usage scenarios that are appropriate for the asset. The scenarios are summarized by the notion of placement, size, duration and extent. In other words, where will the asset be placed (e.g., inside cover of Time Magazine), at what resolution (e.g., two inches square), for how long (e.g., the October issue) and for what size distribution (e.g., 500k copies with international distribution in three languages). Once the usage scenarios are established, the licensing criteria can be enunciated.

License Management refers to the legal terms and conditions that apply to the specific usage scenario. When users determine their usage scenario, the DAM system creates a dynamic price on-line for the specific usage, as well as a legally binding license that is delivered with the asset as it is downloaded. That legally binding license document is generated dynamically by the DAM system based upon the usage choices expressed by the user.

All asset management systems need to be able to track this kind of activity over the lifetime of an asset element. The meta-data associated with an asset also includes the terms and conditions of business for individual suppliers. It is integrated and it is integral to the system itself. The desire to release the commercial potential of the assets is supported by the real-world tools that get suppliers paid. Such rights and licensing management capability must be made a part of a DAM system's architecture.

CONCLUDING REMARKS AND FUTURE STUDY

In the era of e-commerce, Digital Asset Management is emerging as an important topic of study for both practitioners as well as researchers. In this chapter we discuss different concepts and issues of DAM, which include but are not limited to the components and architecture of DAM systems, its basic and desirable features, the taxonomy of DAM systems, protection and distribution sub-systems of

DAM. There are several open issues for research in DAM. A list of these issues includes modeling the storage and organization of digital assets, the digital assets valuation, pricing, rights and licensing models, and methodologies for optimal search and retrieval of digital assets. In a future study, we plan to address some of these open issues.

REFERENCES

Annenberg DAM Conference. (1998). Available on the World Wide Web at: http://www.annenberg.edu/DAM/1998/dam98_1b_transcript.html.

Cravotta, N. (1999). Encryption: More than just complex algorithms. *EDN*, March.

Dipert, B. (2000). Media security thwart temptation, permits prosecution. *EDN*, Available on the World Wide Web: http://www.ednmag.com/ednmag/reg/2000/06222000/13tt.htm. Accessed June 22, 2000.

Faloutsos et al. (1994). Efficient and effective querying by image content. *Journal of Intelligent Information Systems*, 3, 231-262.

Flickner et al. (1995). Query by image and video content: The QBIC system. IBM, Almaden Research Center, San Jose, CA 95120-6099, *Computer*, September, 28(9), 23-31.

Frost and Sullivan. (1998). Available on the World Wide Web at: http://www.frost.com/verity/press/IT/pr584270.htm.

Griffin, J. (1998). Available on the World Wide Web at: http://www.annenberg.edu/DAM/1998/dam98_2a_transcript.html.

Romer, D. (1998). Available on the World Wide Web at: http://www.annenberg.edu/DAM/1998/dam98_2b_transcript.html.

Rosenblatt, W. (1998). Available on the World Wide Web at: http://www.annenberg.edu/DAM/1998/dam98_1b_transcript.html.

Sharples, H. (1999). Sights set on site. *Graphic Arts Monthly*, November, 52-54.

Su, P., Wu, C. and Kuo, C. C. (1999). *Encryption and Watermarking for Media Security*. Available on the World Wide Web at: http://viola.usc.edu/newextra/Research/Scott_Pochyi/Home.htm.

Section II

Marketing

Chapter VI

Pricing and Service Quality in Electronic Commerce

Kemal Altinkemer
Purdue University, USA

Kerem Tomak
University of Texas at Austin, USA

INTRODUCTION

Increased numbers of companies are conducting trade over the Internet. According to a report the AMR Research, we are at the midst of the business-to-business (B2B) growth (as of October 2000). They foresee aggressive growth rates through 2004, causing fundamental changes to the way businesses do business with each other. There is not a day passing without new numbers and forecasts arising about the current state or the future of the Internet Economy. One thing is certain though: the impact of the Internet on the business rules and how they are conducted is tremendous. A recent study from the University of Texas at Austin (Barua and Whinston, 2000) shows that the e-commerce portion of the Internet Economy alone tops the banking, aerospace and drug industries in revenues.

The study divides the Internet Economy into four layers. The first layer consists of the telecommunications companies, Internet Service Providers, Internet backbone carriers, local access companies and manufacturers of end-user networking equipment. In the second layer, Internet Applications Infrastructure involves software products and services necessary to facilitate Web transactions and transaction intermediaries. In addition to the software products that help facilitate Web transactions, this layer of the Internet Economy includes the consultants and service companies that design, build and maintain all types of Web sites, from portals to full e-commerce sites. The third layer, called the Internet Intermediary Indicator, consists of businesses that do not generate transaction-related revenues in the same way as the companies in other layers. There is a distinct type of company that operates in layer three, one that is predominantly an Internet pure-play. While not directly generating revenues from transactions, their Web-based business generates revenues through advertising, membership subscription fees and commissions. Many of the layer three companies are purely Web content providers, while others are market makers or market intermediaries. Finally, the companies that are included in layer four are only those companies that are conducting Web-based commerce transactions (Barua and Whinston, 2000).

In this chapter, we analyze the pricing structures in each of the four layers of the Digital Economy, outlined above, and analyze the relationship between different pricing strategies and customer service quality concept. We provide a selective survey of the vast amount of related literature in the intersection of economics, marketing and computer science as well as point to open research problems and current efforts to understand the pricing and service quality issues in electronic commerce.

PRICING AT LAYER ONE

Layer one consists of networking hardware/software companies, Internet backbone providers and Internet Service Providers. The main focus of research in this area is to use pricing as a strategic tool to allocate scarce network resources among its users in the most efficient way with the assumption that they act selfishly. One of the seminal papers in this area is by Mendelson (1985). A considerable amount of literature that cites this paper forms a branch of literature on pricing and resource allocation in data networks at the intersection of computer science and economics. In general, those who surf the Internet are the ones whose opportunity cost of time is low. For a sustainable network operation with satisfied users, there needs to be a pricing system that is not only socially fair but takes into account the heterogeneous valuation of services by different customers as well. Mendelson (1985) studies the effects of queuing delays and users' related costs, on the management and control of computing resources. The novelty of his approach comes from embedding the representation of performance of computer systems with queuing systems, into the standard microeconomic framework used to study price and capacity decisions, therefore creating an interdisciplinary approach to the problem. He represents quantity of computing per unit of time or, equivalently, the number of standardized transactions (or jobs) processed per unit of time, by q. Associated with this level of usage is the value function $V(q)$, which is an aggregate of users' subsystems. The change in the value function with an additional change in the transaction is equal to the price of that transaction.

$$\frac{dV(q)}{dq} = p$$

The connection to the queuing representation of computer services is made by observing that the transactions in a computer system are actually their arrival rate.

Representing the arrival rate by λ, the value of computer services is $V(\lambda)$ which is twice differentiable and strictly concave. A user's willingness to pay for obtaining processing results one time unit earlier is denoted by v and the expected time a job remains in the system from its arrival time until its processing is completed is given by W. Taking the delay costs into account, and assuming the system is stationary (i.e., no flunctuations in the usage pattern of the computer system), the marginal value of a transaction is equal to the price and expected delay cost of the job:

$$\frac{dV(q)}{dq} = p + vW$$

Depending on whether the capacity of the switch can be changed or not, vW is then computed using standard tools from queuing theory such as Little's Law and representation choice of the behavior of computer systems using a specific type of queuing system (e.g., $M/M/1$, $M/G/1$, etc.). Three optimization problems studied in the paper are given below: given $L = \lambda W$, b: marginal capacity cost, μ :

Net-Value Maximization: $\max_\lambda \{V(\lambda) - vL\}$

Cost Recovery: $\mu b = \lambda p + vL$

Profit Maximization: $\max_\lambda \{\lambda V'(\lambda) - vL\}$

The results obtained in the paper shed light to various issues in the context of computing resource management in organizations. He continues to show that in the presence of delay costs, cost recovery may be quite undesirable and would lead to under-utilization of resources. In fact, if the computing center is required to balance its budget, resulting allocation of resources will not lead to an overall optimum and create incentives to drift away from the optimal solution. The organization as a whole would benefit from reducing congestion by imposing queuing-related charges. Further, he demonstrates that taking users' delay cost into account, seemingly low utilization ratios are often optimal. In the absence of queuing delay accounting, a profit-center approach to computer centers will lead to lower capacity, lower usage rate and similar relative utilization when compared to net-value maximization. Queuing delay is taken as a proxy to service quality in this paper. Another important finding is that the representation of the computing system as a net-value maximizing center as opposed to a profit center leads to higher transaction rates that are more socially optimal.

Tomak, Altinkemer and Kazaz (2000) study the related problem of market segmentation in a computer system using well-established literature on price discrimination. They start with the question of, "Is there an effective segmentation strategy followed by a network manager trying to maximize overall profits while achieving efficient and optimal outcomes?" and arrive at a strategic dependency between the price and capacity. Unlike previous work in this area, a representative network system is modeled as an $M^{(x)}/D/1$ network of queues. Bulk arrival of message cells occurs at the switch. Service time is fixed since the message cells are of fixed length. Using modeling tools from the literature on price discrimination, they show that there is a tradeoff between capacity choice and price discrimination. If the monopoly deliberately chooses to operate under lower capacity ex ante, then ex post price discrimination attempts do not work. Conversely, if the final goal is to provide multiple service levels, then higher ex ante capacity deployment is necessary. In fact, they show that the market is equally divided among different priority classes as the capacity level is increased while keeping all other network parameters constant. With a similar approach, Van Mieghem (2000) studies a setting in which a service provider offers multiple service grades that are differentiated by price and quality. Quality of Service (QoS) is measured by the delay distributions that customers experience in receiving service. The service provider has direct control over the grades, their prices and scheduling. He derives an analytic specification of scheduling, delay distributions and prices under realistic convex delay costs.

On the Internet and in various types of data networks, QoS arises from the concept that transmission rates, error rates and other characteristics can be measured, improved and to some extent guaranteed in advance. It is determined by how well the network design meets customer requirements. As an example, in Asynchronous Transfer Mode (ATM) networks, a user negotiates a traffic contract, which outlines the ATM transfer capability, associated traffic characteristics and the requested QoS. This traffic contract is used to enable efficient operation of the network. In electronic commerce, there is a rich collection of services that require different levels of service quality over the same data communication network. During a telnet session, a user requires a high-speed and low-volume data transfer for real-time interaction with a server. On the other hand, a videoconference needs clarity and coordination in picture and sound, necessitating a much more complex set of service quality attributes, such as synchronization information sent via different interoperable applications (video, audio and text). In addition, audio and video applications require high-volume and high-speed transfers with low variability data transfer rates. Given these diverse application requirements, can pricing

Figure 1: Bridge between the service quality and QoS

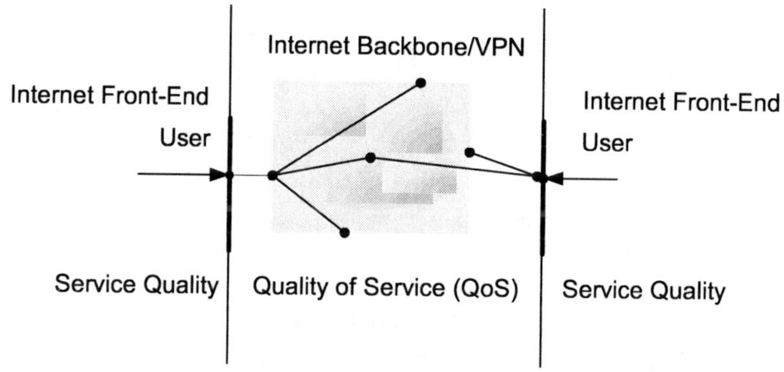

facilitate a given QoS desired by a user in the highly distributed e-commerce infrastructure? How can we best provide different QoS and what role can pricing play in facilitating different QoS?

Seeking answers to these and other related questions, Gupta, Stahl and Whinston (1999) emphasize the importance of QoS match between the network protocols and application/user level service quality requirements. They outline the requirements, characteristics and performance of an ideal price-setting mechanism. They argue that one of the major benefits of having a decentralized computing approach to service provision is that it provides an economic rationale for multiple levels of QoS. It also provides incentives to maintain required QoS levels and will prevent the misuse of the network by redistributing the user demand patterns. A decentralized pricing mechanism can be used when the network is using different protocols for different types of applications, for example, ATM for real-time applications and TCP/IP for applications requiring only best-effort service.

A recent proposal to establish pricing for different applications is Paris Metro Pricing (Odlyzko, 1999). It is a proposal to partition the main network into several logically separate channels in an attempt to provide differentiated services. All channels would route messages using protocols similar to the current ones with different prices. Users choose which channels they would like to send their messages on and pay the corresponding price. This approach builds on a "best effort" setting with no formal quality of service guarantees. More recently, Mason (2000) employs a duopoly model with overall positive network effects to show that flat rate pricing can occur in equilibrium, even when the costs of measuring variable demand are very small. He shows that the possibility of fierce competition when the duopoly firms use two-part tariff pricing leads to flat-rate pricing endogenously arising in equilibrium.

In most of the proposals discussed so far, the network is assumed to have a single link. Gupta et al. (in press) describe a situation where there are sub-networks within larger network structures and only some of them employ usage-based pricing. Other subnetworks are either free or a fixed-pricing is used for access. Even in this situation using usage-based pricing has advantages in spite of free and/or fixed price services in other subnetworks. The socially optimal algorithm in a subnetwork will result in a Pareto improvement even though the other subnetworks are not economically optimal. They identify the users who are going to lose to be those with either little time value or with large size transactions.

A socially optimal resource allocation decision can be made with perfect information about the users' characteristics and the state of the computer systems, but due to the computational burden of collecting and processing this information, it may be prohibitively late to find a solution, if any exists. In ATM-like cell-switched networks, the network manager has to assign priorities to users depending on how much the value of the service is at a given point in time with incomplete information. Altinkemer and Tomak (2000) assume that there is a computer communication network managed by an Information System (IS) department or outsourced to a third party. The department is responsible for the smooth operation of the system and has a network manager who has the right incentives to maximize the net value of the overall system. There are many users from different departments with different preferences in the system. Users know only their own valuations and the network manager knows his/her allocation costs. They bid on the allocation rankings provided to them by the network manager. The model is similar to a double auction mechanism. Each ranking represents a different level of resource allocation with higher ranks corresponding to better transmission speeds. The network system matches true values, including the marginal value and the waiting time, to the rankings through a simple and fast assignment algorithm. They show that this assignment is stable and truth telling (revealing true reservation prices) and is the best strategy for the users.

At the back-end, deploying networks that carry varying levels of traffic is crucial for the future operations of a firm. Designing fault tolerant, efficient and scalable networks is more art than science. Network design problems are typically very complex, involving heuristic computations due to the unlikely nature of finding optimal solutions, varying QoS requirements by heterogeneous users depending on time of the day, changing delay patterns, etc. Managing these network operations is therefore a challenging task. Sophisticated decision and pricing tools are needed to improve usage and service. Inputs to the network routing process are network topology, origin-destination traffic matrix, capacities of existing parallel links and their associated costs in Altinkemer and Bose (2000). Underlying assumptions of this model are Poisson interarrival rate for cells, no node processing delay and negligible propagation delays. In other words, terrestrial fiber optic networks are considered. ATM-based backbone networks are modeled as a network of $M^{(X)}/D/c$ queues where the parallel links are viewed as servers with identical service rate and the cells are viewed as customers. In order to model the links as servers of an $M^{(X)}/D/c$ queue, it is assumed that the cells form a single queue at the nodes and are delivered on the first available link from within "c" parallel links. Another problem is to calculate the prices corresponding to the priority messages providing incentives to the users. This is an important aspect of the network design problem that has not been addressed fully so far. The Lagrangian multipliers for the links are used for the prices. This is just an approximation since the problem is non-linear and there is a duality gap between the primal and the dual problems. However, using the Lagrangian multipliers is a good estimate of the prices. We have to note here that these prices correspond to the shadow prices, which do not necessarily reflect any strategic behavior on the users' part.

The bulk of the literature we have reviewed so far approximates the traffic flow so as to generate the cost structure of the service provider and the network user. This needs to be done in order to allow the modeler to use microeconomic or game theoretic analysis of the economic system. One of the main problems faced by the researchers in this area is the analytical intractability of the models used. It is almost costless to increase the service dimensions in policy-oriented network management software, but a daunting task to replicate the same in an analytical framework. Although simulation has been the preferred approach for realistic performance analysis in computer science and telecommunications research, experimental economics may provide an efficient tool to study the generalizability of many of the economics models used in this area.

Once the network architecture is laid out and pricing method of network services is decided, a new challenge awaits the firms that use this infrastructure to sell digital products. The complementarity and zero marginal cost characteristics of the digital products make it hard to decide on specific pricing strategies. In the next section we discuss pricing of digital products like software, digitized information, etc.

BUNDLING AND COMPONENT PRICING AT LAYER TWO

Diminishing marginal cost of producing and distributing digital goods create new challenges for pricing strategies. Bakos and Brynjolfsson (1999) study the strategic bundling problem and find that when competing for upstream content, larger bundles outbid smaller ones. Bundling may be used strategically to deter entry in the bundler's markets even if the entrants have a superior cost structure or quality. In an earlier paper, Bakos and Brynjolfsson (1997) report that bundling is favored when increasing the number of products within a bundle effectively decreases the heterogeneity of the consumers, which is the case with many information goods. In such cases, bundling reduces the deadweight loss. However, if the consumers' valuations are correlated with one or more common underlying variables, the demand curve continues to reflect the heterogeneity of the consumers' valuations even for large bundles, and the deadweight loss remains. In such cases, it might be profitable to disaggregate the products, and charge the consumers differentially for each product to capture a larger surplus. There is another factor that favors unbundling: Bakos and Brynjolfsson (2000) report that the reduction in transaction and distribution costs tends to make disaggregation of information goods (and by extension, digitized music) more profitable. This is an intuitive result since often goods are bundled just to save on transaction and distribution costs. With a reduction of such costs, it is possible to disaggregate such goods and capture a larger consumer surplus through greater consumer differentiation. They discuss the conditions under which long-term subscription for information goods become feasible. When the product can be costlessly provided over time, it may be profitable to sell a long-term subscription instead of selling individual uses for short periods of time as described above. This is because the user might have high valuations of the goods at some times, and low valuation of the same goods at others. Using arguments similar to bundling, it can be shown that a single subscription fee giving long-term access to the goods might increase profits.

The music industry is directly influenced by the reduction in transaction and distribution costs, and the music albums need to be disaggregated if the arguments in the previous paragraph hold. Altinkemer and Bandyopadhyay (2000) summarize the spectrum of the changes to be considered and start a formal analysis of the underlying issues. Specifically, they consider the effect of unbundling of music items that traditionally came bundled as part of an entire album and present a model for the same. In a music album, the product and its sub-components, the individual songs, are produced by the same company. Denicolo (2000) analyzes compatibility and bundling choices when a generalist firm that offers all the components of a system competes against two specialist firms, each supplying one distinct component only. An interesting finding is that the generalist firm may engage in pure bundling and choose to be incompatible if the differentiation among the components is not high. When systems are more differentiated than their components, the specialist firms will be induced to relax price competition, thus benefiting the generalist firm. At a similar token, Chuang and Sirbu (1999) develop an N-good bundling model with multi-dimensional consumer preferences to study the key factors that determine the optimal bundling strategy. They use analytical and empirical methods to conclude that mixed bundling is the dominant strategy. One of the main results is that pure unbundling outperforms pure bundling, even in the presence of some degree of economies of scale, if consumers positively value only a subset of the bundle components, which is the predominant case in the academic journal context. So, they conclude that academic journal publishers have strong incentives to engage in mixed bundling, i.e., offer both individual articles and journal subscriptions, when selling and delivering over the Internet.

As a newspaper or a journal is a bundle of article components, a software program may be viewed as a bundle of software components. Software component technology that is increasingly used for building applications aims increased efficiency in writing software by providing maximum reuse and dynamic bundling capabilities. Choudhary et al. (1998) study the pricing problem of rentable software components. They concentrate on the effect of network externalities on the pricing strategies of a firm that is renting software as well as selling it. They find a threshold network externality level over which renting becomes strategically desirable for a software company since it increases the customer base. Application Service Providers (ASPs) are good examples of companies building their business models on the very idea of software renting. They offer access to applications through a Web-based interface and provide turnkey software service to customers. There is no custom application development at the end-user's computer system. Businesses are using ASPs' services to outsource the cost of network and server-based application development.

Complementarities, network externalities and entry-deterrence are special areas in the economics literature that may help understand the corresponding characteristics of the software industry. A substantial part of the dynamics of "software economics" remains to be studied as well as the pricing schemes that arise out of the software implementation efforts by the businesses. In the next section, we outline the recent work in customization, personalization and dynamic pricing, especially in on-line content services.

CUSTOMIZED AND DYNAMIC PRICING
IN LAYER THREE

Auctions on the Internet, which are also ways of dynamic pricing, became part of common mantra for the last couple of years. Some treated Internet auctions as revolutionary while others were more cautious. The *Economist* (July 1999) argued that the fixed prices are not going to disappear and auctions will be used when there is uncertainty about what the right price is for a given commodity. *BusinessWeek* (May 1998) was more dramatic a year earlier: "Forget sticker prices. Forget sales clerks too. There is a revolution brewing in pricing that promises to profoundly alter the way goods are marketed and sold. In the future, marketers will offer special deals–tailored just for you, just for the moment–on everything from theater tickets to bank loans to camcorders." Whether it is a revolution or not, one thing is for sure and that is, on-line auctions exhibit some unique characteristics that their physical counterparts do not have. One apparent distinction is that there is a non-negligible probability of interruption during bid submission on the Internet due to technological breakdowns. A software glitch, congested lines or slow connection to the Internet may prevent a bidder from winning an auction. Another interesting characteristic is that the bidding behavior differs even among different auction sites like Amazon and eBay. Depending on the auction closing time rules and the type of the product auctioned, bidders choose to wait until the last second to submit their bids. Roth (2000) shows that this behavior need not result from either common value properties of the objects being sold or irrational behavior. It may occur at equilibrium in private value auctions and may be related to bidder collusion at auctions with fixed end times. Kauffman and Wood (2000) study the opportunistic behavior in Internet auctions. They report that the buyers tend to ignore the reputation score in eBay and base their evaluation of reputation on their own observations of which sellers are interested in long-term relationships with the eBay channel. Lucking-Reiley (1999, 2000) provides exploratory analysis of on-line auctions. He reports that a seller's feedback ratings, reported by other eBay users, have a measurable impact on her auction prices. Furthermore, minimum bids and reserve prices tend to have positive effects on the final auction price and when a seller chooses to have her auction last for a longer period of days, this significantly increases the auction price on average. He sets to test the empirical predictions of recent theories of the endogenous entry of bidders in auctions by using data from a field experiment involving sealed-bid auction for collectible trading cards over the Internet. He observes a participation behavior indicating that bidders consider their bid submission to be costly, and that bidder participation is an endogenous decision. He also notes that a zero reserve price provides higher expected profits. In a similar effort, Bajari and Hortacsu (2000) examine a dataset of eBay coin auctions to explore features of on-line bidding and selling behavior. They find that for a representative auction, a bidder's expected profits fall by 3.2% when the expected number of bidders increases by one. They also document that costly entry is a key component in understanding observed bidding behavior and that items with higher book value tend to be sold using a secret as opposed to posted reserve price with a low minimum bid. In electronic commerce, auctions are not used in selling commodities only. Wellman et al. (in press) suggest using auction for decentralized scheduling of resources to alternate possible uses over designated periods of time. Lazar and Semret (1998) present a progressive second price auction for allocation of variable-size shares of a resource among multiple users. They implement the auction game they propose on the Internet and investigate how convergence times scale with the number of bidders. Weller (1999) proposes the use of auctions for determining which carriers should undertake a universal service obligation and what compensation they should receive for performing this function.

It is important to note that at the brink of major advances in mobile commerce, highly personalized pricing schemes gain further importance. Major consumer portals like Yahoo! already implement mobile auctions. As new applications are developed for distributed computing devices, consumers will increasingly have multiple options for payment. Currently, subscription and usage-based pricing are used in combination. In the next section we discuss the application areas of these two pricing schemes.

SUBSCRIPTION AND TWO-PART PRICING IN LAYER FOUR

Even if large software systems that consist of downloadable applets are practical, they will be available on a subscription rather than a per-use basis. Arguing that this is due to the risk attitude of consumers, Odlyzko (1996) provides a comprehensive overview of various issues in e-commerce including payment methods. The main thrust of his argument is that the users are willing to pay for the software up-front in order to decrease the future additional cost that they would otherwise incur under unforeseen circumstances.

Distribution channels are major components of a production or retailing company's logistics system. Introduction of on-line stores on the Web significantly contributes to the competitiveness of a company, but also requires the optimization of the distribution and operating costs under a logistics system. This phenomenon is best observed when "brick-and-mortar" superstores or general stores evolve to a "click-and-mortar" business model (Aksen and Altinkemer, 2000). Click-and-mortar businesses are sometimes referred to as e-tail businesses as a morph of retail business to electronic-tail business. Amazon.com has recently opened up six new warehouses to serve its customers faster. To ensure a high market share in the new business arena, Amazon.com has to serve potential customers as fast as its giant competitors do. Accordingly, Amazon.com starts to adopt a hybrid structure by resembling more the traditional brick-and-mortar companies. On the contrary, Wal-Mart, trying to quickly respond to this challenge from Amazon.com, already went on-line by opening up a virtual store on the Web. The United States' third largest retailer, Kmart, pursues a similar strategy as well. *USA-Today* announced a $63 million on-line alliance between Kmart and Yahoo! The result of this alliance on behalf of Kmart is the gain of Yahoo!'s on-line expertise and 100 million worldwide users. A new e-commerce firm and a Web site called "BlueLight.com" were also be born from the alliance. The target of these spectacular deals is the same: millions of future on-line customers who are expected to prefer the comfort and convenience of on-line shopping at their homes to on-site shopping. There is a lot of managerial as well as operational dynamics taking place in the background of this entire reshuffling of the marketplace. The effect of multi-channel sales on pricing strategies continues to attract attention from multiple research disciplines.

Fishburn and Odlyzko (1999) investigate the existence and implications of competitive equilibria when two firms offer the same electronically transmitted information goods such as news articles, software, audio and video streams and databases under different pricing policies. The main question they address is whether fixed fee has an advantage over usage pricing, not taking into account the psychological factors and under full information. They find that in the cases that they consider, competition leads to a destructive price war. In the case of a stable equilibrium in which the firms can set prices that lead to non-zero profit outcomes, fixed subscription fee strategy performs better than charging on a per-hit basis.

Zettelmeyer (2000) shows how firms' pricing and communications strategies may be affected by the size of the Internet. If the access to the Internet is limited, firms facilitate consumer search; however, as the number of users increase, he argues that firms' pricing strategies will be closer to the conventional channel. He points to the possibility of firms using information on multiple channels strategically to achieve finer consumer segmentation. In a related paper, Shafer and Zettelmeyer (1999) argue that the ease of information provision on the Internet gives manufacturers an opportunity to communicate their product offerings to consumers directly. This leads to channel conflict, and retailers may be harmed even if it is not used as a direct sales channel. Balasubramanian (1998) considers a model that accommodates the variability of relative attractiveness of retail shopping across consumers, variability of the fit with the direct channel across product categories, competition moderating affect of existing retail presence in local markets and finally, irrelevance of the location of direct marketer to the competitive outcome. The results of his analysis suggest that the traditional focus on retail entry equilibria may not yield informative or relevant findings when direct channels have a strong presence. He points out the strategic aspects of the information made available on the Internet and draws the distinction between the seller efforts to collect information versus the consumers' initiatives. Jain and Kannan (2000) examine the various issues involved in pricing information products using an economic model to analyze the conditions under which the various pricing schemes may prove optimal for the on-line servers. They show that the variation in consumer expertise and valuation of information affects the choice of a pricing strategy by the server. They also find that given the cost structures characterizing the market, undifferentiated on-line servers can compete and coexist in the market while making positive profits.

Off-line sales channels are increasingly using the on-line channel as a complementary revenue source. Advances in distributed computing will further decrease the boundaries between these seemingly unrelated retail venues. It is a big unknown whether the mobile devices will live up to their hype in the marketplace during the next decade.

ISSUES, CONTROVERSIES, PROBLEMS

There are many issues related to pricing and service quality at layer one. One of these is the flat-rate pricing of Internet services versus differential or per-use pricing. The argument for the flat-rate pricing is that it is easy to comprehend. Since most of the users do not care about what is taking place at the nodes in between the transmission, but care much more about the speed of transmission, reliability and availability of the services, simplicity of price schemes is crucial for acceptance. Mental accounting works to the benefit of upfront payment mechanisms in this case. Nobody wants to be worried about the amount they will have to pay in the future for their use of network services. When it comes to using the Internet, we are very risk averse.

Proponents of differentiated services argue, in general, that the current best-effort level of service provided by the Internet is inefficient since it cannot allocate priority-based service to those applications that require it. A videoconference transmission enjoys the same service as a mission-critical application that a business needs to use daily, like an ERP system. In order to control network flow, a smart pricing mechanism is necessary. However, standard price differentiation models from economics and marketing literatures tend to be too complex for application in the network area.

Service quality is another matter of utmost importance for electronic commerce. Increased attention to the customer relationship management solution providers justifies this assessment. The interaction between the user and the network can be decomposed into ex-ante and ex-post stages. Ex-ante, a typical user becomes aware of his/her needs for network services and starts shopping around for different service providers. Once a service provider is spotted through more information, reputation, word of mouth or other means, the match between the expectations of the customer and perceived fit of the service described by the seller is assessed. After the payment is made for the services of a particular provider, experience with the network hardware/software reveals the ex-post evaluation of the company by the customer, and actual satisfaction level is attained. Depending on whether this experience is positive or negative, a network user either decides to change the level of services, keep the current one or discontinue completely. Research is underway in the Center for Research in Electronic Commerce at the University of Texas at Austin to address these problems using tools from economics and operations research (Tomak and Whinston, 2000).

At the second layer, efficiency gains and user acceptance of using micropayments for accounting and charging of software component use is still an open problem. Strategic aspects of using software components' pricing to deter entry in the ASP market deserves attention from an interdisciplinary point of view. The effect of network externalities (positive or negative) on the market entry and exit decisions is an interesting problem to study. There is an ongoing research effort to solve these problems from an economics perspective (e.g., Fudenberg and Tirole, 1999; Parker and van Alstyne, 2000; Bhargava et al., 2000; Tomak, 2000), but much more needs to be done in order to understand the fundamental characteristics of products and markets at this layer of the digital economy.

On-line auctions have unique characteristics that require new techniques to analyze various strategic and behavioral aspects. Participants' overbidding behavior, length of an on-line auction and strategic choice of an on-line selling mechanism by the seller are some of the interesting problems that are in the research agenda of various researchers from different fields (Barua and Tomak, 2000; Bapna, Goes and Gupta, 2000).

The final layer of the digital economy carries importance especially in the business-to-business (B2B) electronic commerce relationships nowadays. With business models still evolving, a sound pricing model that is commonly accepted and used needs to emerge. Further research needs to be done in the context of on-line market structures, partnerships and trade mechanisms in the B2B world. Supplier trust and information sharing across these electronic platforms present vast opportunities for continuing research in this exciting field.

CONCLUSION

There is not a single day that we do not hear about new ways of doing business on the Internet. We also started to realize that not all business ideas are viable on the Internet, no matter how innovative and promising they sound. As the focus of the business world shifts from hype to reality, there are interesting problems waiting to be solved in the electronic commerce area that are inherently interdisciplinary. In this chapter, we brought to attention current research efforts for the last couple of years in pricing and service quality using the framework of the Internet economy as laid out by Barua and Whinston (2000). While providing references to current and ongoing work, we suggested several issues that should spur further interest in research communities around the world. We believe that the pricing and service quality problems we have briefly outlined in this chapter require a unified effort from the member of businesses involved in electronic commerce and academia in related fields.

REFERENCES

Aksen D. and Altinkemer, K. (2000). Metamorphosis from brick-and-mortar to click-and-mortar business model. *Working Paper*, Krannert Graduate School of Management, Purdue University.

Altinkemer K. and Bose, I. (2000). Asynchronous transfer mode networks with parallel links and multiple service classes. *Working Paper*, Krannert Graduate School of Management, Purdue University.

Altinkemer K. and Bose, I. (1998). A queuing model for the World Wide Web servers. *Proceedings of the 3rd INFORMS Conference on Information Systems and Technology*, 28-34.

Altinkemer, K. and Bandyopadhyay, S. (2000). Bundling and distribution of digitized music over the Internet. *Journal of Organizational Computing and Electronic Commerce*, 10(3), 209-224.

Altinkemer, K. and Tomak, K. (2001). A distributed allocation mechanism for network resources using intelligent agents. *Information Technology and Management*, 2(2).

AMR Research. (2000). Special B2B report. Available on the World Wide Web at: http://www.amrresearch.com. Accessed April 2000.

Bajari, P. and Hortacsu, A. (2000). Winner's curse, reserve prices and endogenous entry: Empirical insights from eBay auctions. *Working Paper*, Stanford University. Available on the World Wide Web at: http://www.stanford.edu/~bajari/wp/auction/ebay.pdf.

Bakos Y. and Brynjolfsson, E. (1997). Aggregation and disaggregation of information goods: Implications for bundling, site licensing and micropayment systems. *Working Paper*, MIT, June.

Bakos, Y. and Brynjolfsson E. (1999). Bundling information goods: Pricing, profits and efficiency. *Management Science*, 45(12), 1613-1630.

Bakos Y. and Brynjolfsson, E. (2000). Bundling and competition on the Internet. *Marketing Science*, 19(1), 63-82.

Balasubramanian, S. (1998). Mail versus mall: A strategic analysis of competition between direct marketers and conventional retailers. *Marketing Science*, 17(3), 181-195.

Bapna, R., Goes, P. and Gupta, A. (in press). On-line auctions: Insights and analysis. *Communications of the ACM*.

Barua, A. and Tomak, K. (2000). Buy now or bid?: Optimal choice of an on-line selling mechanism. *Workshop on Information System Economics*, Australia, December 14-16.

Barua, A. and Whinston, A. B. (2000). Measuring the Internet Economy. Available on the World Wide Web at: http://www.Internetindicators.com/june_full_report.pdf.

Bhargava, H., Choudhary, V. and Krishnan, R. (1999). Pricing and product design: Intermediary strategies in an electronic market. *Working Paper*, Carnegie Mellon University.

Business Week. (1998). *Good-bye to fixed pricing?* May, 59.

Choudhary, V., Tomak, K. and Chaturvedi, A., (1998). Economic benefits of renting software. *Journal of Organizational Computing and Electronic Commerce*, 8(4), 277-305.

Chuang, J. C. and Sirbu, M. (1999). Optimal bundling strategy for digital information goods: Network delivery of articles and subscriptions. *Information Economics and Policy*, 11(2), 147-76.

Denicolo, V. (2000). Compatibility and bundling with generalist and specialist firms. *Journal of Industrial Economics*, 48(2), 177-88.

Economist. (1999). The heyday of the auction. Available on the World Wide Web at: http://www.economist.com/editorial/freeforall/24-7-99/fn8116.html. Accessed July 24, 1999.

Fishburn, P. C. and Odlyzko, A. M. (1999). Competitive pricing of information goods: Subscription pricing versus pay-per-use. *Economic Theory*, 13, 447-470.

Fudenberg, D. and Tirole, J. (1999). Pricing under the threat of entry by a sole supplier of a network good. *Working Paper*, Harvard University.

Gupta, A., Stahl, D. O. and Whinston, A. B. (1999). The economics of network management. *Communications of the ACM*, 42(9), 57-63.

Gupta, A., Linden, L., Stahl, D. O. and Whinston, A. B. (in press). Benefits and costs of adopting usage-based pricing in a subnetwork. *Information Technology Management*.

Gupta, A., Stahl, D. O. and Whinston, A. B. (1997). A stochastic equilibrium model of Internet pricing. *Journal of Economic Dynamics and Control*, 21(4-5), 697-722.

Jain, S. and Kannan, P. K. (2000). Pricing of information products on on-line servers: Issues, models and analysis. *Working Paper*, Purdue University.

Kauffman, R. J. and Wood, C. A. (2000). Running up the bid: Modeling seller opportunism in Internet auctions. *MISRC Working Paper*, University of Minnesota.

Lazar, A. A. and Semret, N. (1998). The progressive second price auction mechanism for network resource sharing. *The 8th International Symposium on Dynamic Games*, Maastricht, The Netherlands.

Lucking-Reiley, D. (2000). Auctions on the Internet: What's being auctioned, and how? *Journal of Industrial Economics*, 48(3), 227-252.

Lucking-Reiley, D. (1999). Using field experiments to test equivalence between auction formats: Magic on the Internet. *American Economic Review*, 89(5), 1063-1080.

Mason, R. (2000). Simple competitive Internet pricing. *European Economic Review*, 44, 1045-1056.

Masuda, Y. and Whang, S. (1999). Dynamic pricing for network service: Equilibrium and stability. *Management Science*, 45(6), 857-869.

Mendelson, H. (1985). Pricing computer services: Queueing effects. *Communications of the ACM*, 28(3), 312-321.

Odlyzko, A. (1996). The bumpy road of electronic commerce. Maurer, H. (Ed.), *WebNet 96-World Conference of the Web Soc. Proceedings*, *AACE*, 378-389.

Odlyzko, A. (1999). Paris metro pricing: The minimalist differentiated services solution. *Proceedings of the 7th International Workshop on Quality of Service*, 159-161.

Parker, G. G. and van Alstyne, M. W. (2000). Information complements, substitutes and strategic product design. *Proceedings of the International Conference on Information Systems*.

Roth, A. and Ockenfels, A. (2000). Last-minute bidding and the rules for ending second-price auctions: Theory and evidence from a natural experiment on the Internet. *Working Paper*, Harvard University.

Shaffer, G. and Zettelmeyer, F. (1999). The Internet as a medium for marketing communications: Channel conflict over the provision of information. *Working Paper*, University of California at Berkeley.

Simon, H. (1992). Pricing opportunities and how to exploit them. *Sloan Management Review*, Winter, 55-65.

Tomak, K., Altinkemer, K. and Kazaz, B. (1999). Priority pricing in cell switched networks. *Seventh International Conference on Telecommunication Systems Modeling and Analysis*, 72-82.

Tomak, K., Altinkemer, K. and Kazaz, B. (2000). Externalities and market segmentation in data networks. *Working Paper*, University of Texas at Austin.

Tomak, K. and Whinston, A. B. (2000). Incomplete digital markets for service quality in electronic commerce. *Working Paper*, University of Texas at Austin.

Tomak, K. (2000). Strategic entry and exit to the application service provider market. *Working Paper*, University of Texas at Austin.

van Mieghem, J. A. (2000). Price and service discrimination in queuing systems: Incentive compatibility of Gc mu scheduling. *Management Science*, 46(9), 1249-1267.

Weller, D. (1999). Auctions for universal service obligations. *Telecommunications Policy*, 23, 645-674.

Wellman, M. P., Walsh, W. E., Wurman, P. R. and Mackie-Mason, J. K. (in press). Auction protocols for decentralized scheduling. *Games and Economic Behavior*.

Zettelmeyer, F. (2000). Expanding to the Internet: Pricing and communications strategies when firms compete on multiple channels. *Journal of Marketing Research*, 37(3), 292-308.

Chapter VII

Delivery and Tracking of Rotating Banner Advertisements on the World Wide Web: An Information System Model

Subhasish Dasgupta
George Washington University, USA

Rajesh Chandrashekaran
Fairleigh Dickinson University, USA

In this chapter we propose a framework for the delivery and tracking of rotating banner advertisements on the World Wide Web (WWW). The proposed conceptual framework attempts to improve upon traditional approaches by utilizing both client and server resources. In addition to being able to track clicks, it allows for other non-traditional measures like exposure time and opportunities to see.

INTRODUCTION

According to the Internet Advertising Bureau (IAB), banner ads accounted for almost 55% of all advertising on the Internet. A typical banner advertisement consists of short text and/or graphic that is hyper-linked to an advertiser's Web site. That is, when a user clicks on the button or banner, s/he is directly transported to that site.

As an advertising medium, the World Wide Web (WWW) has several characteristics that make it similar to both print and broadcast media. Although banner advertisements on the WWW can, in many ways, be equated with advertisements in traditional print media (newspapers and magazines), the Web offers a unique environment in which advertisers can include animation and interactive features to enhance the effectiveness of banner ads. Of course, greater interactivity demands greater bandwidth. In addition, the WWW offers selective targeting, flexibility and the ability to track effectiveness. Recent statistics (Li, 1999) suggest that, despite its many unique advantages, on-line advertising accounts for only a small portion of total media spending ($2.8 billion versus $117 billion in 1999). According to the Internet Advertising Bureau (http://www.iab.net), a large portion of Internet advertising dollars was devoted to consumer products and financial services.

Although traditional media like television continue to consume a major portion of the advertising budget, marketers have recognized the potential of the World Wide Web to communicate with their target market, and are focussing on using the power of this new medium to communicate with "net savvy" consumers. This is evidenced by the fact that the amount spent on net advertising has increased almost five-fold between 1996 and 1997 (*Business Week*, 1997). Advertisers, who have been constantly looking out for newer and better ways to get their ads noticed, find that the WWW offers them with a very unique environment in which to "sell their wares." As noted by Berthon, Pitt and Watson (1996, pg. 53), "The World Wide Web is characterized by ease of entry, relatively low set-up costs, globalness, time independence and [most importantly] interactivity." Unlike other traditional broadcast media (like television and radio), the Web offers advertisers a chance to communicate with consumers when they are highly involved, and when they are in an information-gathering and -processing mode.

Evaluating and Pricing On-Line Banner Advertisements

To be able to evaluate the Internet's potential as an advertising medium, advertisers and Web sites must be able to develop valid and reliable ways of measuring effective reach (percentage of people from a given target market who have the opportunity to see the ad), frequency (average number of times a user in the target is exposed to the ad in a specified time period) and overall impact (behavioral and/or attitudinal changes produced). Ways of assessing the impact of on-line ads include the number of times the banner was served by the ad server (impressions), number of unique visitors (eyeballs), hits, click-through percentage, conversion rate, page views and duration of stay (sight stickiness). Although many firms (e.g., Media Metrics, Neilsen) have made significant progress in audience measurement and tracking ad effectiveness using a combination of several consumer-centered and site-centered measures, several issues need to be addressed before Web ad effectiveness can be assessed at the individual user level.

Although click-through and subsequent purchase behavior are popularly used as indicators of banner ad effectiveness, recent research has indicated that, in addition to eliciting behavioral responses (e.g., clicking), banners may be used to build awareness, create and change users' attitudes towards advertised brands (Briggs and Hollis, 1997). It is estimated that only about 4% of visitors click on banners the first time they are exposed to it. Therefore, pricing Internet banner ads using measures based on click-through may be sub-optimal (Hoffman and Novak, 1996).

As many researchers have noted, click-through rate essentially measures the audience's "behavioral" responses to the Web advertisement (Briggs and Hollis, 1997). Thus, only the short-term effects of advertising are examined. However, extant research has shown that advertising has the potential of eliciting other non-behavioral responses as well (Batra, Myers and Aaker, 1996). For example, advertising (in other traditional media like television and magazines) can be used to affect consumers' attitudes, which may or may not translate to immediate behaviors. The advertising literature offers several cognitive measures of effectiveness such as aided and unaided-recall (recognition), which have been used to examine the effects of advertising exposures on audiences' top-of-the-mind awareness. However, the effectiveness of advertising on the Web has been evaluated purely on behavioral grounds, but other cognitive and attitudinal effects of Web advertising have not been addressed.

Despite the crucial role of the WWW as an information source for consumers, there is surprisingly little research on the entire range of effects produced by banner advertisements on the Web. Towards this end, the Internet Advertising Bureau (IAB) and MB Interactive engaged in a joint research effort (see IAB On-Line Effectiveness Study, 1997), in which they addressed several important issues related to the use of banner advertisements. In particular, most of the emphasis is on click-through rates, but knowledge about whether and how advertising on the WWW affects consumers' perceptions, beliefs, attitudes and behaviors towards the products and services being advertised is limited. Although the use of the Internet as an advertising medium has exploded in recent years, advertisers are not aware of how this medium can be used in synergy with other traditional media.

Finally, the issue of pricing needs to be addressed. How should Web sites bill advertisers for advertising time/space on the World Wide Web? Traditional media vehicles bill advertisers on the basis of paid (guaranteed) circulation, program ratings, etc., which measure the "reach" of the media vehicles. Thus, television shows (like Seinfeld) and events (like the Super Bowl), which have large audience shares (i.e., high program ratings), can charge premium prices. Similarly magazines bill advertisers on the basis of the number of audience members reached. Here, "reach" may be defined in terms of the paid circulation multiplied by the pass-along rate (i.e., average number of number of readers per issue). However, Web sites selling advertising space to interested advertisers have not been able to formulate pricing strategies based on any systematic research. A commonly used method of billing is in terms of the popularity of the Web site (measured in terms of the number of hits). Some advertisers pay Web site owners on the basis of the number of people who actually click on the ad and link to the advertisers' Web pages to seek out more information. This measure is commonly referred to as the "click-through rate."

From the advertiser's perspective, a "click" offers unequivocal proof that the ad was indeed noticed. Thus, it is based on accountability.

The most popular ways of assessing the efficiency of the Web as an advertising medium is using traditional CPM (cost per thousand impressions delivered), which averaged around $33.75 in 1999 (Strauss and Frost, 2001, p. 259), and CPC (cost-per-click). However, several researchers and practitioners are not comfortable with evaluating on-line ads solely on the basis of these figures. Better understanding of users' Web surfing behavior have enabled Web sites (e.g., DoubleClick) to deliver customized and highly targeted messages (banners) from their ad-servers based on several demographic, geographic and psychographic characteristics.

STATIC VERSUS ROTATING BANNER ADVERTISEMENTS

Static banner advertisements are defined as those in which the banner space is utilized by a single advertiser, whose banner appears along with a Web page through the duration of client's visit. Each such ad provides a link with the advertiser's home page via a "button." Note that the term static simply refers to the fact that the ad belongs to a single advertiser. However, each ad may include moving or animated elements (text, graphics or both) and other features that attempt to draw attention to the ad.

In contrast, rotating banner advertisements refer to ads belonging to different advertisers that can share the same banner space for the duration of the page visit. That is, two or more advertisements appear in succession on the user's screen in the same banner space. Each ad appears on the user's screen for a predetermined duration, and is then replaced by another ad belonging to a different advertiser. Thus "rotation" continues as long as the page is being displayed on the user's screen. Again, each ad may contain moving elements. Furthermore, similar to static ads, each ad in the rotation provides a link to the advertiser's page for the duration of display. Rotating banner ads can be thought of as being similar to rotating billboard advertising during sports events (e.g., basketball games). Currently, most banner ads on the Web are static ads.

Why Examine Rotating Ads?

The motivation for this study is based on research, albeit limited, on the impacts of stadium billboard advertisements (Hansen, Bay and Friis, 1997). Although increasing the number of ads has the potential of reducing the effectiveness of Web ads by introducing the problem of "advertising clutter," advertisers might agree to share the advertising time and space with other advertisers for several reasons. First, the sheer novelty of rotating banner ads might arouse audience interest resulting in greater reach. Second, even if there is a decline in effectiveness due to clutter, it might be offset by reduced cost of advertising, resulting in more profitable allocation of advertising budgets. Third, the possibility of time, space and cost sharing using rotating banners will allow smaller advertisers with smaller advertising budgets to benefit from the power of the Internet.

IS MODELS FOR AD DELIVERY AND MEASUREMENT

At a very fundamental level, there are five steps involved in an ad delivery system: (1) user or client requests a page from the Web site, (2) Web site requests an ad to be placed on the page, (3) ad is inserted into the page, (4) page and ad are downloaded by the user and (5) ad is displayed on the user's screen. Let's look at the entire process of page and ad delivery using an example. A user starts the process by entering a Web address like http://cnn.com into their browser's location bar. The user's browser then requests the first, also called home, page from the Web site http://cnn.com. The page may contain a banner advertisement and the Web site requests the ad to be placed on the page, which is generally done using an insert image HTML tag in the homepage. Then the ad is inserted into the page and both the ad and the page are downloaded to the user's computer. The page and ad are displayed on the user's screen using a browser. Although this is the basic process of delivering ads to a user, there are a number of different variations depending on how ads are placed on the page and what places them there. Each variation constitutes a different ad delivery and measurement model. In the following paragraphs of this section, we look at different models.

Browsers have a set up in which they store the most recently used pages in the client computer hard drive. This is called the browser cache. One of the challenges of Internet advertising is to measure ad delivery even when the corresponding ad banner is not downloaded from the server but is displayed from the browser cache. For example if a user requests a page from http://cnn.com, the homepage may be downloaded with the ad banner associated with it. If the user visits the page again and if the page content is changed but the associated ad is not, the old ad banner may not be downloaded by the client computer but may be displayed directly from the client's cache. In this case the server may not be able to count that the ad associated with the page was delivered. Since some advertisers pay per 1,000 ad impressions, this may be a loss for the Web site.

Some companies use cache more effectively by setting up a proxy server on the client side. The server serves as a Web cache for a number of different clients. This proxy server caches recently used pages by the Web clients and these pages are not subsequently downloaded. This constitutes a serious problem for the ad delivery system. Some ad delivery systems now use cache-busting mechanisms to prevent proxy servers from repeatedly caching pages and banners, but these methods have met with limited success. Figure 1 shows the mechanism used in cache-based ad delivery systems.

We classify ad delivery and measurement models into three types: Static Ad Model, Dynamic Ad Model and Measurement-Focused Ad Model. ABC Interactive

Figure 1: Proxy Server-Cache Mechanism

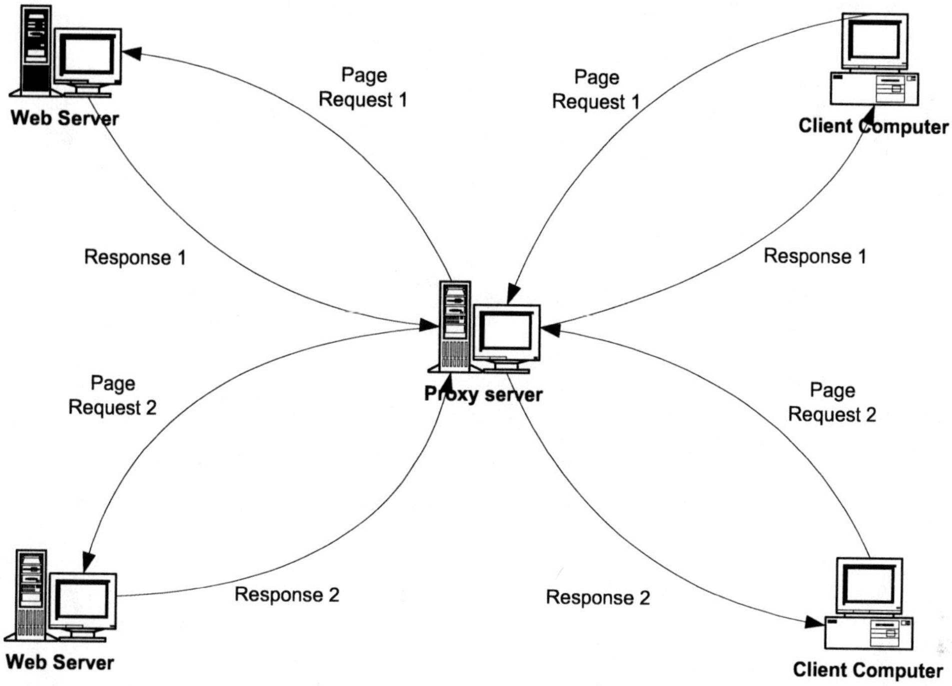

proposed five models for ad serving and tracking (Bennett, 1998). We consolidated their five model types into three categories by combining variations of similar model types. We believe that our classification is more realistic and it groups similar models together.

The Static Ad Model

In the Static Ad Model when a user requests a page, the Web server responds with the requested page. The page has content and HTML code to insert a banner image into the Web page. This banner image is the advertisement. The server finds the requested banner image for the Web page. The page content and the banner image are then transmitted to the user's computer, that is, the client, over the Internet. The Web server log records the transfer of the content page as a "hit" in the server's log. When the ad file is sent out to the client, the server also records that the user's browser successfully downloaded the advertisement. In this model each page has only one ad associated with it and this ad is changed in batches, either once per day or once per week. Figure 2 provides a graphical representation of the process.

The basic model consists of the following computer components: client computer (including browser, cache, log), proxy server and Web server (including Web server log). Table 1 provides brief descriptions of each of the different components of the basic ad delivery model.

Figure 2: Static Ad Model

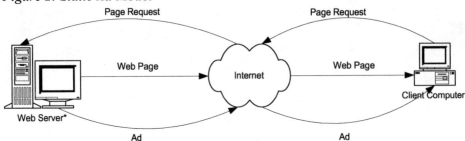

* The Web server has both content and the ad

Table 1: Ad delivery model components

System	Component	Description
User or client computer	Browser	A computer program that requests web pages and other associated applications over the Internet and that can display these files using the right format
	Cache	A storage area on the user computer's hard disk where recently viewed web pages are stored
	Browser Log	All requests for individual files and ads are logged by a software program running on the client's browser.
Proxy server (also called web cache)		This is a server that lies in between the organizational network and the Internet. It has its own disk storage and stores copies of recently requested objects. (Kurose and Ross 2000)
Server	Web server	A computer that is addressable by a URL and that houses objects. Objects include web pages (HTML files), JPEG images, and other applications or programs.
	Web server log	Also called an Access log, this is a list of all requests for individual files and ads that users (or clients) have made from a web site (from Whatis.com 2000)

For example, a user requests a particular page at http://cnn.com/news.html, a site that uses a static ad model. In this case both the page content, that is, the news text as well as the advertisement banner at the top of the page are stored in the same Web server. The server log is updated as soon as the user downloads the content and the advertisement image. If the user requests the same page a number of times during the day, the user may receive the same advertisement because only one ad banner is associated with the page. This is a serious flaw of the Static Ad Model, and has been rectified in subsequent ad delivery mechanisms. The fact that the entire content and ad delivery is done by only one Web server can be an advantage, as well as a disadvantage. The advantage is that content and ad banners are centralized on a single system. The disadvantage is that images like ad banners are large in size and the space available or capacity of the Web server may limit the number of banners that can be stored.

The Dynamic Ad Model

The Dynamic Ad Model is very similar to the Static Ad Model described above. In addition to the Web server, there is a separate server called Ad server which stores all the banner advertisements that are delivered to the client. The Ad server also has special software that makes a decision regarding which ads should be served to the client or user. Figure 3 graphically represents the ad delivery mechanism of the Dynamic Ad Model.

For example, a user visits the same page http://cnn.com/news.html but the site now uses a Dynamic Ad Model. The process starts with the user's browser sending a request for the page news.html on the server cnn.com. The Web server finds the page news.html and finds an HTML tag in it, which mentions that a banner image should be included in the page. The information is passed to the Ad server, which determines the banner that should be inserted into the page. Banner selection is done using a combination of different criteria based on user preferences. The Web page with the content and the banner ad are then transmitted over the Internet to the user's browser where it is displayed.

Bennett (1998) called this mechanism, in which banners are inserted into a Web page based on user preferences or other criteria, an Ad Insertion Model. This model is used by many ad management software products like Accipter, NetGravity and RealMedia. According to Bennett, there are many inaccuracies in the measurement of ads delivered using the Ad Insertion Model. The measurement is inaccurate when browsers have graphic files turned off and cannot make a request for the ad even when the page is downloaded to the browser. Also, if a Web site's page is served from client computer cache or proxy server, the ad server may not get an opportunity to provide its customized ad.

FIgure 3: Dynamic Ad Model

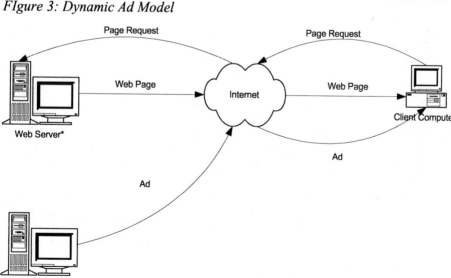

* Content is stored on the Web server and ads are on the Ad server

Another variation of the Dynamic Ad Model is a delivery mechanism in which the ads assigned to Web pages are constantly changed. Unlike the Static Model in which only one ad is associated with a Web page when it is requested, the Dynamic Model uses server-management software to dynamically assign ads to the Web page. In such a delivery system, although only one ad is delivered at a time to any particular user, different banners may be delivered to the same user on different visits. Similarly, different banners may be delivered to different users requesting the page at the same time. Using the Dynamic Ad Model approach on an earlier example, the user requests the page http://cnn.com/news.html then the user's browser requests the page news.html from the Web server cnn.com. Since a dynamic model is used in this system, the Ad server dynamically assigns an ad to be displayed with the page. Both, the content and the ad assigned are then downloaded to the user's browser. In this case, if the user clicks to reload the same page, thereby repeating the download sequence, the user may receive a different ad along with the page. This model enables the server to provide different advertisements for the same page content.

Measurement-Based Models

The previously mentioned models are based on the type and method by which an ad is inserted into a Web page. The remaining two models address measurement of ad delivery. The first, cache-measurement, "allows for the appropriate measurements of ads stored and provided from cache by a proxy server or browser, as well as those ads actually provided by the ad server" (Bennett, 1998). The second, browser measurement, allows for the recording of ad-related activity using software (e.g., Java) that runs on the requesting browser.

Two companies, the Internet Advertising Bureau and MB Interactive, conducted a study in 1997 of the effectiveness of Internet advertising. They pointed out that ad delivery measurement is primarily based on the 'click-through' rate generated by the banner advertisement. However, a number of unobservable effects of banner advertising like "opportunities to see" have been ignored.

Table 2 provides a summary of the three Ad delivery and measurement models discussed above. The table provides a comparison of ad delivery mechanism used in each of the ad delivery models considered in this chapter. We find that the Static Ad Model uses a centralized process in which both the content and ad are stored and delivered by a single Web server. On the other hand, in the Dynamic and Measurement-focused Ad models a separate server handles the delivery of ads. These models concentrate on the delivery and tracking of single banner ads, and cannot manage the delivery of rotating ads. Therefore, in the next section, we provide a new information systems model for the delivery and tracking of rotating ads.

Table 2: A comparison of three Ad delivery models

MODEL	CONTENT DELIVERED BY	AD DELIVERED BY	DELIVERY MECHANISM
Static Ad Model	Web server	Web Server	One ad associated with each page. These ads are changed in daily or weekly intervals
Dynamic Ad Model	Web server	Ad server	Different ads are dynamically associated with each page. This can be done based on the user
Measurement-focused Models	Web server	Ad server	Two types: Cache –measured: In which the emphasis is on counting ads provided from cache by a proxy server Browser-measured: In which a browser run program keeps track of Ads downloaded

A FRAMEWORK FOR DELIVERY AND TRACKING OF ROTATING BANNERS

Rotating ads provide the ability to deliver multiple ads to users by associating many ads with a single Web page. Most Web sites have popular pages that users visit often. Rotating banners allow companies to deliver more than one advertisement for these pages thereby increasing their yield from the page. In this section we develop a theoretical framework to examine how rotating banner ads may be delivered and evaluated. Figure 4 shows the proposed framework for the delivery and tracking of rotating banners.

The proposed system consists of two components: Ad delivery and Ad tracking. The following sections describe each in turn.

Ad Delivery

When a Web page is downloaded from the server, it downloads the contents of the page (containing the Java Script for the rotation of the ad images), the ad images and a program to keep track of time spent on the page (T_p) and click status of each ad (C_i). Once the page and the ads have been loaded on the client's browser, the Java Script program that is built into the Web page is executed using the client-computer's resources. This provides the ad rotation, and is essentially the same as the one discussed earlier. This program is crucial to the implementation of the rotating banner system.

Figure 4: Ad delivery and tracking system

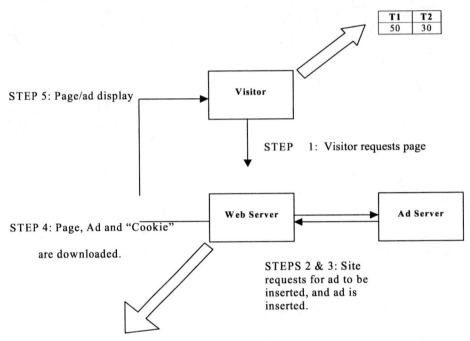

CLIENT-SIDE LOG

T1	T2
50	30

STEP 5: Page/ad display

Visitor

STEP 1: Visitor requests page

Web Server

Ad Server

STEP 4: Page, Ad and "Cookie"

are downloaded.

STEPS 2 & 3: Site
requests for ad to be
inserted, and ad is
inserted.

SERVER-SIDE LOG

Client	Time (T)	S1	S2	C1	C2
1	0	1	0	0	0
	30	1	1	0	0
	60	2	1	0	0
	80	2	1	1	0

Note:
T = Time elapsed since page and ads were downloaded
S1 and S2 = Number of opportunities to see ads 1 & 2 respectively
C1 and C2 = Click status of ads 1 & 2 respectively
T1 and T2 = Total time of display of ads 1 & 2 respectively

Ad Tracking

The tracking system consists of two sub-systems. The one that resides on the Web (or Ad) Server is called the Server Side sub-system, and the other, which utilizes the user's computing resources, is called the Client Side sub-system. Each sub-system is further described below. For explanation purposes we consider a system that consists of two rotating ads: Ad 1 and Ad 2.

Server Side Sub-System. This sub-system is responsible for maintaining a log of the time (T) elapsed since the page was sent (start of the download by client). In addition, it maintains counts (S_1 and S_2) of the number of opportunities that the user has had to see each ad (Ads 1 and 2 respectively). S_1 and S_2 are incremented based on the frequency of rotation, i.e., how many seconds (t) each ad is displayed for. The log file also maintains a record of the "click status" of each ad using counters C_1 and C_2 for Ad 1 and Ad 2 respectively. Initially, all counters are set to zero. When the client clicks on a particular ad (say Ad 1), the respective counter (here, C_1) is incremented by one, but C_2 remains unchanged (refer to Server Side Log in Figure 4).

The Server-Side Log might also contain additional fields. For example, it may contain a code that uniquely identifies both the advertiser and the version of the ad being sent. This information is crucial for advertisers who want to test the performance of multiple executions (such as is used in split run testing). These and any other additional fields are not shown in Figure 3.

Using the above program, the Web server cannot only measure the click-through rate of each ad, but can also measure the number of opportunities the client has had to see each ad. The latter measure can be used to determine reach, gross impressions and other variables that may be used in sophisticated pricing models. This additional information also allows the server to estimate an ad's effectiveness on dimensions other than those that are behavioral in nature. Existing models concern themselves only with click-through rates (see IAB and MB Interactive study, 1997).

Client-Side Sub-System. This sub-system is responsible for maintaining a log on the client's side. This log contains such information as the client code, duration of display for each ad (T1 and T2). The sub-system uses a program which is downloaded to the client's computer along with the Web page requested. The code in the program creates a time stamp when the ad was received using the client's own computer clock and stores it in the hard drive. This mechanism operates like a "cookie," and can be implemented using programs like Java applets.

Consider the scenario when the client clicks on one of the rotating banners. At this time, the data in the cookie (i.e., the entire log from the client's side) is transmitted back to the server log, which then updates the appropriate fields. In this case, the time is noted based on when the click-through was made. Based on the start time and end time transmitted to the server log, the actual time duration (T_1 and T_2) for which each ad was displayed on the client's browser can be calculated and stored in the server log.

Consider another scenario in which the client does not click on any of the ads on the page, but moves to a different page on a different server. In this case, as soon as the user moves to a different page, the end time is noted from the computer's internal clock and stored on the hard disk as a "cookie" by the client–side program. The next time the same client connects to the Web site (server), the data in the cookie is transmitted back to the server log, and the actual ad display times are recorded in the log.

It is important to note that there may be differences between the server-side and client-side logs because the server-side log does not consider the time taken to transmit data and images from the server to the client and back. The client program will be more accurate since its time logs are not affected by the time taken to transmit data and images. To reconcile these differences, the client side data is used to calculate the final values of S1, S2, T1 and T2.

A possible limitation of this system is that a client may not visit the site after the first visit or the browser may be set to refuse cookies, in which case ad display information is lost. However, in cases where the client-side information is not available or cannot be retrieved, the server may use its own logs.

IMPLICATIONS AND DIRECTIONS FOR FUTURE RESEARCH

Implications for Researchers

As mentioned earlier, although there is ample research about ads in other traditional media, there have been no systematic efforts to examine the effectiveness of banner ads on the WWW. Current research on banner advertising has examined only static ads and has focused mainly on click-through rates. The proposed system allows for the tracking of banners on additional dimensions–both display duration and click-through rates, which may be used by advertisers and Web media for optimal pricing decisions. To our knowledge, few studies have examined the issue of rotating banners. Thus, this study represents a pioneering effort in that direction.

Implications for Advertisers

This study raises several issues for Web advertisers to consider. First, advertisers should be clear about what they hope to achieve, i.e., what are the objectives of the advertising strategy? Rotating banner ads also offer reduced cost, thus making more efficient use of the advertising budget and the banner space. Many companies like America Online (AOL) have a backlog of advertisements. The use of rotating banner advertising helps companies get the maximum yield from their most popular pages. Therefore, the use of rotating banners should be carefully managed based on the company's overall advertising strategy.

Implications for Information Systems Personnel

There are a number of Web-specific technical issues that should be considered by advertisers considering rotating banners. The speed of the modem used may hamper the effectiveness of using rotating banner advertisements. Rotating banners include multiple image files. Over a slow modem these files may take a long time to download, thus affecting effectiveness of the advertisement. Another aspect that should be considered is the tool used for making the banners rotating. Here we used Java Script as the language to rotate the banners. This enabled us to utilize the client resources (rather than server resources) to show multiple banners to the customer. Java Script as a language is not standardized any more. Microsoft and Netscape browsers implement and support different versions of Java Script. This means that the Java Script code, which works well in one browser, may not work at all in the other. Fortunately, there are other methods of rotating banners like incorporating multiple banners in a single image file using the principles used in creating animated image files on the Web. Another solution to this problem is using a programming language like Java to design and run an applet that changes the banner. Advertisers may want to be aware that Java Script and other programs utilize client computer resources. This is something that is disliked by a number of Internet users.

This study can be extended and improved in several ways. First, it is important to test our model for delivery and tracking of rotating banner advertisements on a sample group. Second, future research could examine the effects of varying the exposure time and the number of ads per rotation. It is possible that ad awareness increases up to a point and decreases thereafter, thus suggesting an inverted U-shaped relationship between recall and exposure time. The same could be expected for increasing the number of different ads per rotation. Finally, product categories and other respondent characteristics (age, income, education, etc.) need to be examined for their effect on rotating banner advertising. We hope that this study will stimulate much needed work in examining the potential of the Internet as an advertising medium.

REFERENCES

Business Week. (1997). Web ads start to click. *Special Report*, October, 128-140.

Batra, R., Myers, J. and Aaker, D. A. (1996). *Advertising Management*, Fifth edition, Upper Saddle River, NJ: Prentice Hall.

Bennett, R. (1997). How Internet ads are delivered and measurement information. *ABC Interactive*, White Paper. Available on the World Wide Web at: http://www.accessabvs.com/Webaudit/admeasurement.html.

Berthon, P., Pitt, L. F. and Watson, R. T. (1996). The World Wide Web as an advertising medium: Toward an understanding of conversion efficiency. *Journal of Advertising Research*, January-February, 43-54.

Briggs, R. and Hollis, N. (1997). Advertising on the Web: Is there response before click-through? *Journal of Advertising Research*, March-April, 33-45.

Hansen, F., Bay, H. and Friis, L. (1997). The effect of moveable stadium billboard advertising and some factors influencing it. In Fred van Raaij, W., Woodside, A. G. and Strazzieri, S. (Eds.), *Proceedings of the 2nd International Research Seminar on Marketing Communications and Consumer Behavior*, Institut d'Administration des Entreprises d'Aix-en-Provence: 164-182.

Hoffman, D. L. and Novak, T. P. (1996). Marketing in hypermedia computer-mediated environments: Conceptual foundations. *Journal of Marketing Research*, July.

IAB On-Line Advertising Effectiveness Study. (1997). San Francisco, CA: Millard Brown Interactive. Available at http://www.mbinteractive.com.

Kurose, J. F. and Ross, K. W. (2000). *Computer Networking*. New York: Addison-Wesley Longman Inc.

Li, C. (1999). Internet advertising skyrockets. *The Forrester Report*, August.

Strauss, J. and Frost, R. (2001). *E-Marketing*. 2nd edition. Upper Saddle River, NJ: Prentice Hall.

Turban, E., Lee, L., King, D. and Chung, M. (2000). *Electronic Commerce: A Managerial Perspective*, Upper Saddle River, NJ: Prentice-Hall.

Chapter VIII

The On-Demand Delivery Services Model for E-Commerce

Merrill Warkentin
Mississippi State University, USA

Akhilesh Bajaj
Carnegie Mellon University, USA

Traditional business models are increasingly being replaced by newer business models based on relationships enabled by information technologies. In this chapter, we survey and categorize many of these new business models enabled by electronic commerce (e-commerce). The main contribution of this chapter is the proposal and analysis of a new business model enabled by e-commerce: the On-Demand Delivery Services (ODDS) model. The ODDS model of e-commerce is one in which the physical products for sale are delivered directly to the customer without the use of a third-party logistics provider, such as a common carrier. For purpose of analysis, we sub-categorize the ODDS model into three submodels: The ODDS Model A applies to business-to-consumer (B2C) online sellers of physical goods who own or control their own delivery vehicles and may provide further services to extend the value proposition for the buyer. The online grocer is a typical example of businesses in this category. The ODDS Model B applies to business-to-business (B2B) sellers of physical goods, who also own a significant portion of their delivery fleet and deliver goods on demand to local distributors or business customers. Office supply eMerchants provide an example of this model. The ODDS Model C applies to businesses that typically provide virtually instantaneous delivery of third-party goods to consumers or businesses. Businesses in this category own or control their own delivery fleet and add value by delivering items within very short periods of time, usually one-hour delivery.

In order to analyze these models, we conducted a structured interview with key senior managers of one representative business in the ODDS Model A and Model B categories. We extensively surveyed recent literature on companies in the ODDS Model C category. We use the results of our study to analyze different aspects such as revenue streams, cost structure and operational peculiarities of businesses following the ODDS model, and finally discuss the long-term viability of the sub-models.

BACKGROUND: E-COMMERCE BUSINESS MODELS

Electronic commerce (e-commerce) is the electronic exchange (delivery or transaction) of information, goods, services and payments over telecommunications networks, primarily the World Wide Web (WWW). e-commerce activities include the establishment and maintenance of online relationships between an organization and its suppliers, dealers, customers, strategic partners, regulators and other agents related to (or in support of) traditional delivery channels. These activities may be business-to-consumer ([B2C] such as direct book sales to the general public by Amazon.com), business-to-business ([B2B] such as corporate procurement or supply chain management using a secure extranet), consumer-to-consumer ([C2C] such as a public auction at ebay.com) or within a business (such as an employee intranet or an enterprise resource planning [ERP] system). This environment enables organizations to reengineer their internal and external functions and activities, increasing both efficiency and effectiveness. Firms can automate existing processes and dramatically reduce cycle times throughout the supply chain. They can enhance communication, collaboration and cooperation between knowledge teams (including virtual teams) using intranet technologies as well as between the organization and members of its external constituent organizations using extranet technologies. This taxonomy has been more recently extended with B2G (business-to-government), A2B (unattended appliance-to-business) (Charny, 2000), B2E (business-to-employee, as in the corporate intranet), and others.

As with traditional ("brick-and-mortar") markets, e-buyers must find sellers of products and services; they may need expert advice prior to purchase and for service and support afterwards. Similarly, e-sellers must find buyers and they may provide expert advice about their product or service. Both buyers and sellers may automate handling of their transaction processing and "electronic financial affairs." Several categories of new types of businesses have evolved to take advantage of the unique opportunities within this new environment. There are a number of ways these new business models can be viewed. The following sections categorize these emerging business models.

Content, Community and Commerce Strategies

Business models that have emerged in this era of e-commerce activity have been categorized in a number of ways. Most models explicitly leverage the ubiquitous and universal availability of the WWW as a platform for communication between and among organizations and individuals. One fundamental taxonomy of Web-based e-commerce models is based on whether they are oriented toward the purpose of content, community or transactional commerce as shown in Figure 1.

The content category includes sites offering news, reports, publications ("e-zines"), clipart, music, information or other soft goods. Classic examples include NYtimes.com, Yahoo.com and activebuyersguide.com. Many such sites "give away" the content for free, and generate revenue by displaying banner ads. Others charge a subscription. Sites with a community purpose include those that provide focused niche discussions, fora, newsgroups, message boards or chatrooms plus sites that offer filesharing or image sharing. Community sites may display banner ads, charge a subscription or generate revenues through affiliate programs or other advertising. An active community site offers dynamic content which draws virtual visitors back frequently at a low cost, given that the visitors provide the content! Classic examples include deja.com, tripod.com and myfamily.com.

Sites for the purposes of commerce include all sites that directly sell either "soft goods" (documents, reports, clipart, music, software, etc.) or "hard goods" (requiring common carriers or shippers) by implementing order-entry, order-fulfillment and payment processing online. Classic examples include Amazon.com, Dell.com and Egghead.com. Commerce-oriented sites usually seek to generate revenues by selling items at a price marginally higher than the total associated cost (fixed plus marginal) for each item.

However, in today's environment, most e-commerce site managers feel compelled to satisfy all three objectives. For example, visit www.garden.com and find content (articles about gardening, advice from the "garden doctor," etc.), community (24 live chats about gardening with people around the world, celebrity chats and

Figure 1: Fundamental Web-based e-commerce models

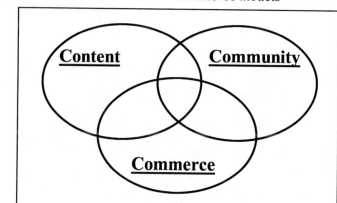

a forum to get advice from other gardeners or to showcase your gardening photographs) and commerce (with help for buying the right plants for your soil, sun and other conditions).

Strategies for Organizational Structure and Linkages

One classification scheme identifies business models by the inter-organizational structure and linkages which are facilitated. Examples include intermediaries, infomediaries, disintermediaries, auctions, buyers' unions, aggregators, consolidators and others. Timmers (1998) has identified 10 e-commerce business models, which are extended here to include several other models:

1. E-shop (individual seller at one Website)
2. E-procurement (direct or through exchanges organized by seller, buyer or third-party intermediary)
3. E-auction (for B2B or for C2C purposes)
4. E-mall (consolidates many sellers under one umbrella which handles payment processing, billing, shipping, etc.)
5. 3rd-party marketplace
6. E-communities
7. Value chain service provider
8. E-integrators
9. Collaboration Platforms
10. Third-Party Business Infrastructure sites: information brokers, trust and other services, ratings, standards certifiers, comparison sites, agents, etc.
11. E-exchanges or industry spot markets for commoditized products
12. E-reverse auctions that allow buyers to request competitive pricing offers from multiple sellers
13. "Name your own price" sites
14. E-aggregators that consolidate demand (group purchasing), quantity discounters

In Figure 2, we place these models into a framework which identifies each as a B2C model, a B2B model or a C2C model.

Having surveyed selected e-commerce business model, we next present a new business model, which we call the On-Demand Delivery Services (ODDS) model.

THE ON-DEMAND DELIVERY SERVICES
BUSINESS MODEL

Most enterprises engaged in e-commerce practice a large degree of outsourcing. While concentrating on core competencies, they develop strategic alliances with partner firms in order to provide activities such as payment processing, order fulfillment, outbound logistics, Website hosting, customer service and so forth. Many "etailers" are virtual organizations with nothing more than a marketing function under direct control. Partyka and Hall (2000) suggest that the Internet has

Figure 2: E-commerce business models. (Warkentin et al., 2001)

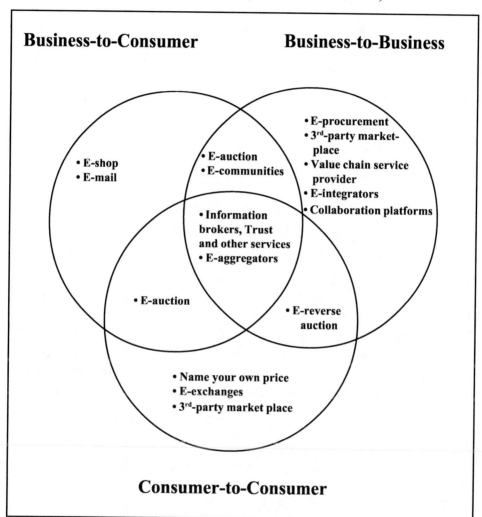

created three classes of home delivery models, based on route characteristics–substitute, next day and same day. The On-Demand Delivery Services (ODDS) model of e-commerce is one in which the physical products for sale are delivered directly to the customer without the use of a third-party logistics provider, such as a common carrier. This implies the ownership or control of a fleet of delivery vehicles by the business, which has several very important implications for the business. First, it may offer the ability to exercise greater control over a significant cost of conducting business. Second, the delivery function can be used as a source of distinct competitive advantage–promising next-day delivery, for example, can be a powerful value proposition for the customer. Finally, the direct connection to the customer may enable stronger connections, which in turn may enable a greater ability to understand the customer, provide improved services to the customer or create a sense of loyalty. This leads to "stickiness" and switching costs for some customers. Despite the added costs associated with ownership of a delivery fleet, it must not be outsourced if it is central to the value proposition of the firm–if it constitutes one element of the firm's core competence.

The following sections subcategorize the ODDS model into three different forms called the ODDS Model A, ODDS Model B and ODDS Model C. A case study of each is presented and discussed. The ODDS model is diagrammed in Figure 3, which indicates the control the organization extends over the outbound logistics function, a major connection to the customer.

ODDS Model A

The ODDS Model A applies to B2C online sellers of physical goods who own or control a fleet of delivery vehicles, and who may provide further services to extend the value proposition for the buyer. Online grocers like ShopLink.com, Streamline.com and PeaPod.com are examples of businesses in this category. In this first form of the ODDS model, the firm integrates on-demand delivery as an added service to channels they may already use (such as a brick-and-mortar storefront or a catalog business).

ODDS Model B

The ODDS Model B applies to B2B sellers of physical goods, who also own a significant portion of their delivery fleet and deliver goods on demand to local distributors or business customers. Office supply eMerchants like Staples.com or onVia.com provide examples of this model.

ODDS Model C

The ODDS Model C applies to businesses that typically provide virtually instantaneous delivery of third-party goods to consumers or businesses. Firms in this category own or control their own delivery fleet and add value by delivering third-party items within very short periods of time such as one-hour delivery. Examples of businesses in this category include Kozmo.com and UrbanFetch.com.

Having introduced the three types of ODDS e-commerce business models, we now present an analysis of these models, based on in-depth field research.

Figure 3: The On-Demand Delivery Services business model

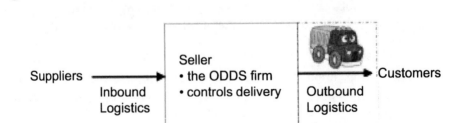

RESEARCH STUDY: THREE ODDS FIRMS

To analyze the three ODDS models, this project utilized a comparative case study methodology to evaluate three e-commerce organizations, each employing one of the ODDS business models. Structured interview data from key senior managers was used in two cases, and extensive secondary data was compiled and evaluated for the third case. The key managers (Chief Operating Officer and Director of E-commerce at Shoplink.com and VP of Operations for Staples.com) were interviewed at length to identify key integrating factors related to their separate business models. The list of questions that were asked of each manager is presented in Table 1. These questions represent dimensions of the ODDS model that in our judgment differentiate the ODDS model from other business models. This list is based on our earlier interactions with employees of companies that followed this model (these interactions are not reported in this study).

Each interview used in this study lasted approximately 45 minutes. As can be seen from Table 1, the questions were relatively open-ended in nature, so that the managers were free to voice their own insights. The interviews were then transcribed, and analyzed by the authors for insights from the part of the subjects, who had many years of experience at senior management level in the area. These insights are used in this work to analyze the ODDS models.

The first business, ShopLink.com, provides unattended weekly delivery of groceries and other items to tens of thousands of consumer households in New England and New York. Customers pay a monthly subscription, and order once (or occasionally twice) per week over the Web. ShopLink.com's fleet of trucks deliver the orders the next day in chillpacks to the customers' garages, using a numeric keypad to open the garage door, taking away dry cleaning, refundable bottles and cans, UPS packages and the empty chillpacks from the week before. Thus, ShopLink.com is an ODDS Model A type of business. The authors have worked closely with ShopLink.com, and have developed extensive material on the business model of this firm and its competitors.

The second organization also offers next-day delivery, but for business customers. This firm, Staples.com, is a B2B office supplies delivery provider which owns and operates its own fleet of trucks, but also uses third-party logistics providers. Their clearly stated value proposition is "next day delivery guaranteed." Staples, Inc., the second largest office supply superstore company in the U.S., sells office products, computers, supplies, furniture, and printing and photocopying services at more than 110 stores in the U.S., through telephone catalog sales, and with their Staples.com Website. They offer over 8,000 office products primarily to small- and medium-sized businesses (Hoovers, 2000b). The Staples.com Website creates greater flexibility for these business customers, and values its brand and repeat business from these customers. Staples.com is an ODDS Model B type of business.

The final organization, Kozmo.com, provides one-hour delivery of CDs, DVDs, ice cream, juice, videotapes, candy, snacks and other items to individuals in

Table 1: Specific structured interview questions

Could you briefly describe your Customer Relationship Management (CRM) operations? What kind of software do you use to enhance your CRM? How do you see your organization's business model as being different from other business models, as far as the use of CRM is concerned?
Could you briefly describe your outbound logistics management? What kind of software do you use for outbound logistics management? How do you see the your organization's business model as being different from other business models, as far as the use of outbound logistics are concerned?
What are your sources of revenue? Where do you see the company making revenue in the long term? What are your sources of cost? Which are fixed? Which are variable? How do you see the cost/revenue model in your organization as being different from other business models?
Suppose your customer base were to triple. How would that affect: • your operations, • your revenue/cost model, and • your ability to provide service?
Where do you see yourself 5 years from now? What are the top 3 factors (in descending order of importance) that make your organization unique, in your opinion?

many large cities. They also operate "drop boxes" in convenience stores and StarBucks coffee retailers throughout these cities for individuals to return rented movie videotapes and DVDs or borrowed chill-bags. This firm's business model is also based on the on-demand delivery services value proposition, but Kozmo.com often satisfies demand for impulse buying ("want" not "need") for consumers, and employs less customer-relationship management activity. Many purchases are one-time events, rather than part of a pattern of ongoing purchases. Kozmo.com is an ODDS Model C type of business.

Analysis of ODDS Model A

The domestic grocery market is valued at over $300 billion annually. Online grocery sales will exceed $5 billion this year and Andersen Consulting projects the market to top $85 billion by 2007, capturing about 15% of U.S. households (Taylor, 1998). There are more than a dozen competitors in the grocery e-tail business. The most notable are Peapod.com, HomeGrocer.com, ShopLink.com, Streamline.com, WebVan and NetGrocer. All offer the ability to order items online and have them delivered to the consumer's house. Some offer regular "unattended" weekly delivery (to your garage, for example) based on a monthly subscription model. Others offer on-demand deliveries (if you are home) with a surcharge on the grocery bill (and sometimes an additional delivery charge). Many offer additional services, such as dry cleaning pickup and delivery. One sells only nonperishable items shipped via common carrier. Other unique features include "don't run out" automatic continual ordering of weekly staples, fresh flower delivery, movie rental and pickup, shoe shines, meal planning, recipe tips, multimedia information and nutritional information.

An extensive survey conducted by the Consumer Direct Cooperative (Orler, 1998) (which included Peapod, Coca-Cola, Streamline.com, Harvard Business School, and others) pointed to six major groups of potential online grocery shoppers, some of whom are more likely to use online grocers than others. These include:

1. shopping avoiders, who dislike grocery shopping;
2. necessity users, who are limited in their ability to shop;
3. new technologists, young, comfortable with technology;
4. time starved, will pay to free up time in their schedules;
5. responsibles, gain sense of self-worth from shopping; and
6. traditionals, older individuals, enjoy shopping in stores.

ShopLink.com, incorporated in 1996, is an online provider of groceries, household consumables and services. They utilized an "unattended" direct home delivery logistics plan, which means the consumer does not have to be home (as with other online grocers). Its two facilities in Massachusetts and Connecticut currently serve 175 suburban communities. They plan to operate 22 facilities by the end of 2002. Recently, Gomez Advisor, Inc. (www.gomez.com) ranked the company first of 11 online grocers in the "Selective Shopper" and "Online Resources" categories, and number three overall. Their value proposition is providing a total solution for today's busy consumer by creating a pleasant experience for time-starved, stress-laden, or supermarket-averse shoppers.

ShopLink customers are generally repeat customers who order week after week in a tight ongoing relationship with the grocer. The interaction with the Website is much more substantial than with other B2C Websites and user feedback is also more prevalent than for most Websites. "It's a very sophisticated purchase versus if you're going to Amazon you might be buying one to three to four items— our average order has 54 different items in it cutting across five temperature zones" (Kruger, 2000).

After a series of information conversations with ShopLink.com's Director of Marketing and Director of E-commerce, we conducted a structured interview of the Chief Operating Officer, with additional customer relationship management information provided by the Director of E-commerce. We next describe the insights provided as a result of the interviews, following the sequence in Table 1.

It is clear that CRM is very important to ShopLink.com. Their "Delivery Specialists" are a critical link in the communication chain that starts at different parts of the organization and extends to the customer. Delivery Specialists are often used to learn more about customers' needs and behavior, and this information is used by departments such as customer service and operations to modify their activities to provide better CRM. A number of different software systems are used to capture different information about their customer, and information from customer records is given to Delivery Specialists en route. The buying process of groceries is different from buying other retail items such as books or music, for example, because the customer typically purchases many items together (often 50 or 60 items). Furthermore, the customer has an ongoing relationship with ShopLink.com, characterized by routine weekly purchases automatically charged to the credit card account on file, weekly communication to the customer, and personalization of the interface with shopping lists and suggestions. The product quality and selection is of vital importance to customers since food is a basic need. Since most customers order nearly all their groceries online, ShopLink.com can mine the data to create valuable information, which is aggregated and sold to food manufacturers. (Individual data is never disclosed to third parties.)

Further, since all online activity is captured, the level of detail is finer than that developed by traditional grocers, enabling ShopLink.com to create even more value to customers in the form of personalization of customer interaction and information. Ongoing efforts in the area of CRM include better integration of systems and providing customers the ability to track their drivers so as to be able to estimate their own personal delivery time more accurately for that particular day. ShopLink.com will further enhance their ability to evaluate customer needs as they expand their use of data mining. (A brick-and-mortar store doesn't know if you pick up a can, read the nutritional label, then put it back on the shelf without purchasing it, but the online grocer does!)

The outbound logistics model for ShopLink.com starts with the customer placing an order online for groceries by 2 p.m. on a business day, in order to get delivery the next business day. ShopLink.com currently delivers on Tuesdays through Fridays in eastern Massachusetts and parts of Connecticut and New York. ShopLink's commitment is to deliver groceries the next business day before a pre-determined time (usually 6 p.m.). Delivery Specialists are routed using intelligent routing software. Important parameters that determine the cost of delivery include: a) the latest time promised for delivery (extending the promised delivery time to 8 or 10 p.m. can significantly reduce delivery costs), b) the geographical distribution of customers and c) the mean time taken by a Delivery Specialist to physically transfer the groceries from his or her truck to the customer's door. (Most customers give ShopLink.com the code to the garage door keypad, and chillpacks are placed within the garage.) Employment of their own Delivery Specialists allows for greater reliability in the delivery process—something that is important to consumers of online grocers. Tight control of delivery costs is critical to the success of their business model. Controlling their own outbound delivery system (consisting of a fleet they own and Delivery Specialists they employ) is critical because it allows flexibility in routing intelligently, in making changes en route and for the provision of ancillary services like dry cleaning and package pickup. These factors combine to allow greater control of cost, while also allowing the offering of extra services, reliability and timeliness. For example, the dynamic routing algorithm plans the delivery schedules each day using current statistics to ensure maximum route efficiency. The routes form concentric circles, with distant routes dispatched first, followed by closer routes. In some cases, Delivery Specialists can deliver nearby routes and return to pick up and deliver a second or third truckload of groceries in one day. Capacity utilization is a critical cost component contributing to profitability.

ShopLink.com offers a guarantee of "next-day delivery" as one value proposition. Other online grocers will deliver the same day, but only if the customer is home to receive the groceries. The interview data provides evidence for a clear cost/benefit tradeoff between promised delivery time and total cost for delivery. Thus, while delivering groceries in an hour or the same day may be marginally more valuable to the customer, the costs associated with such a model make it prohibitively expensive. (The costs must be borne by the customer or absorbed by the grocer into the overall operating costs.) The optimal time for delivery seems to be in the range of 18-36 hours after ordering, which necessitates an unattended delivery model. While some customers are home for deliveries and speak with the Delivery Specialists, others frequently communicate with ShopLink's Customer Service specialists and leave notes in the return bins. The Website also facilitates communications by providing a categorized message area with each order and a menu item to communicate with ShopLink about any issue.

The revenue sources for ShopLink.com include an industry-standard markup on the actual sale of grocery goods, a subscription fee of $25-$35 per month and the sale of aggregated data on consumer buying practices (without revealing information on any particular customer) to well-known manufacturers of consumer goods. Its primary cost components include the cost of goods sold, labor, the cost of delivery, warehousing costs, and Website and database maintenance. The delivery costs are very sensitive to fuel costs, so that increasing fuel prices may require some adjustment in the other cost factors. The inventory maintenance and warehousing costs are significantly lower than for brick-and-mortar grocers, because demand is better understood. In fact, since orders are submitted by 2 p.m. on the day before delivery, there is sufficient time to acquire many items from third parties, eliminating the need for any inventory of those items! Fixed costs include the purchase of delivery vehicles, office infrastructure, a Website and a warehouse. Variable costs include the cost of goods sold for each order, delivery costs and holding costs for their limited inventory. Overall, the firm is growing very rapidly, and is quickly reaching the economies of scale necessary for break-even. A ShopLink goal it is close to achieving is to cover the variable delivery costs through the subscription revenues.

From a capacity fulfillment standpoint, it is clear that warehouse capacity and fleet capacity are crucial to meeting increased demand and growth. Possible methods of dealing with increased demand include the construction of new warehouses (a large fixed cost), increasing the size of the fleet, limiting the geographic area that can be serviced and hiring more personnel. The reality is that it is essential to be constantly aware of market size and market share, so that there are no surprises with regard to suddenly increased demands on capacity. This also allows us to conclude that the ODDS Model A is probably less suitable for the sale of seasonal goods like holiday items, which are characterized by sharp increases in demand, unless customer expectations are lowered with regard to delivery schedules and price competitiveness.

The sources of competitive advantage amongst firms in the online Grocer industry appear to be in: a) the adoption of methods to maximize the value of services to busy customers, including the unattended delivery model; b) the maintenance of high standards for delivery quality while controlling total costs outbound logistics; c) the accurate execution of order fulfillment to ensure that customers accurately receive the correct 50 or so items per order; and d) the product quality and selection of the groceries sold.

The managers thought that wider adoption of "broadband" Internet access by consumers and the increasing number of Web users meant that the overall market for online grocers would increase, so that it consists of late technology adopters as well as early adopters. They felt it was imperative to adopt financially responsible models by charging for delivery or requiring minimum order size, so that the number of customers required to break even is in the tens of thousands and not the hundreds of thousands. Over the next five years, the most likely areas for penetration appear to be major metropolitan areas in the USA.

Analysis of ODDS Model B

Staples.com, a wholly owned subsidiary of Staples, Inc. is a B2B office supplies delivery provider which operates its own trucks, but also uses third-party logistics providers. Staples.com provides an alternate business channel to the firm's business customers, in addition to their extensive nationwide chain of brick-and-mortar stores and their mature catalog sales channel. Their clearly stated promise to their customers is "next-day delivery" of office supplies. We conducted a structured interview of the Vice President for Operations of Staples.com, asking the open-ended questions listed in Table 1. This section presents the findings and reports the insights obtained from this research.

CRM forms a key component of Staples.com's strategy. Data relating each customer's shopping patterns are gathered and stored in a central database that links information from all channels of Staples, Inc., including their telephone catalog services, Staples.com and their brick-and-mortar stores. In all, information on about six million customers is stored. This aggregation of data across channels allows key managers to see customers as they change channels, and allows them a complete picture of each customer. The overall profitability of each customer is also interpolated from statistical analysis of purchase patterns. It also allows them to see the comparative strength of each channel and to set rational incentives for managers of different channels, so that they are not penalized if the customers in their area shift to another channel (for example from brick-and-mortar to Staples.com). Staples, Inc. also incorporates CRM with their outbound logistics, by providing information on every unfulfilled order to customer service, so that customers can call in and get complete information. Problem orders are logged permanently, so that customers can be offered better service in the future. High levels of customer service are key to Staples.com's strategy. Their system also enables their small business customers to market their own products and services to each other in a virtual marketplace (Internet.com, 2000).

In the area of outbound logistics, Staples.com owns and operates 29 warehouses, called "order fulfillment centers," through which all orders flow. Merchandise sold by Staples.com is either inventoried at these centers or ordered from a third party. Since Staples.com promises next-day delivery, third-party vendors will often ship their part of an order directly to the customer, so the customer receives all the parts of an order the next day. This means that customers may receive their orders in multiple packages. The entire outbound logistics are controlled by a sophisticated system built in-house by Staples. Staples, Inc. maintains its own delivery fleet, and in some cases outsources delivery to third-party common carriers such as United Parcel Service (UPS). They view the growth of their own fleet as important, and also try to control delivery costs by restricting Staples.com to densely populated areas. Staples.com also views as advantageous their long-term relationships with third-party carriers, though they see their own delivery fleet taking a larger share of deliveries in the densely populated areas in the future. However, the fact that their customer can be a small business anywhere (including a rural area out of reach of their fleet) necessitates their continued use of third-party carriers for the future. Senior management at Staples.com has carefully evaluated the costs and benefits of same-day or one-hour delivery mechanisms and has determined that such delivery options are not economically feasible. The optimum delivery period appears to be next day, in terms of value to customers and current estimates of costs for such delivery. It should be noted that one of their smaller competitors, W.B. Mason, has recently begun same-day delivery of certain office supplies–orders must be placed by 9 a.m. and they are delivered before 5 p.m. This competitive development and potential reactions will be observed in the next year.

The revenue sources for Staples.com include the actual sale of office supplies and the delivery fee that is added to each order. The cost sources include the cost of goods sold and the cost of delivery. The fixed costs are the creation and maintenance of the order fulfillment centers and the delivery fleet. Variable costs include the cost of goods for each order, as well as the cost of delivery. Their business is a low-margin, high-volume business, and is therefore highly dependent on customer retention, necessitating a strong customer-orientation throughout the organization.

From a capacity standpoint, it is clear that Staples.com believes in steady, planned growth and careful monitoring of past trends and sales, so as to manage demands on capacity. Since their value proposition is next-day delivery and accurate fulfillment of orders, they avoid marketing schemes that cause sudden short-term spikes in demand. This approach has been successful to date, and is likely to ensure continued controlled growth and profitability.

The sources of competitive advantage amongst firms in this industry appear to be: a) the successful offering of complementary multiple channels; b) the ability to control total costs and purchase inventory at a discount due to the low-margin, high-volume nature of the business; and c) offering value-added services and a brand that their businesses' customers can trust. The latter may be instrumental in enabling somewhat higher margins than competitors, thereby achieving greater profitability.

Analysis of ODDS Model C

Kozmo.com competes in the convenience food and entertainment retail industry. It is a consumer-oriented (B2C) Website that sells and provides one-hour delivery of CDs, DVDs, ice cream, juice, videotapes, magazines, snacks and other items to individuals in many large cities. They also operate "drop boxes" in convenience stores and StarBucks coffee retailers throughout these cities for individuals to return rented movie videotapes and DVDs or borrowed chill-bags. Traditional in-store shopping offers consumers immediate access to desired items, but often with problems associated with driving, parking and loss of valuable time. Founded in 1997 "with a handful of bike couriers delivering goods ordered online by New Yorkers, Kozmo.com has grown into an army of 'Kozmonauts' that serves about a dozen major cities" (Hoovers, 2000a). It has attracted significant funding from several high-profile Venture Capital firms and from Amazon, but recently withdrew its planned Initial Public Offering.

Kozmo's business model, which is also based on the on-demand delivery services value proposition, is primarily built on the satisfaction of consumer demand for impulse purchases or cravings, and not planned, repeating purchases like ShopLink. The firm has fewer overall repeat customers and employs less customer-relationship management activity.

Kozmo.com employs carriers generally known as "Kozmonauts" who own their own vehicles. Kozmo.com's roots as a bicycle courier service in New York City offers some insights into their corporate culture. While there are some repeat customers, a large percentage of purchasing is "single time" or nonroutine purchasing, conducted to satisfy cravings or impulses. While impulse purchasing is a powerful and proven driver for marketing, it does not provide sustained and reliable customer purchase patterns and income streams necessary for capacity planning and long-term growth.

Our analysis, based on numerous independent articles that describe the failure of Kozmo.com, indicates some factors that contrast with ODDS Models A and B. Key lessons include finding an optimal delivery schedule that is sustainable by revenues (mainly delivery charges or added cost of product), and being the delivery agent for one or two businesses. Thus, Kozmo is now evolving from being a delivery agent for several businesses to being one only for Starbucks.com. Cost control will be critical to make the model viable.

Because order sizes are significantly smaller than for the two previous ODDS models, the cost of delivery as a percent of sales is much larger. Yet, Kozmo.com does not charge its customers any delivery charge! The entire outbound logistics system of personnel represents a major cost component, but their lack of ability to recover costs from this major source will jeopardize their future profitability.

Urbanfetch.com is another firm providing one-hour delivery of selected items throughout central New York City and London until recently. The planned merger between Kozmo.com and Urbanfetch.com ("instant gratification archrivals") was withdrawn (Muehlbauer, 2000), and it appears that Urbanfetch.com cannot continue to operate according to this ODDS C Model. Urbanfetch's CEO, Ross Stevens, told the *Wall Street Journal* that they didn't think Kozmo.com's business model was profitable (Muehlbauer, 2000). Indications are that Urbanfetch will revert to being a traditional courier service, and industry analysts are also predicting that Kozmo.com will become a specialized delivery extension of Starbucks Coffee, one of it major investors.

iToke (www.itoke.co.uk) is a British delivery service promising to make deliveries in Amsterdam within 30 minutes. The twist is that their deliveries will be able to order marijuana using computers, fax, phone or WAP-enabled wireless phones (Evangelista, 2000). The Website, designed after Starbucks Coffee's Website, accepts smart credit cards that can be refilled at Amsterdam kiosks. The "iTokkerista" couriers ride green-and-white bicycles. Amsterdam brick-and-mortar coffee shop owners are concerned with the "Amazon-ization" of their business.

Another development to watch is the national emergence of PDQuick (formerly called Pink Dot), a Los Angeles-based company that has operated a fleet of Volkswagen Beetles to deliver goods since 1987 (Helft, 2000). It plans to clone itself in other parts of the country, starting with a 30-minute delivery service in Washington and Baltimore before the end of 2000. It is targeting music CDs and food delivery, and currently makes between 3,000 and 4,000 deliveries per day to about 150,000 active customers in LA. They state that the key is to implement strict financial controls and never provide free delivery. Free delivery "drives down average order size and drives up the price of the product for the consumer" (Helft, 2000). They charge a flat $2.99 delivery charge per order, and customers are expected to tip the couriers, who own their own vehicles. This is expected to drive down employment costs, in contrast to rivals who offer free delivery.

It seems evident that cost control is a key factor for the success of ODDS-based businesses in the future. Same-day delivery is suspect itself as a long-term strategy for success. Laseter et al. (2000) suggest that WebVan, Urbanfetch and other same-day transporters are based on economic models that "won't deliver for long." Furthermore, despite focusing on a limited number of high-margin products, Kozmo.com might seek to expand their product selection further in order to appeal to a broader audience, and enter new markets. They must increase the average order size in order to approach profitability.

Having presented the insights from the research study, we next discuss the findings and provide recommendations for managers of e-commerce organizations.

DISCUSSION AND RECOMMENDATIONS

The growth of the volume of electronic commerce activity will rely not only on the continued growth in the size of the online community and the increase in Internet access, but also in the confidence of consumers and business customers in the ability of online firms to provide clear value propositions vis-à-vis brick-and-mortar sellers. Such value propositions will come from technological innovations in some cases and in other cases from traditional business practices modified for the online experience. For the purchase of ongoing or routine products, purchasers will demand consistency and reliability in the delivery mechanism as well as personalized services. The development of highly unique customer interaction experiences will be a key component to retaining loyal customers that build a solid base for growth and profitability.

Our research indicates that the ODDS model, when implemented correctly, can constitute a strong basis for customer retention, growth and profitability. From our findings above, it is clear that while the three ODDS models have clear differences, they also have common features that differentiate them from other e-commerce models. The key common features of all the ODDS models include:

a)   The control of delivery costs is necessary to make the business model viable. Factors that play a major role in controlling the delivery costs include the minimum order size, a delivery fee, a subscription fee, the density of customer population, fuel costs and the "time to delivery" deadline. One key manager said they looked at one-hour and same-day delivery options and "it doesn't make sense to us … You'd have to charge a significant delivery fee to make it work."

b)   The importance of CRM in general, and its linkage to outbound logistics. The control of one's own delivery personnel and/or fleet presents a unique opportunity for face-to-face customer interaction and information gathering which can be utilized to enhance CRM if a feedback loop from delivery to CRM is incorporated in the company. Further, strong incentives for loyalty will ensure a strong basis for a reliable income stream. This is extended with a variety of value-added services that enhance the interaction experience, contribute to the convenience of online purchasing and create "switching costs" as barriers to entry by potential competitors.

Friedman (2000) suggests that another key to success for businesses in this sector is the ability to develop "networks of cross-industry partners that provide products and services that relate to the customer's basic life objectives." He emphasizes the personalized point of interaction and expertise at assimilating and leveraging customer information. He says the use of the Web enables network partners (such as ShopLink and the grocery product manufacturers) to collect and refine information about each customer to create customer intelligence for all partners. The Web also enables interactive, continuous and real-time customer dialog.

Several key differences between the ODDS models are summarized in Table 2.

Based on our findings, we propose a set of recommendations for organizations that wish to adopt an ODDS model for e-commerce:

a)   The control of delivery costs is crucial to the long-term viability of the model. Some methods of controlling these costs include: targeting only densely populated areas, requiring a minimum order size, extending the promised

Table 2: Strategy dimension for on-demand delivery services Models A, B and C

Dimension	ODDS Model A	ODDS Model B	ODDS Model C
Customer Base	General Consumers. Geographically confined (usually metropolitan and densely populated)	Businesses. Geographically dispersed across the country.	Usually consumers but sometimes businesses. Usually metropolitan and densely populated
Outbound delivery mechanism	Usually ownership of delivery personnel and/or fleet	A mixture of own delivery personnel and/or fleet, and third party carriers for geographically scattered customers in rural areas.	Usually ownership of delivery personnel and/or fleet.
Delivery deadline	Usually Next Day	Usually Next Day	Usually same day
Type of purchase	Frequently recurring purchase like groceries, or other regularly consumed items	Business purchase, less frequently recurring than in Model A, like office supplies.	Impulse purchase like Pizza or ice cream or DVD rental, usually not frequently recurring.
Cost of Delivery	Small as a percentage of overall purchase	Small as a purchase of overall purchase	Large as a percentage of overall purchase.

delivery deadline and using intelligent routing software. Further, geographic growth into areas with demographic characteristics consistent with larger order sizes or lower delivery charges will contribute to profitability.

b) An important benefit is the information that delivery personnel can get on face-to-face interaction with the customers. This information can be fed into the CRM system to provide better service. It can also be combined with purchasing behavior information, aggregated and then sold to third parties (while preserving individual anonymity of customers) to yield significant revenue.

c) It is useful to link the ODDS model to existing channels in the organization (such as retail outlets, catalogs and field sales forces). This gives the customer flexibility and convenience. If this is done, it is important to change the organization's incentive structure so that all the channels work together to provide a positive experience for the customer, rather than compete with each other. One way to avoid channel conflict is to reward managers in all channels based on the zip code of customers through a sharing of credited revenues.

In the future, there may be even greater opportunities for tight linkages between the ODDS provider and the customer. One technological development that may enable this customer intimacy is the wireless or mobile Internet access device. In the future, customers will be able to "access the routing program and their data on a remote server" (Partyka & Hall, 2000). Accessing each order anytime from anywhere will enhance the loyalty and value proposition for ODDS customers.

The business models developed for success on the Internet are appearing as fast as the technologies to support them. Many will not be successful models in the long run, while others will create entirely new marketspaces and industries. The On-Demand Delivery Services model for customer satisfaction, when implemented according to strict cost-benefit guidelines and with tight cost controls, will likely become a profitable long-term model for conducting certain business online. Its strength is the provision of reliable delivery of essential products and valuable related services to consumers or business customers. When combined with a personalized interaction experience and expertise at assembling and analyzing customer information for customized offerings, it should contribute to the retention of a loyal, predictable customer base, which will lead to overall profitability.

REFERENCES

Charny, B. (2000). *A2B: Eliminating the Human Element.* Available on the World Wide Web at: http://netscape.zdnet.com/framer/hud0022420/www.zdnet.com/zdnn/stories/news/0,4586,2646086,00.html: ZDNET News.

Evangelista, B. (2000). Founders dream of high demand on iToke net size. *San Francisco Chronicle.* August. Available on the World Wide Web: http://itoke.co.uk/pressdown.html. Accessed November 2, 2000.

Friedman, J. (2000). Best Intentions: A Business Model for the E-economy. Retrieved November 2, 2000 on the World Wide Web: http://friedman.crmproject.com: Anderson Consulting.

Helft, M. (2000). *Expand and Deliver.* Available on the World Wide Web: http://www.thestandard.com/article/display/0,1151,18925,00.html: *The Industry Standard.* Accessed November 2, 2000.

Hoovers. (2000a). Kozmo, Inc. Available on the World Wide Web: http://www.thestandard.com/companies/display/0,2063,61706,00.html: *Hoover's Company Capsule.* Accessed November 2, 2000.

Hoovers. (2000b). Staples, Inc. Available on the World Wide Web: http://www.thestandard.com/companies/display/0,2063,14790,00.html: *Hoover's Company Capsule.* Accessed November 2, 2000.

Internet.com. (2000). *Staples.com Enhances its Marketplace for Small Businesses.* Available on the World Wide Web: http://e-commerce.Internet.com/ec-news/article/0,,5061_325921.00.html: www.Internet.com. Accessed November 2, 2000.

Kruger, J. (2000). Reponses Given During Structured Interview.

Laseter, T., Houston, P., Chung, A., Byrne, S., Turner, M. and Devendran, A. (2000). *The Last Mile to Nowhere.* Available on the World Wide Web: http://www.strategy-business.com/bestpractice/00304/: *Booz-Allen and Hamilton.* Accessed November 2, 2000.

Muehlbauer, J. (2000). *Delivery Merger Couldn't Go the Last Mile.* Available on the World Wide Web at: http://www.thestandard.com/article/display/0,1151,19270,00.html: *The Industry Standard.* Accessed November 2, 2000.

Orler, V. (1998). *Early Learnings From the Consumer Direct Cooperative.* Anderson Consulting.

Partyka, J. G. and Hall, R. W. (2000). On the road to service. *OR/MS Today*, August, (27), 26-30.

Taylor, R. (1998). Online grocery shopping on track for rapid growth. *Anderson Consulting News*, December 1.

Timmers, P. (1998). Business models for electronic markets. *Electronic Markets*, 8, 3-8.

Warkentin, M. and Bajaj, A. (2000). An investigation into online grocer selection criteria. *Proceedings of the 2000 Annual Northeast Conference of the Decision Sciences Institute*, 155-157.

Warkentin, M., Sugumaran, V. and Bapna, R. (2001). Intelligent agents for electronic commerce: Trends and future impact on business models and markets. Chapter 7 in Rahman, S. and Bignall, R. J. (Eds.), *Internet Commerce and Software Agents: Cases, Technologies and Opportunities*. Hershey, PA: Idea Group Publishing, 101-120.

Section III

Finance

Chapter IX

Electronic Payment Systems: An Empirical Investigation of Customer and Merchant Requirements

Pat Finnegan
University College Cork, Ireland

John Kilmartin
Deloitte and Touche Consultants, Ireland

INTRODUCTION

The advantages of electronic trading are numerous, with benefits for both users and merchants. However for electronic trading to reach its full potential, factors such as ease of use and improving customer confidence will have to be addressed in relation to many aspects of electronic business. Indeed an important stumbling block for widespread adoption of electronic trading, from a convenience perspective, is the ability to complete transactions electronically at payment and delivery stages. The delivery stage is dependent on the type of product or service, but electronic payments are possible even if many payment options are not widely used. Conventional payment instruments are not well equipped for the speed and cost effectiveness required by electronic commerce. The marketing ploy of the Internet is its ease of use and convenience. Many therefore deem it unacceptable that customers have to utilize conventional payment mechanisms due either to the complexity of existing payment systems or the customer's fear of conducting financial payments electronically.

Many would argue that the most important stakeholders are customers and merchants. This stems from the fact that unless these stakeholders accept and use a system, the financial institutions and developers will have no reason to implement the system. The objective of this chapter is to investigate customer and merchant requirements for electronic payment systems in order to predict the types of payment systems that emerging electronic business applications will require.

ELECTRONIC PAYMENT SYSTEMS

Merchant site designs are moving from simply offering product information to enabling the full order process, including payment. However, in many cases payment is often completed in the traditional way using the telephone or mail to send details. Clearly this does not meet consumer needs for convenience or merchant needs for an integrated order and payment process (Europay, 1998).

Arguments for electronic payment systems can be made on many fronts. Digital money makes it possible to collect payment immediately. For example payment for electricity or phone usage can be collected every hour rather than at regular intervals (Hammond, 1996). Many firms are finding that accepting debit is less expensive than accepting cash. Firms are also attracted to electronic payment options, because consumers appear to spend more when using cards than when spending cash (Kalakota and Whinston, 1996). Also, the increased velocity of transactions that the Internet is stimulating may increase economic growth (Panurach, 1996; Hammond, 1996). Digital money gives the individual the chance to 'level the playing field' with the banks and major corporations. Software agents allow people to pay bills precisely when the best discount is available and choose the currency that saves most money at the time (Hammond, 1996).

Banks may also gain from making electronic money a reality because paper currency and coinage is proving increasingly expensive to handle ($60 billion annually in the U.S. for money transportation in 1996). It is also assumed that crimes related to cash would be reduced (Hammond, 1996). However, the question is, what will replace cash and what characteristics does it, will it and should it have?

In order to develop an acceptable payment system, it is imperative to identify issues that are important to stakeholders involved in the business transaction. Identifying the needs of stakeholders may be of use to developers when designing new payment mechanisms and also to businesses implementing electronic commerce solutions.

EXISTING ELECTRONIC PAYMENT SYSTEMS

There are five main categories of payment systems in development or operation at present: credit card payment, electronic check, electronic cash, smart cards and micro-payments. Within each of these categories, various companies have developed different strategies and models, but essentially each model revolves around the similar operational principles within each category.

Credit Card-Based Systems

Credit card payment is the most common way of paying on the Internet. A survey of Internet / electronic shopping centers showed that 58% of customers paid by sending their credit card details over the Internet (Cockburn and Wilson, 1996; Salmi and Vahtera, 1997). However, the risk of losing the card number to fraudulent persons on its way through the network frightens many people (Salmi and Vahtera, 1997). However, credit card payment is seen by some as a wasteful, inefficient method and not the means to enable the billions of daily electronic commerce transactions (Hammond, 1996). The advantages and disadvantages of credit card systems are shown in Table 1.

Electronic Cheque Systems

The electronic cheque is based on the idea that electronic documents can be substituted for paper and that public key cryptographic signatures can be substituted for hand-written signatures (Anderson, 1998). Like paper checks, electronic checks are legally binding promises to pay. In place of the hand-written signature on a paper check, the electronic cheque uses a digital signature that can be automatically verified for authenticity. The electronic cheque is embedded in a secure electronic file that contains user-defined data regarding the purpose of the check. It also includes information found on a paper check, such as payee name, payer account information, amount and date (Anderson and Checota, 1998). Electronic cheques can replace paper cheques without the need to create a new payment instrument, avoiding the necessity of legal, regulatory and commercial practice changes that a new payment instrument would imply. Examples of electronic cheques are FSTC

Table 1: Advantages and disadvantages of credit card systems

Advantages	Disadvantages
• Secure with the use of encryption. • Third party authenticates users. • Credit card numbers need not be passed over the network in some systems. • Basic financial system in place already. • Card company's indemnify customers in the case of fraud. • Existing system is accepted by users. • Over the counter and Internet transactions possible. • Portable.	• Costs too high, especially for low value transactions. • No anonymity. • Does not allow micro-merchants. • Involves several connections over the net in-order to complete a payment. • No standardized process. • Traceability through third party.

and NetCheque. The advantages and disadvantages of electronic cheque systems are shown in Table 2.

Electronic Cash Payment Systems

Electronic cash is digital coinage for online transactions. Client software allows customers to withdraw electronic cash from a bank and store it on their computer. The bank that mints coins validates existing coins and exchanges 'real' money for electronic cash. Merchants accept the electronic cash as payment for goods and services, and redeem the electronic cash at participating banks in return for traditional monitory value (Anderson and Checota, 1998; Panurach, 1996; O'Mahony et al., 1997; Kalakota and Whinston, 1996). Client 'wallet' software allows customers to withdraw electronic cash from and deposit to transaction demand deposit accounts. No physical coins are involved. Messages include strings of digits, and each string corresponds to a different digital coin. Examples of electronic cash systems are DigiCash and NetCash. The advantages and disadvantages of electronic cash systems are shown in Table 3.

Table 2: Advantages and disadvantages of electronic cheque systems

Advantages	Disadvantages
Clearing process already in place	High costs of involving third parties to an already cost process.
Secure with the use of encryption.	No anonymity.
Third party authenticates users.	Does not allow micro- merchants.
Basic system in place already.	Involves several connections over the net in-order to complete payment
Risk is limited to the value of the cheque and if cashed without proper ID, bank indemnifies the customer	Slow method , no immediate transfer of funds
Existing system is used and trusted by consumers.	Just using the internet as a method of delivery. Payment is still made via traditional payment methods
Migration form paper cheques to electronic cheques is not huge	Costs are too high for low value transactions
	Only senders bank can issue value for the cheque
	Traceability through third party.
	No anonymity.
	Internet use only
	Not portable
	No immediate confirmation
	No guarantee of payment upon receiving a cheque

Table 3: Advantages and disadvantages of electronic cash systems

Advantages	Disadvantages
Eliminates the third party	Uses proprietary currencies thus depend on issuing companies to honour their internet cash
Secure with the use of encryption.	Consumers are slow to trust such a system
Allows micro-merchant payments	Tied to specific machines (wallet on hard drive)
Allows anonymity	For internet use only
Mirrors cash so easy acceptance	Not portable
Fast	
Low cost perfect for low value transactions	
Once received it has value immediately	
Software solution no extra hardware required	

Smart Cards

Smart cards are plastic cards enhanced with microprocessors capable of holding more information than the traditional magnetic strip. There are two basic kinds of smart cards. The first type of card is often called a memory card. These cards are information storage units that contain stored values. The user can spend this value in pay phones, retail vending machines or related transactions. The second type of card is an "intelligent" smart card, which contains an embedded micro-processing chip. This type of card contains a central processing unit that has the ability to store and secure information, and to make decisions as required by the card's issuer's specific application needs (Mc Elroy and Turban, 1998; Kalakota and Whinston, 1996). In order to facilitate payments, the microprocessor is programmed to function as an 'electronic purse.' The electronic purse can be loaded with monetary value, where it is stored until it is used as payment for goods or services at retailers or service outlets (Mondex, 1998). Electronic-purse-enabled smart cards are aimed at replacing coins and low denomination currency notes and have already been used extensively as stored value fare tickets on transport systems, as phone cards and in vending machines. The key word for customers is convenience, "...with one simple swipe, no signature, no remote checking, no change, the transaction is complete" (Preston, 1998). Table 4 identifies some of the advantages and disadvantages of smart-card systems.

Micro-Payment Systems

Transactions that involve less than the value of the smallest coin or denomination of value have caused problems for payment systems. Micro-payment payment systems can efficiently transfer very small amounts, less than a penny, in a single transaction. The low value per transaction means the profit made on each transaction also has to be small. This implies that communications traffic must be kept to a

Table 4: Advantages and disadvantages of smart-card systems

Advantages	Disadvantages
Flexibility in adding applications giving extra value to consumers.	Hardware specifications pose a problem.
Secure with the use of passwords/pins.	Does not allow micro- merchants.
Over the counter and Internet transactions possible.	Uses proprietary currencies thus depend on issuing companies to honour their internet cash.
Low costs.	Anonymity.
Ideal for low value transactions.	
Risk is limited to the value of the cash sent on the network.	
Mobile source of money.	
Can be used for online and offline transactions.	
Immediate transfer of funds.	

minimum, and the transaction server has to be able to process transactions at a high rate (O'Mahony et al., 1997; O'Dea, 1998; Brown, 1997). Micro-payments have not been available in conventional commerce and thus their introduction opens many new areas of business. Examples of micro-payment systems are Millicent, PayWord and CyberCoin. Table 5 identifies some of the advantages and disadvantages of micro-payment systems.

The most important factor in the development of a payment system is to gain wide acceptance by the general public. A system could gain market dominance and remain in that position by virtue of its being the ad hoc standard (e.g., First to market). Sellers would use it because most customers use it; customers would use it because most sellers use it (Panurach, 1996). In order to get to that position the needs of users have to be taken into account. But instead of the user being at the centre of the discussion so far, the focus has been on payment instruments and how to solve technical issues. This results in public policy and corporate decisions being taken, often without an understanding of how this new form of money will shape and be shaped by social relations and cultural values (Singh, 1996).

RESEARCH APPROACH

The objective of this study is to investigate customer and merchant requirements for electronic payment systems. The study took a three-pronged approach to data gathering: first, a questionnaire designed to capture customer reaction to electronic payment systems was distributed to two distinct categories of customers; technical and non-technical users. One hundred and ten (110) questionnaires were distributed, with a response rate of 56%. Questionnaires were administered in the town of Ennis, County Clare, Ireland, which is the site of a six-month trial of the electronic payment system VisaCash. These respondents were classified as non-technical. Questionnaires were also dispensed to systems development professionals in a U.S. company. The development professionals were classified as technical customers. This categorization allowed any differences between those experienced with technology and those with little experience to be highlighted. However when responses were studied, there turned out to be very little difference of opinion

Table 5: Advantages and disadvantages of micro-payment systems

Advantages	Disadvantages
Allows low value transactions.	Coins are vendor specific does not allow flexibility.
Secure with the use of encryption.	Not mobile.
Verification of user is not important as there is immediate transfer of funds.	Uses proprietary currencies thus depend on issuing companies to honour their internet cash.
Low costs.	No extra hardware required.
Risk is limited to the value of the cash sent on the network.	Internet use only.
Software solution.	

between non-technical and technical customers. Thus in the analysis of customer responses, the results were aggregated and dealt with as one category.

The merchant study comprised of: 1) pre-interview surveys which captured merchant reaction to characteristics identified by previous researchers and 2) follow-up interviews which were conducted to establish why merchants had selected various characteristics. Three categories of merchant were selected for interview: large merchants, small merchants and Internet merchants. The large merchant survey group comprised of large supermarkets. Smaller merchants could best be described as convenience stores. The third merchant group included in the study were online traders. The online traders interviewed were general traders operating over the Internet. They were not participating in the Ennis trial, as Visa-Cash's operation was exclusively off-line. They used secure credit card systems to allow payment.

CHARACTERISTICS OF ELECTRONIC PAYMENT SYSTEMS

High-Priority Requirements

Table 6 shows the characteristics that had highest priority for stakeholders. Our study reveals that customers will not use a system unless it possess all these characteristics. As can be seen from Table 6, each of the characteristics--security, liquidity and convertibility, confidentiality, trust, simple and easy operation, cost and acceptability--are of top priority to all stakeholders. However security of the system is by far the most important feature of any payment system, and trust in a system is only gained where users feel secure in transferring information, especially financial information, over the network.

Table 6: High-priority requirements

Characteristics	Customers	Retail Merchants	Internet Merchants	Description
Security	High	High	High	Security of information and protection against fraud has to be infallible.
Liquidity and convertibility	High	High	High	Value in a system needs to be liquid and convertible.
Confidentiality	High	High	High	Confidentially of customer information is vital.
Trust in the system	High	High	High	Stakeholder trust in a system is obligatory.
Simple and easy operation	High	High	High	System operation needs to be simple and easy to use.
System acceptable to stakeholders	High	High	High	Systems need to be acceptable to stakeholders.
Low set up and transaction costs	High	High	High	Low set up and transaction costs are required by stakeholders
Accessibility	High	High	High	A payment system should be open to every one to use

Security can be accomplished by the use of proper procedures, through the use of encryption on the data transmission or software side and with the use of secure lines on the hardware side. There is a lack of trust in the security in place at present. Figures issued by Visa International Inc. demonstrate that 2% of their credit card business is related to Internet transactions, yet 50% of its disputes and discovered frauds are in the area of Internet transactions (Legard, 1999). Customers' fear of Internet commerce is perhaps best highlighted by the fact that 90% of customer respondents purchased from catalogues while only 54% of customer respondents purchased over the Internet.

Large merchants believe that electronic payments reduce the risk of employee and criminal theft, making over-the-counter electronic payment desirable from a retailer's perspective. Forty-nine percent (49%) of customer respondents fear merchant fraud. This fear is not substantiated according to Visa. Mark Cullimore, Director of emerging technology at Visa International Asia-Pacific, asserts that *"Consumers are responsible for most of the disputes and fraud, not merchants, and blamed the problem of authentication for this"* (Legard, 1999). Our study found that the authorization process of the credit card system is popular with merchants because of the security it ensures. Also the indemnity offered by credit card companies is an advantage to merchants.

The ease and simplicity of use and administration of a system is of tremendous importance to large merchants. The existing credit and debit card system is very popular with merchants. Ninety-five percent (95%) of customer respondents saw ease of use as important while 93% sought simplicity in a systems use. Small merchants linked ease of use and the speed of the transaction; these were seen as the most important aspects for small merchants who saw customer convenience as the number one concern.

People's accessibility to a payment system is important, as both customers and merchants want it to be possible to spend money ubiquitously using the system. This is a problem with credit card systems, as only certain people can get cards and only some merchants can redeem value. For instance children, who potentially have vast purchasing power, are excluded from present systems as most children do not have a bank account and cannot hold a credit card. Thus this potential market is lost to electronic commerce. A similar issue relates to the convertibility and liquidity of electronically transacted funds. Parties do not want to have funds tied up in one form of money, which they are unable to spend elsewhere.

Costs related to the system are a major concern and can in some instances be the determining factor in system choice and use. However, if customers feel they are getting value for money, then they will be happy with a system. Low set-up and per-transaction costs are very important to merchants. However, if there is demand from the public for higher cost systems, then merchants will accommodate the demand. The Visa Cash system while on trial did not charge for merchants' use of the system. However, small merchants stressed if charges were introduced, they would get the system taken out. This was directly related to the low volume of use, which they claimed to be less than 1% of daily transactions. This volume would not make it worthwhile to hire the reader and pay deposit costs. Internet merchants interviewed were not happy with credit card charges, which are a percentage of sales, and say they have to absorb the charges rather than passing it on to the customer.

The confidentiality of payer information is of great importance to merchants so that customers are comfortable shopping with them. Customer respondents also expressed a strong desire for confidentiality in relation to their transactions. Confidentiality is linked to office procedures and staff professionalism as well as technological issues. No matter how secure the collection and transmission of information is, if office procedures or staff discipline break down, information can fall into the wrong hands. The need for non-traceability of payments was expressed by 74% of respondents. Trust in a payment system is a major requirement for customers. Simplicity and ease, coupled with trust in sponsoring institutions and knowledge that information will be dealt with confidentially, help allay customer fears of the electronic environment.

Medium-Priority Requirements

Table 7 shows the characteristics which were of medium priority for stakeholders. These characteristics affect peoples' use of a system rather than their selection of it. It is suggested that customers may discontinue use of a system based on these characteristics. Some of the characteristics in this and the next category may also be referred to as 'nice to have' characteristics and are not a determining factor in a system's use.

Convenience is the word that best describes the level of service sought by stakeholders from electronic payment systems. Convenience is made up of various aspects of systems operation from speed to reliability, flexibility to integration. For electronic payment systems to be a success, the procedure needs to be easy, the customer should know and understand what is taking place and have confidence in the reliability, security and accuracy of the transaction.

Speed is identified by customers and merchants as an important aspect of any system, more so however for over-the-counter customers than Internet customers. Payment system hardware needs to be widely available, reliable, flexible and allow integration *with existing systems*.

Seventy five percent (75%) of customer respondents said speed of transactions would influence their use of a system, but interestingly 50% did not think transactions at present were too slow. The speed of the transaction was of moderate importance to large merchants, due to the uniqueness of supermarket operation. As pointed out in the interview with the management of a Newsagent, "Once people are in line in a supermarket, they do not mind a delay of seconds as it is part of the process. There are specific checkout lanes and people allow a certain amount of time to shop in such places as opposed to the operation of small merchant shops where there is a limited number of cash tills and servers." According to the site developer of one Website studied, "Speed is not so important to either the customer or the merchant in Internet transactions, as most are quick to use and administer. The main

Table 7: Medium-priority requirements

Characteristics	Customers	Retail Merchants	Internet Merchants	Description
Flexibility of system	High	High	Medium	A system should not be tied to particular equipment, it should allow multi-purpose payments and be portable.
Hardware: widely available, reliable and integrate with present systems	Medium	High	High	Hardware needs to be widely available, reliable and integrate with systems currently in use.
Confirmation of transactions	Medium	High	High	Confirmation of a transaction by receipt or acknowledgement is essential.
Payments on an international basis	High	Medium	High	Payments should be possible on an international basis.
Customer base	Medium	High	High	An established customer base is required to encourage sceptical participants.
Merchant base	High	Medium	High	Customers need great numbers of places to use electronic payment
Speed	High	High	Low	The speed of the transaction has to be commensurate with present financial transactions if not faster.
Administration	Low	High	High	The ease of administration of the system.
Defined purpose	High	Medium	Medium	There should be a defined purpose for systems, a specific purpose for their operation.
Dual operation	High	Low	Medium	Systems ought to allow online and offline operation.
Counter space	Low	High	N.A	Electronic card readers will have to also be portable
Cash back	High	Low	N.A	People can get cash as well as purchase items with the one system
Ability to track spending	High	Low	Low	A log of spending, where, when, and how much.

advantage of Internet payment (speed wise) is that once the customer has passed the number details over the network, the rest of the payment process does not involve his engagement."

The down side of speed is mistakes. Large merchants acknowledged that if all payment was effected electronically, the payment process would be quicker and administration would be simplified. However the management of a large supermarket pointed out that *"If the transaction were faster, it may mean more mistakes."* They felt that the Visa cash system gave people time to see the transaction operation, thus they knew what was happening and gained trust. Management felt that excessive speed could lead to mistakes due to customer or attendant error, which in turn would lead to time delays when remedying errors. This points to the need for a balance between speed and a correct process.

Users should have the ability to use a system in a wide range of places and for a wide range of payment types. Open standards and easy integration with other systems are important to allow systems made by different manufacturers to work together. Widely available hardware, merchant base and customer base are crucial in order that customers and merchants adopt a system. For payment systems to become popular, the required hardware has to be available on standard equipment, whether that turns out to be smart-card readers or wallets of some kind. Also any storage mechanism must allow for recovery from crashes of the system or individual PCs. Thus the onus is on the developer or sponsor to ensure that all the enabling devices are in place so that a customer and merchant user base develops.

Large merchants suggested building electronic payment hardware into existing cash and credit card acceptance systems. This would reduce duplication of entry, which is done at present. Seventy percent (70%) of customer respondents desired hardware integration. This desire was in terms of payment systems allowing operators to effect different types of payments, for instance over the counter and over the Internet, in large and small denominations. Large merchants acknowledged that electronic cash systems added extra work for till operators and cash office staff. However, if the system were built into the present accounting system, then there would be no noticeable difference in the process. Thus the till read out would include cash, credit card and any other electronic payment methods.

Administration was a concern for small merchants. However most of the concern related to the duel system in place in the Ennis trial with cash tills and card readers having separate printouts adding extra work in reconciliation. There was extra work also in reconciling bank statements due to separate lodgements. However the point was made on the issue of extra administration that if customers used the system in adequate numbers, merchants would adjust quickly and accept the extra work.

The flexibility of any payment system is of utmost importance to customers, giving them the option to use the electronic payment system as a legitimate replacement to other forms of payment. Seventy-two percent (72%) of customer respondents do not want a system tied to particular equipment, while 81% would like to make payments both over the counter as well as over the Internet. Seventy percent (70%) of customer respondents believe systems should allow multi-purpose payments. Part of the flexibility of any system needs to be its portability. Seventy-six percent (76%) of customer respondents believe a payment system needs to be portable.

Confirmation of the transaction aids in assuring customers that transactions are processed correctly. It also acts as proof of purchase and assists in the settlement of disputes. Forty-three percent (43%) of customer respondents see issuing receipts as critical in respect to non-refutability of payment.

Getting the system out into the public domain 'en masse' should be a priority for developers. However it would seem that although it may be an issue for developers and promoters, the size of the customer base is not of tremendous importance to customers. Only 45% of customer respondents wished to see a large customer base while 32% are unconcerned with customer base. Merchants advocate making a system available to the widest possible audience and recognize that widespread adoption of electronic payments would only come with increased opportunity for customers to use systems. A customer base is very important for small merchants, as without numbers using a system, there is no incentive for merchants to offer the service, especially if the cost of offering the service is high. Internet merchants also stressed they would not consider a system that did not have large numbers of people using it or global coverage.

Low-Priority Requirements

Table 8 shows the characteristics which were of low priority for stakeholders. Low-priority requirements are those which stakeholders have least interest in seeing as part of a system. These characteristics have very little bearing on stakeholders' choice of system.

Scalability is an aspect that demands the efforts of most developers (Seitz and Stickel, 1998; Baldwin and Chang, 1997). Systems have to have the capacity to allow large numbers of customers and merchants to use the system when it goes live. Large-scale use is important to ensure customers have a wide range of opportunities to use the system and to secure profit for developers and implementers. For Internet merchants in our study, scalability was not a problem as the levels of use were low. Should an increase in use come about, their attitude was to regularize procedures in the work place to administer payments, which at present was ad hoc.

Although thought to be an essential characteristic, anonymity and traceability are of little concern to large merchants. They just need to insure that payment is going to be affected. For Internet companies, anonymity is not practical, as for delivery purposes, the customer's name and address have to be tendered.

Settlement is an area which concerns large merchants, as does the issue of float and who holds it, especially where large quantities of money are lodged on a daily basis. Float is the money that has been removed from the payer's account but has not yet been credited to the payee's account. Coupled with this is liquidity and convertibility of payment. Merchants need to have access to funds almost immediately due to the close management of stocks, especially in the 'just in time' supermarket trade.

Table 8: Low-priority requirements

Characteristics	Customers	Retail Merchants	Internet Merchants	Description
Scalability	Medium	Medium	Medium	System is capable of dealing with increased numbers of users
Anonymity	Medium	Medium	Low	Customer anonymity needs to be guaranteed.
Settlement	Low	Medium	Medium	Settlement of customer payments needs to be accurate and fast.
Third party involvement	Medium	Low	Low	Trusted third parties influence the participation of stakeholders.
Peer to peer payments	Medium	Low	Low	Person to person payments should be possible.
Regulation	Low	Low	Low	Government regulation needs to be put in place.

Lack of government regulation in the area of electronic payment is not an issue for large merchants, although they acknowledge that there is little recourse if something goes wrong. Perhaps a deterrent to customers making payments over the network is the belief supported by 46% of customer respondents that there is a lack of government regulation in the area. Sixty-six percent (66%) of customer respondents would like to see regulation in regard to Internet trading. This is compounded by the belief on the part of 49% of customer respondents that there is little recourse if something goes wrong with an Internet transaction. However it does not seem to be the international aspect of the Internet that worries customers, as there is mixed reaction to the fact that Internet companies operate outside the jurisdiction of the state.

Although person-to-person payments are not of importance to merchants, 63% of customer respondents desire peer-to-peer payments. Merchants acknowledged that any characteristic which would make a system more popular with customers is of interest. They acknowledged that such a feature would increase a system's popularity but would not be of any direct use to them except in cases of refunds.

Centralization of the payment process in certain financial institutions is of little concern to merchants, as for the most part they deal with one financial institution. Large merchants suggested however that any system should be supported by all banking institutions. This would allow everybody to use the same system and ensure a customer and merchant base.

Trusted third-party involvement can combat customer fear. Eighty-seven percent (87%) of customer respondents believe the reputation of the sponsoring firm was important, while 85% of customer respondents felt the reliability of sponsoring institutions was critical. However, only 59% indicated they required existing institutions' participation in any payment system.

CONCLUSIONS

The ease of use and the global nature of the Internet make it a perfect vehicle for electronic commerce. However, users are still not fully content conducting transactions in electronic form. A fear of the electronic environment is evident from results obtained which suggest that customers use the Internet for research purposes and do not view it, or trust it, as a purchasing tool. Fear for the security of information passed over the Internet, and in particular financial information, has become a major impediment for people purchasing electronically.

Regardless of the priority stakeholders give characteristics, there are dependencies across categories. From the customer perspective the interface has to be easy and fast to use. Hardware has to be widely available and reliable. Security and confidentiality is a given, and if not foolproof, customers want to be indemnified against any losses. A systems operation has to be ubiquitous and allow over-the-counter, online and person-to-person payments. International payments will also need to be catered to. Cost is linked to value for money, thus it is dependent on the usefulness of the product and obviously the demand.

A comparison of customer and merchant requirements with characteristics of existing payment systems is shown in Table 9.

Table 9: Stakeholder characteristics which existing payment systems satisfy

System Type	Credit-Cards		Electronic Cheques		Electronic Cash		Smart-cards	Micro-payment		
	SET	Cyber-cash	FSTC	Net-Cheque	Digi-Cash	Net-Cash	Mondex	Cyber-Coin	Milli-cent	Pay-Word
High Priority Characteristics										
Security	*	*	*	*	*	*	*	Light security		
Liquidity and convertibility	*	*	*	*	?	?	*	*	*	?
Confidentiality	?						*	*	*	
Trust in the system	?						* *			
Simple and easy operation	*	*	*	*			* *			
System acceptable to stakeholders	*	*	*	*	?	?	* *	?	?	?
Accessibility		?	?	?			*	?	?	?
Low set up and transaction costs					Low					
Medium Priority Characteristics										
Hardware: widely available, reliable and integrate with present systems	*	*	*	*	*	*	*	*	*	*
Confirmation of transactions	*	*	?	*	Potentially	*	*	*	*	*
Payments on an international basis	*	*	?	*	?	?	*	?	?	?
Customer base	*	*		?	?		*	?	?	?
Speed of the transaction	*	*	?	?	?	?	*	?	?	?
Ease of administration	*	*					*	*	*	*
A defined purpose	*	*					*			
Cash back	*	*		*	*	*	*	*	*	*
Counter space										
Allow tracking of spending	*	*	*	*			*			
Merchant base	*	*	*				*	*		*
Online and offline operation	*	*								
Low Priority Characteristics										
Customer anonymity	*	*	*	*	*	*	*	*	*	
Settlement process	*	*	*	*	?	?	*		*	
Third party involvement			*		* *	* *	*			
Person to person payment					* *	* *				
Regulation	Card Regulation		Cheque Regulation		?					*

Credit card systems at present offer most promise. SET and CyberCash are both specifically for use over the Internet. However drawbacks of the systems include the lack of anonymity and the fact that liquidity is dependent on the merchant's bank. Nevertheless, the major disadvantage of credit card purchases is their high cost, both to the customer and merchant. This makes them unsuitable for low-value purchases. However, at present, credit card payment systems offer the most practical payment method and have become the de facto payment methods for Internet and over-the-counter electronic payments.

Electronic checks do not seem to offer a solution to stakeholder desires for cashless payments. Again high cost is a major drawback, as are: not facilitating low-value payments, no anonymity, not being portable, no confirmation, slow transaction speed, and liquidity problems. However, because the process is familiar to users, electronic cheques may act as a stepping stone to the introduction of more dynamic payment methods.

Electronic cash offers the greatest possibilities for electronic trading but has many flaws to be addressed. The lack of open standards between systems is one of the major obstacles, but portability and permitting macro-payments also have to be worked out. Perhaps smart cards can be used as an enabling device for electronic cash to overcome these difficulties. Smart cards offer huge possibilities due to their capability to store vast amounts of information in a portable form. The major drawback to smart-card use is the extra hardware that is needed to introduce such a system and also the fact that smart cards are just an enabling device and not a payment method in itself.

Micro-payment systems may play a role in advancing electronic payments but their inability to allow macro-payments and the fact that they are vendor specific suggests they will not provide the ultimate solution, as they would be administratively difficult to regulate and would not allow experimentation on the part of customers.

It is evident that credit card and smart-card systems satisfy stakeholder requirements best, as both offer dual payment options and both concepts are not alien to users. Cost will have a major bearing and credit card systems do not fare well on that score. Other systems lack the flexibility to allow on- and off-line payments, as most are specifically designed for Internet use. It can be extracted from the study that people want fewer, more simplified payment systems. Thus developers will have the task to incorporate all types of payment into one system, which is available for everybody's use.

REFERENCES

Anderson, K. and Checota, N. (1998). Survey of Internet payment systems. *Owen Graduate School of Management.* Vanderbilt University.

Anderson, M. (1998) The electronic check architecture. *Financial Services Technology Consortium.*

Baldwin, R. and Chang, V. (1997). Locking the e-safe. *IEEE spectrum*, February, 40-43.

Brown, E. (1997). *Micropayment Schemes Promise to Make the Web Profitable-One Penny at a Time. Newmedia*, June. Available on the World Wide Web at: http://www.newmedia.com/newmedia/97/08/fea/micropayments_small_change.html. Accessed June 23, 1998.

Cockburn and Wilson. (1996). Business use of the World Wide Web. *International Journal of Information Management*, 16(2), 83-102.

Europay. (1998). Available on the World Wide Web at: http://www.Europay.com/e_commerce/html/index_commerce.html. Accessed June 6, 1998.

Hammond. (1996). *Digital Business: Surviving and Thriving in an Online World.* Hodder & Stoughton. Available on the World Wide Web at: http://www.hammond.co.uk/digitalbusiness/. Accessed June 24, 1999.

Kalakota, R. and Whinston, A. B. (1996). *Frontiers of Electronic Commerce*, Reading, MA: Addison Wesley.

Legard, D. (1999). *Visa: Ecommerce is Major Fraud Source*, Visa Int. Inc. March.

McElroy, D. and Turban, E. (1998). Using smart cards in electronic commerce. *International Journal of Information Management*, 18(1), 61-72.

Mondex. (1998). *How the Technology Works*. Available on the World Wide Web at: http://www.mondex.com. Accessed September 9, 1998.

O'Dea, A. (1998). Net revenue. *Business and Technology*, February 2-4, 33.

O'Mahony, D., Pierce, M. and Tewari, H. (1997). *Electronic Payment Systems*. London: Artech House.

Panurach, P. (1996). Money in electronic commerce: Digital cash, electronic funds transfer and ecash. *Communications of the ACM*, 39(6), 45-50.

Preston. (1998). Available on the World Wide Web: http://195.153.248.3/cthe-32qmde.htm.

Salmi, H. and Vahtera, P. (1997). Payment systems. *Proceedings of the 10th International Bled Electronic Commerce Conference*, 1, 101-113.

Seitz, J. and Stickel, E. (1998). Internet banking-An overview. *Journal of Internet Banking and Commerce*. Available on the World Wide Web at: http://www.arraydev.com/commerce/JIBC/9801-8.html. Accessed September 9, 1998.

Singh, S. (1998). The use of Internet money. *Journal of Internet Banking and Commerce*. Available on the World Wide Web at: http://www.arraydev.com/commerce/JIBC/9604-5.html. September 9, 1998.

Chapter X

E-Commerce in the Financial Services Industry

RIchard Holowczak
Baruch College, City University of New York, USA

INTRODUCTION

The financial services industry consists of retail financial services such as retail banking, consumer lending and mortgage banking, insurance (life, health, property) and financial markets. Each of these sectors has seen tremendous growth in the services and products delivered over public internetworks such as the Internet. The recent signing into law (November 1999) of the Gramm-Leach-Bliley Act in the U.S. has enabled firms such as retail banks to provide an unprecedented array of financial services. As competition within the industry increases, firms of all sizes are looking to achieve competitive advantage through Electronic Commerce (EC). According to a recent study by the Securities Industry Association and the TowerGroup, securities firms in North America spent $3.9 billion on Internet-related information technology (21% of their total IT spending) in 1998, and this is expected to double by 2002 (SIA, 1999).

Implementing such services is not a trivial task, however. Concerns over security, privacy, legal compliance and other sources of risk must be addressed. While specific enabling technologies have been developed to address some of these issues, innovations in technology and policy will still be required. For example, some interesting issues arise from the application of Internet technologies, such as cookies and Web advertising, to financial services such as online banking and bill payment, and investment advertising.

In this chapter, we will present an overview of some of the current services and products provided by the financial services industry through EC. We will then discuss some important issues specific to the application of EC in financial services. Finally, we will present business strategy issues facing companies in the industry.

PRODUCTS AND SERVICES IN THE FINANCIAL SERVICES INDUSTRY

Virtually every aspect of financial services has been affected by the growth of the Internet, World Wide Web and EC. In this section, the main sectors of the industry will be outlined, along with an overview of how firms within these sectors make use of EC to interact with customers.

Retail Banking

Account Maintenance

Most major retail banks now offer a set of services via the Internet. As personal computers became more commonplace in the home in the late 1980s and early 1990s, many banks developed proprietary "PC banking" systems with custom software running on personal computers that would connect over private networks to the bank's central information systems. Such an architecture required each bank to maintain a private, secure network. Software distribution was also an issue as bug fixes and new features had to be distributed via floppy disk or CD-ROM to customers who were then responsible for upgrading.

Today, the Internet and Web-based applications have displaced these PC-based systems. With enabling technologies such as Web browsers and encryption implemented in protocols such as Secure Sockets Layer (SSL) over the Web, online banking applications have migrated to Web-based applications. The burden of establishing a connection to the Internet and for installing a standard Web browser is placed on the customer while the bank can more easily maintain and update the applications that reside on their servers.

The basic set of consumer-oriented personal banking services are directed at basic checking and savings account maintenance. Such services include checking account balance, check clearance, account transaction history, stop-payment on checks, check re-ordering and so on. Many banks also offer basic search tools to locate checks or other transactions by date or amount. This set of services is generally also provided via Automated Teller Machines (ATMs) and via touch-tone telephone in addition to proprietary PC banking and Web-based banking applications.

Another interface to this set of services comes from the integration of online banking and personal or small-business accounting software packages (often called Personal Financial Management (PFM) software) such as Quicken®, Microsoft Money® and QuickBooks®. In this case, the personal accounting software includes a module that provides access to personal banking transactions via the Internet. Transactions initiated via the PFM software are also recorded locally in that software's internal database for future reference. In this fashion, the PFM software can act like an aggregator of one's financial information by accessing the relevant data from one or more banks.

While most retail banks offer a few basic types of accounts such as savings, checking, money market and certificates of deposit (CDs), they differ widely in the conditions, fees and interest rates associated with such accounts. Several Web sites have been established that poll both online banks and traditional brick-and-mortar banks and then post the relevant characteristics. One such site is FinanCenter.com, an independent site that obtains information on a variety of financial services including online and off-line bank accounts and rates on CDs (see Figure 1 below). In a recent report by *TheStandard*, it was found that the data collected by FinanCenter.com suggested that purely Internet-based banks were offering higher interest rates than traditional banks that have just started extending their services onto the Internet (Mowrey, 2000). According to FinanCenter.com's Web site (see Figure 1), as of October 6, 2000, pure Internet banks such as AmericaBank and First Internet Bank of Indiana were offering six-month CD rates as high as 7% Annual Percentage Yield (APY) with minimal penalties for early withdrawal and minimum deposits of $1,000 or less. During this same time period, First Union, a major U.S. bank now offering services online, offered a six-month CD with a $1,000 minimum balance at a rate of 4.10% APY.

Figure 1: FinanCenter.com comparison of CD rates as of Oct. 6, 2000 (Courtesy, FinanCenter.com)

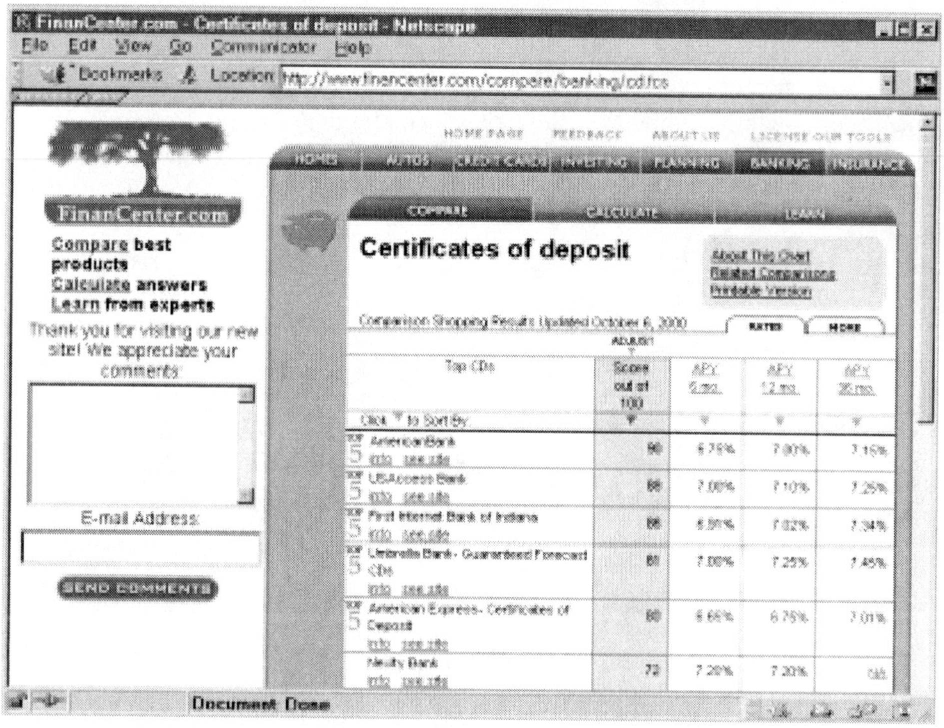

Bill Payment

A second major service offered by retail banks is online or automated bill payment. This service provides the ability to transfer funds to a third party in much the same way funds are transferred to settle a personal check. Online bill payments represent a significant per-transaction savings over check processing as virtually every aspect of the process can be automated.

According to PSI Global, 18 billion bills were sent in the U.S. in 1999, however only about 5% of institutional billers offered electronic bill payment. According to PSI Global and the U.S. Federal Reserve, 68 billion checks were written in 1999 with roughly one-third of those used to pay bills. Given the tremendous opportunity for savings, and additional 24% of institutional billers plan to offer such services by 2001 (Lawrence, 2000). One reason for the current lack of interest in electronic bill payment may be due to the limited revenues generated by transaction cost savings. IDC estimates that revenues should increase steadily until 2002 when the industry will reach critical mass, and both transaction volume and revenues should increase significantly.

Online bill payment can be implemented in several variations according to how bills are presented and how they are paid: Four variations are shown in Table 1.

The upper left quadrant (Paper Presentment/Paper Payment) represents the traditional way in which bills are paid. The method represented in the lower left quadrant is generally rare.

In cases where the customer directs their bank to issue an electronic payment to a third party, the third party must be prepared to accept such an electronic payment. Such preparations may include participation with an automated clearing house (ACH) also used by the customer's bank. If this is not the case, the customer's bank may be able to issue a check on the customer's behalf that is then sent to the payee.

Electronic bill presentment requires the payee to establish a relationship with the customer's bank under which it will agree to present the customer's bills in electronic form.

Table 1: Comparison of bill presentment and bill payment options

		Bill Payment	
		Paper	**Electronic**
Bill Presentment	**Paper**	1) Bill sent to customer. 2) Customer pays with check or money order	1) Bill sent to customer. 2) Customer enters payment authorization in service. 3) Service transfers funds to payee's account or issues a check to the payee.
	Electronic	1) Bill sent electronically to service. 2) Customer pays with check or money order and uses the service to keep track of payments.	1) Bill sent electronically to service. 2) Customer authorizes payment. 3) Service transfers funds to payee's account or issues a check to the payee.

Organizations considering accepting automated bill payments are likely to begin by first accepting electronic payments from customers' banks. The banks representing large organizations such as utility companies are almost certain to already participate with some ACH making the funds transfer form of payment a relatively easy first step.

Consumer Lending and Mortgage Banking

Retail banks and loan brokers offer a number of different loan services for the purposes of purchasing a home or vehicle, home improvements, education, small business development and many others. Typically such loans are categorized according to the ultimate use of the funds. The intended use of funds is also related to the risk the financial institution must take on when financing the loan. Such risk is reflected in the terms of the loan such as the rate of interest charged to the customer and the qualifications of the customer.

There are three general categories of Web sites that offer information, advice, applications and loan services. Information sites provide general loan information, calculators and other materials intended to help educate a customer. Such sites often provide links to sponsoring financial institutions that actually handle the application process. As described above, retail and commercial banks offer a variety of loan products directly to the consumer. Finally, loan brokers such as eloan.com and lendingtree.com aggregate timely information about loans and bring together consumers and financial institutions (Strand, 2000).

Online loan services generally consist of online applications, approvals and purchasing assistance. The online application process consists of submitting personal information such as social security number, address, current and past employer information and other related information. This sensitive information is transmitted over the Internet using encryption. Based on this information, the bank will perform a credit check to ensure the relative financial health of the customer. Once a loan has been approved and processed, the bank may require periodic loan payments according to the terms of the loan. Such payments may be automated as described in the previous section, and is especially likely in cases where the customer also maintains a savings or checking account with the same bank.

Financial institutions may offer different loan terms including interest rates depending upon the current market rates, level of risk exposure and many other factors. Consumers contemplating a loan are likely to comparison shop among institutions in an effort to minimize the costs of obtaining and paying back a loan. A growing number of Web sites poll various institutions and provide a means to compare rates and other loan features. Such comparison is typically done for financial institutions serving specific geographic areas. One example of this is the Yahoo! Finance Loan Center. Figure 2 illustrates the mortgage rates for national averages, metropolitan areas and specific states.

In addition to national averages, rates in specific states or regions are also available. For example, Figure 3 illustrates the mortgage rates offered by several major financial institutions for mortgages in the New York City metropolitan area.

Figure 2: Yahoo! Finance Loan Center mortgage rates as of October 5, 2000 (bankrate.com, a publication of Bankrate, Inc. N. Palm Beach, FL. Copyright 2001)

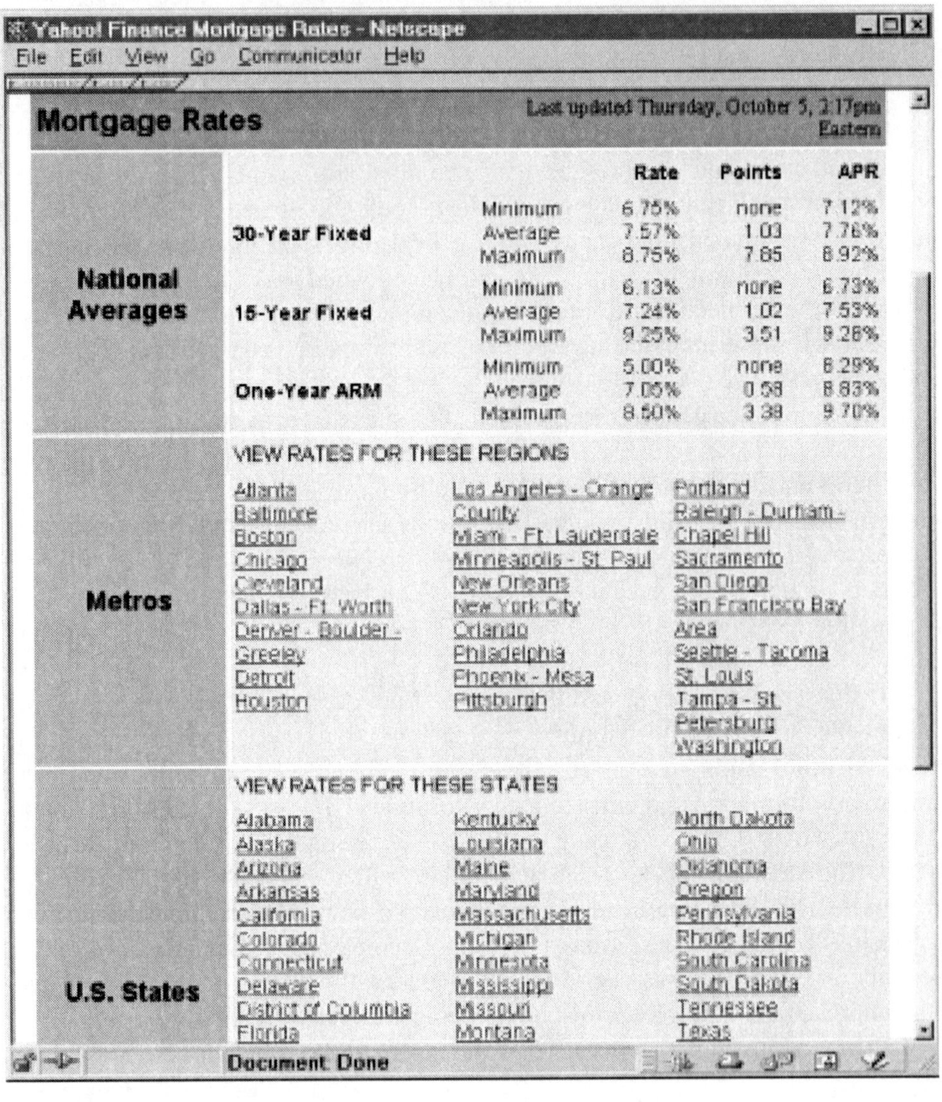
Yahoo! Finance Mortgage Rates - Netscape
File Edit View Go Communicator Help
Mortgage Rates
Last updated Thursday, October 5, 3:17pm Eastern
Rate Points APR
National Averages
30-Year Fixed
Minimum 6.75% none 7.12%
Average 7.57% 1.03 7.76%
Maximum 8.75% 7.85 8.92%
15-Year Fixed
Minimum 6.13% none 6.73%
Average 7.24% 1.02 7.53%
Maximum 9.25% 3.51 9.28%
One-Year ARM
Minimum 5.00% none 8.29%
Average 7.05% 0.58 8.83%
Maximum 8.50% 3.38 9.70%
Metros
VIEW RATES FOR THESE REGIONS
Atlanta
Baltimore
Boston
Chicago
Cleveland
Dallas - Ft. Worth
Denver - Boulder - Greeley
Detroit
Houston
Los Angeles - Orange County
Miami - Ft. Lauderdale
Minneapolis - St. Paul
New Orleans
New York City
Orlando
Philadelphia
Phoenix - Mesa
Pittsburgh
Portland
Raleigh - Durham - Chapel Hill
Sacramento
San Diego
San Francisco Bay Area
Seattle - Tacoma
St. Louis
Tampa - St. Petersburg
Washington
U.S. States
VIEW RATES FOR THESE STATES
Alabama
Alaska
Arizona
Arkansas
California
Colorado
Connecticut
Delaware
District of Columbia
Florida
Kentucky
Louisiana
Maine
Maryland
Massachusetts
Michigan
Minnesota
Mississippi
Missouri
Montana
North Dakota
Ohio
Oklahoma
Oregon
Pennsylvania
Rhode Island
South Carolina
South Dakota
Tennessee
Texas
Document: Done

Many institutions now offer or plan to offer information and loan applications online. Jupiter Communications surveyed 50 top companies in 1999 and found that while less than one-quarter currently offered online loan and credit applications, more than half planned to add such capabilities by 2001. However, few consumers are currently actively applying for and taking out loans using this medium. Nielson/NetRatings suggests several factors that contribute to this current status. Loans generally involve sums of money several orders of magnitude larger than most retail product purchases. Loan products are also tightly integrated with the sales process for high-cost items such as homes and vehicles. In particular, the approval of a

Figure 3: Yahoo! Finance Loan Center mortgage rates for NY City area as of October 5, 2000 (bankrate.com, a publication of Bankrate, Inc. N. Palm Beach, FL. Copyright 2001)

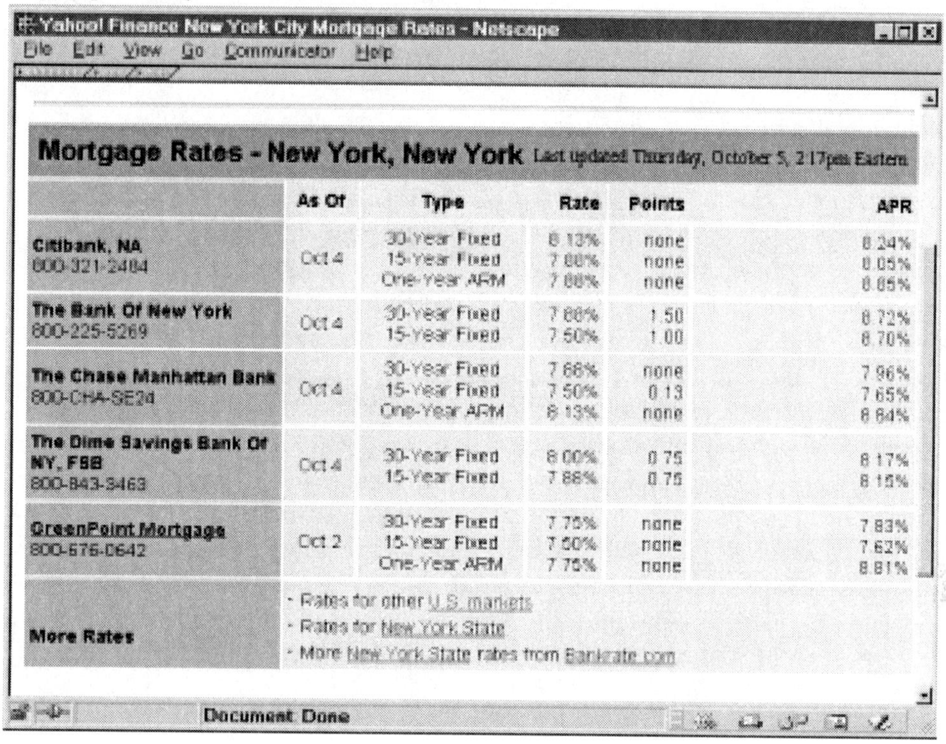

	As Of	Type	Rate	Points	APR
Citibank, NA 800-321-2484	Oct 4	30-Year Fixed 15-Year Fixed One-Year ARM	8.13% 7.88% 7.88%	none none none	8.24% 8.05% 8.85%
The Bank Of New York 800-225-5269	Oct 4	30-Year Fixed 15-Year Fixed	7.88% 7.50%	1.50 1.00	8.72% 8.70%
The Chase Manhattan Bank 800-CHA-SE24	Oct 4	30-Year Fixed 15-Year Fixed One-Year ARM	7.88% 7.50% 8.13%	none 0.13 none	7.96% 7.65% 8.84%
The Dime Savings Bank Of NY, FSB 800-843-3463	Oct 4	30-Year Fixed 15-Year Fixed	8.00% 7.88%	0.75 0.75	8.17% 8.15%
GreenPoint Mortgage 800-676-0642	Oct 2	30-Year Fixed 15-Year Fixed One-Year ARM	7.75% 7.50% 7.75%	none none none	7.83% 7.62% 8.81%
More Rates	· Rates for other U.S. markets · Rates for New York State · More New York State rates from Bankrate.com				

mortgage with a reputable loan broker or financial institution is often a key negotiating component for home purchases (Strand, 2000).

Looking forward, Jupiter Communications presents the case that if the current refinancing climate continues, the number of mortgages originating online could increase to 1.1 million with a value of $155 billion by 2003. This would represent a near 40-fold increase in the value of online mortgages (Jupiter, 1999).

Insurance

The insurance industry offers a wide range of products and services, including property (e.g., home, vehicle), casualty (e.g., fire, flood, weather), health and life insurance. Consumers purchase a policy in which they may pay premiums over time. In response to an event, a claim may be filed wherein the consumer is reimbursed partially or fully for the costs incurred by the event. Insurers' products can generally be compared based upon their premiums (how much the policy costs) and the benefits.

The insurance industry has well-established business models that involve the insurance companies themselves comprised of agents that sell and administer policies. Home and vehicle insurance are two such products where personal interaction with an insurance agent is the norm. The industry as a whole is heavily regulated at the state and federal levels in the U.S.

Online insurance services presently take one of two forms. Existing, well-established insurance companies have started to bring some of their services online while a new breed of purely online companies have started to offer education, comparison and referral services to consumers. The top five legacy insurance companies include American International Group, Allstate, Metropolitan Life, Prudential and State Farm. Each of these firms now provides education and information about their various policies and most include or plan to offer online policy quotes for some types of policies.

Purely online companies such as insWeb.com and the insurance arm of Quicken called Quicken Insurance (hosted on insuremarket.com) offer a wide range of articles and advice on various aspects of insurance policies. Their main feature, however, is a rate comparison service. Visitors to the site can register and provide relevant information (such as driving history for an auto loan). The service then polls several participating insurance companies and provides quotes for the requested policy. Due to regulatory restrictions, however, very few sites can actually carry through the process to actual policy purchase at this time. In virtually all cases, the customer is referred directly to a local insurance agent to complete the purchase process. It should also be noted that not all insurance companies are able to provide quotes and/or policies in all states in the U.S., again due to regulatory restrictions.

Capital Markets

The past decade has seen a major shift in the destination of consumers' savings and investments. In the U.S. in the 1980s, more than half of consumer's savings were allocated in basic savings accounts, money market accounts and CDs. Today, such deposits have shifted significantly towards more active investment accounts. In 2000, more than half of all Americans owned shares either through direct investments or through mutual or retirement funds.

Much of this new direct investment by consumers has been facilitated by online brokerages such as E*Trade, Ameritrade, Schwab, Fidelity, Datek, TD Waterhouse and over 100 others. According to a report by the U.S. Securities and Exchange Commission, the number of online brokerage accounts tripled from 3.7 million in 1997 to 9.7 million in the second quarter of 1999 (SEC 1999). Jupiter Communications, predicts that online brokerage assets will grow to $3 trillion by 2003 (Jupiter, 1999).

Online brokerages are most often differentiated as either "pure play" brokerages such as E*Trade, Ameritrade and Datek that were originated in, and operate only in an online fashion, and traditional firms such as Schwab, Fidelity and Merrill Lynch which have significant legacy brokerage businesses that have been extended into the online world. Entering into this mix is a large number of retail banks which are now able to offer brokerage services to their account holders.

Most online brokerages provide a similar set of services. Typically, delayed market quotes, basic historical pricing and other market data with charting capabilities, analysts' reports, news and portfolio tracking are offered to any registered visitor. Several financial information portals such as America Online Personal Finance, Yahoo! Finance and SmartMoney.com also offer similar services. Once an account has been established at an online brokerage, often real-time quotes and proprietary research and analyses become available in addition to the ability to place orders for equities, mutual funds, options and other investment instruments.

Brokerage firms are typically segmented according to the level of support and investment advice given to investors. Full-service brokerages typically offer the most comprehensive financial planning and investment advice but may charge a premium (in terms of commission on transactions) for these services. Discount brokerages compete by offering much lower commissions but may provide much less hand-holding than their full-service counterparts. Online "pure plays" such as E*Trade and Datek tend to fall into the latter category of discount brokerages.

FINANCIAL SERVICES E-COMMERCE ISSUES

Financial services continue to evolve at a rapid pace due to the rapid introduction of new online systems and services. With such new systems, however, come a number of issues that also must evolve and keep pace with changes in the online world. In this section, we describe selected issues related to brokerage firms and the banking industry and outline some of the directions in which these issues are evolving.

Suitability, Internet Advertising and Privacy

The suitability doctrine was first specified in 1939 by the National Association of Securities Dealers and stipulates that a broker/dealer must advise an investor/client by recommending investments that are best suited to the client's needs and tolerance of risk. While this fuzzy principle is difficult to define precisely, counter examples are ample and many abuses by brokerage firms have been prosecuted. In a recent report (SEC, 1999), the SEC outlined several issues related to the suitability doctrine when applied to online firms. Because online firms provide a wide range of services from basic transaction processing to full-service recommendations and portfolio management, a consistent suitability benchmark is difficult to establish across all online industry participants.

On the World Wide Web, assimilating Web access logs (the pages that were viewed), referrer logs (pages visited before the current page), cookie logs (data about prior visits) and other Web visitor information can provide advertisers with opportunities to target specific advertising to individuals. Ad serving networks such as DoubleClick have recently been investigated for suspected breaches of privacy with respect to gathering and selling collections of visitor log data.

With respect to brokerage firms, a possible suitability issue may arise if the firm targets advertising to specific types of individuals and such advertising promoted investments that are not suitable for the type of individual. A trivial example illustrates the point: by examining referrer data, a brokerage could potentially promote investments according to the sites the user visited previously. For example, if the referrer data indicates a previous Web page located on "seniors-net.com" (presumably a portal for senior citizens), unsuitable advertising would include extremely risky investments such as penny stocks that promise significant returns.

Because of the lure of significant returns on investment, senior citizens often fall victim to unsuitable promotions. The Securities and Exchange Commission routinely monitors brokerage advertising and sales tactics and has the authority to bring suit against offending firms. On the Web, however, monitoring a growing number of brokerage sites, as well as the thousands of other sites on which such improper advertising might be displayed, is a significant problem.

In concluding remarks in their report, the SEC relates a number of scenarios where the suitability doctrine applies. In general, the more customization and personalization features a firm provides (special alerts, targeted recommendations based on prior trading behavior, etc.), the more concrete the suitability issues become. By contrast, firms and financial information portals that provide uniform services to all customers are less likely to have suitability issues.

Many firms are now employing data mining and collaborative filtering systems that can examine previous trading behavior and page views of particular research reports and advice, and then automatically recommend additional investments or strategies (McMillan, 1999). Such automated systems may trigger an issue with respect to suitability. In addition, consumers are generally leery of such practices and many online users consider their privacy a primary concern (Federal Trade Commission, 1999).

Best Execution

Best execution is the obligation of a broker/dealer to place a client order in a market with the most advantageous pricing. For a sell order, such a market would be one in which the best price could be taken. Given an order, a broker/dealer has at their disposal several options. First, the order may be internalized, meaning the broker/dealer handles the transaction by either buying or selling shares within the brokerage. Another option is for the order to be placed in a traditional exchange such as the NASDAQ or NYSE. A third option is to place the order on an Electronic Communications Network (ECN). A broker/dealer who perhaps internalizes an order when a more advantageous price could have been taken on a marker or ECN would be in violation of the best execution doctrine.

With the proliferation of ECNs and with interconnections between exchanges, systems have been developed to automate the flow of orders to specific markets for execution. Such systems may take into account current bid and ask prices and block sizes as well as historical information such as recent order fill rates. Orders are generally not executed instantly, and in the time between when an order is placed and when it is executed in an exchange, available prices might change. As price competition forces commissions lower, online investors are slowly becoming aware that quality execution of their transactions is of perhaps more importance than commission charges.

Market Data

Market data constitutes price information from recent trades that is originated by the major financial exchanges and distributed by the Securities Industry Automation Corporation (SIAC). Broker/dealers subscribe to market data from exchanges and utilize this data in making investment decisions. Market data is generally supplied in a delayed form (anywhere from 15 to 20 minutes) for free, or in a real-time form for which subscribers pay a monthly fee. Fee schedules are generally based on either unlimited use per user terminal (or workstation), unlimited user per individual user or on a "per-quote" basis. Such fees represent a significant source of revenue for the exchanges.

Under the present practices, a broker/dealer with a terminal-based subscription can relay unlimited real-time quotes to clients via telephone. If, however, the same broker/dealer provides such quotes via an Internet service, they are charged on either a per-quote basis or on a per-user basis (SEC, 1999). As market data services continue to evolve, whether or not per-quote fees are appropriate or excessive, and how to encourage the widespread dissemination of market data are two questions the SEC is currently investigating.

Screen Scraping, Privacy and Proprietary Data

As Web-based access to banking, bill payment and brokerage accounts proliferate, consumers demanding efficiency and ease of use are driving the need for access to all of their account information from a single location. Bill payment portals and financial information portals are two such examples of Web sites and systems that are addressing this need. Such portals require a user to register and then provide account information such as bank account numbers, user names, passwords and other security-related information for each of the bank accounts, bill payment systems and brokerage account information. The portal will then carry out transactions against the individual accounts by feeding the proper account and password information directly to the Web sites as if the consumer were interacting directly with the site. Account reports can also be aggregated and displayed on one screen. Such a system has become known in the industry as "screen scraping" and has become a major issue in baking and finance. An example is outlined in Figure 4.

Examples of such portals include Ameritrade's OnMoney.com, PayMyBills.com and CheckFree. Two of the largest companies that provide aggregation technology and services that banks and portals use are Yodlee and VerticalOne.

From a financial services firm's perspective, when a consumer registers at their site to engage in online banking, trading or bill payment, they are entering into an agreement with the firm in which they are obligated to keep account information

Figure 4: Interaction between consumer, portal and financial services sites

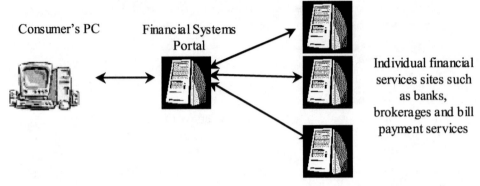

Consumer's PC   Financial Systems Portal

Individual financial services sites such as banks, brokerages and bill payment services

1. Consumer   2. Portal Maintains   3. Portal Logs into each financial
Logs into portal   account information   services site and processes transactions

such as user names and passwords private. If such information is shared with the portal, is this considered a breach of the agreement? Another issue concerns security. If the consumer's portal account were to be compromised, potentially a large number of systems would be at risk. Because the individual firms do not control nor guaranty the security of the portal, their systems are indirectly placed at risk. A third issue concerns the ownership of consumer account data. Banks may maintain that a consumer's account numbers, balances and transaction history are the property of the bank and that such information can only be manipulated by transactions controlled by the bank under stipulated conditions. From the consumer's perspective, such data represents his or her own funds and as such it should be the consumer who dictates who the information should be shared with. The Securities and Exchange Commission is presently investigating these issues.

FINANCIAL SERVICES E-COMMERCE STRATEGY

The financial services industry is evolving at a rapid pace. Firms that are decades old are finding themselves competing for market share with year-old startups. In countless ways, technology continues to remove certain barriers to entry. In this section, we introduce four complementary e-commerce business strategies for firms in the financial services industry.

Strategy I: Build

Existing firms are being pushed to innovate and complement their existing lines of business with online services. With the build strategy, such firms invest in in-house IT development to provide these services.

Strategy II: Aggregate

Financial services portals aggregate content from a variety of sources and present them under a common brand name. Content most often includes delayed or real-time stock quotes; financial news from Reuters, Dow Jones, Bloomberg and other sources; analysts' reports and recommendation and ratings; and financial calculators and other tools. Revenues to pay for such content are typically raised through advertising. The aggregation site generally does not provide any original content or other services. Some examples of such an aggregation strategy are America Online Personal Finance, Yahoo! Finance and SmartMoney.com.

Strategy III: Partner

In a partnering strategy, firms offering complementary services form an agreement to share each others' services and content. For example, E*Trade provides transaction services while its market data, news and analysis content is provided by Standard & Poor's. The partnering strategy allows firms specializing in a particular aspect of the financial services industry to compete with full-service firms without the need to develop additional applications and services in-house.

Strategy IV: Focus

Firms that specialize in one particular aspect of financial services such as initial public offerings (IPOs), order matching (ECNs) and bond issuing constitute the fourth strategy called focus. Such firms are typically market leaders in a narrow aspect of financial services and choose to compete based on a superior level of service and support rather than attempt to offer a broad range of services.

Services, Support and Strategies

Firms also differ in the type of investor they aim to service. Two such dimensions are the service orientation and the breadth of services offered. In terms of service orientation, a distinction can be drawn between firms providing extensive investment advice and expertise, and those firms who target more self-directed investors.

In terms of the breadth of services offered, firms such as Island and other Electronic Communications Networks (ECNs) offer very specific tools such as order processing. By contrast, full-service brokerages offer a much wider range of services.

Many first-time investors require assistance, advice and in general more "hand holding" than more experienced online investors. Full-service brokerage firms with an online presence already maintain the staff and support systems to assist novice investors with investment advice and expertise. Historically, revenues from commissions have supported such services. Examples of such full-service firms include Merrill Lynch and Goldman Sachs.

By contrast, firms such as Ameritrade and Datek target investors who are less likely to require investment advice and expertise. The lower commissions and fees such services require often reflect this difference. Self-directed investors are more likely to be price sensitive in terms of commissions and other brokerage fees.

In terms of the four business strategies discussed previously in this section, firms that focus on a narrow range of specific services aimed at self-directed investors may consider an aggregation strategy which allows their services to be aggregated with others. Such low-margin, high-volume businesses typically cannot provide a wide range of services or support for investors, so an aggregation approach allows such focused complementary services to be bundled.

Firms with a narrow range of services that provide a more robust service orientation may consider focusing on vertical applications that enable specific types of investing across the entire value chain. Full-service firms oriented towards self-directed investors may consider partnering with online investment information sites in order to complement their services with additional support and investment advice and expertise. Finally, traditional full-service firms may consider a build strategy wherein online services are created to complement existing lines of business.

CONCLUSION

In this chapter, a variety of financial services E-commerce applications have been introduced and a number of issues specific to this industry were presented. As in many industries, E-commerce technologies and strategies are fueling rapid growth in the services firms are able to offer. This rapid growth brings with it several interesting issues such as privacy concerns and suitability, and also calls into question who owns an individual's financial information.

ACKNOWLEDGEMENTS

The author wishes to acknowledge the assistance of Dr. Bruce Weber, Baruch College, CUNY, who provided key ideas and feedback on the Financial Services E-Commerce Strategy section.

REFERENCES

Federal Trade Commission. (1999). *Self-Regulation and Privacy Online: A Report to Congress*. Available on the World Wide Web at: http://www.ftc.gov/os/1999/9907/privacy99.pdf. Accessed July, 1999.

Jupiter Communications. (1999). *$3 Trillion in Assets by 2003 in Online Brokerage Accounts, But Customer Service Still Lacking*. Available on the World Wide Web at: http://www.jup.com/company/pressrelease.jsp?doc=pr990901. Accessed September, 1999.

Lawrence, S. (2000). Still waiting for the big bang. *TheStandard*. May 8. Available on the World Wide Web at: http://www.thestandard.com/research/metrics/display/0,2799,14778,00.html.

McMillan, A. F. (1999). *Data Mining Goes Online: Online Brokers Want to Get to Know You, Track You and Give You What You Want*. Available on the World Wide Web at: http://cnnfn.cnn.com/1999/09/24/investing/q_datamine/. Accessed September 24, 2000.

Mowrey, M. A. (2000). You'd better shop around. *TheStandard*. Available on the World Wide Web at: http://www.thestandard.com/research/metrics/display/0,2799,14793,00.html. Accessed May 8, 2000.

Securities and Exchange Commission. (1999). *On-line Brokerage: Keeping Apace of Cyberspace*. Available on the World Wide Web at: http://www.sec.gov/pdf/cybrtrnd.pdf. Accessed November, 1999.

Securities Industry Association and the TowerGroup. (1999). *Technology Trends in the Securities Industry: Spending, Strategies, Challenges & Change*. Available on the World Wide Web at: http://www.sia.com/surveys/html/technology_trends.html.

Strand, L. A. (2000). Lending a hand. *Nielson NetRatings E-Commerce Strategy Spotlight*, June.

Chapter XI

E-Capital Budgeting: Managing Strategic Investments in a World of Uncertainty

Parvez Ahmed
Penn State Harrisburg, USA

Over the last five years, firms with strong presence on the Internet have seen increases in the value of their firms to what some consider obscene levels. The "new era" economy has led to "irrational exuberance" in the stock market. This era of uncertainty has also unleashed numerous valuable opportunities for firms. The world in general and e-commerce ventures in particular are dominated by strategic investments with lots of uncertainty that require huge capital outlays. Moreover, these projects must have the ability to adapt to changing conditions that evolve as new information becomes available. The failure of traditional discounted cash flows (DCF), such as NPV, in valuing e-commerce projects is partially due to meager cash flows relative to required investments and high discount rate due to unknown risk in the projects. This chapter will show how techniques used in valuing financial options can be used to value project or firms under conditions of extreme uncertainty.

E-COMMERCE: NEW ECONOMY OR IRRATIONAL EXUBERANCE

E-retailing has continued a steep upward climb with online sales that were a mere $13 billion in 1998 tripling to over $40 billion in 1999. With close to 100 million Americans expected to cruise the Web by the year 2000, the expectation of growth is truly staggering. However, Rosen and Howard (2000) warn that the "Internet will not change everything." Only a few products are suitable for e-retailing, as online shopping is suitable for certain product types that do not require 'touch and feel' and require detailed information about it (that can be better obtained online). Some examples of products that are suitable for online retailing are sporting goods, computers and books. While the success of e-retailing may be somewhat limited, its greatest impact is perhaps being felt in the manufacturing sector where the benefits are much more tangible. Ken Vollmer, Research Director of Giga Information Group, identifies four main areas where the Internet is helping manufacturers. Some of the key areas are: product design (companies can share information more quickly), procurement (business-to-business e-marketplace initiatives), customer service (by improving post-sales support) and supply chain management.

In the last five years, firms with strong presence on the Internet have seen increases in the value of their firms to what some consider obscene levels. Wilshire Associates, which tracks the performance of more than 400 Internet stocks, reports that as of June 30, 2000, these firms had a market capitalization of $1.5 billion. This market capitalization is less than 1% of the total market cap of the entire stock market. However, while the overall stock market has averaged about 23% for the years 1998-99, the Internet stocks have produced dizzying average returns of 150%. The extraordinary valuations of the Internet stocks are viewed by many a result of irrational individual day trading of any stock that "begins with e- or ends with .com" (Schwartz and Moon, 2000). Others view that the high valuations of Internet firms are due to investor optimism on the growth potential of these firms.

The "new era" economy has led to what many believe to be "irrational exuberance" in the stock market. Shiller (2000) notes that the market has been heading up fairly uniformly ever since it bottomed out in July of 1982. It is clearly the most spectacular bull market in U.S. history. The upward trend in price-to-earnings (P/E) ratio has been even more dramatic. While real earnings have remained flat, the real stock prices have increased by more than 300%. This era of uncertainty has also unleashed numerous valuable opportunities for firms. According to John Seely Brown, Director of Palo Alto Research Center, "Fundamental changes are underway in the world of business...With this shift, we are finding many of our background assumptions and time-honored business models inadequate to help us understand what is going on, let alone compete." The first six months of the year 2000 witnessed some impressive reversals. While the broad stock market as measured by the Wilshire 5000 had a return of -0.80%, the Internet stocks were down -14%.

THE WORLD OF UNCERTAINTY

In this world of uncertainty, how does a firm go about valuing its investment projects and how can investors in turn find out the fair value of the stocks?

Introductory courses in corporate finance teach about valuation techniques such as net present values (NPVs) which work well under conditions of certainty. However, e-commerce ventures are dominated by strategic investments with lots of uncertainty that requires huge capital outlays, and these projects must have the ability to adapt to changing conditions that evolve as new information becomes available. The failure of traditional discounted cash flows (DCFs), such as NPVs, in valuing e-commerce projects is partially due to meager near-term expected cash flows relative to required investments and high discount rate due to unknown risk in the projects (Amram and Kulatilaka, 1999). Further, traditional NPVs make implicit assumptions about the "expected" cash flows under different expected "states." Also, the NPV method assumes the management's passive commitment to a certain "operating strategy" (Trigeoris, 1993).

Under conditions of uncertainty and change, the actual cash flows will differ from management's expectations. As new information arrives, management may even have the flexibility of altering its operating strategy to capture the benefits or reduce losses from the new information. Common examples of such change in strategy are to defer, expand, contract or abandon a project at different stages during its useful life. This flexibility has a value. More specifically, this value has an unlimited upside and a limited downside. This asymmetry, resulting from managerial flexibility, is like an option which gives the management the right but not the obligation of pursuing new "paths" when confronted with new information which can only be known ex post. Under such circumstances, the "expanded or strategic NPV" must reflect the traditional NPV from estimation of direct cash flows and the option of operating and strategic adaptability.

This chapter will show how techniques used in valuing financial options can be used to value projects or firms under conditions of extreme uncertainty. An option gives the buyer the right, but not the obligation to take an action in the future. Uncertainty makes option more valuable. Investments in e-commerce create subsequent opportunities that may be undertaken at a future date contingent on the information available then. In this framework, an investment opportunity is not just a stream of cash flows but is a stream of cash flows plus a set of options. The main reason for the failure of any DCF technique in explaining current stock prices is because "standard discounted cash flow techniques will tend to understate the option value attached to growing profitable lines of business. Corporate finance theory requires extension to deal with real options" (Myers, 1984).

WHAT IS AN OPTION?

An option is a right, but not an obligation, to either buy (invest) or sell (disinvest) in the future. This right belongs to the owner of the option. Under uncertainty options become more valuable. Real options are an extension of financial options that trade on organized exchanges such as the Chicago Board of Options Exchange. While financial options have standardized contract terms that are detailed, real options embedded in strategic investments have to be identified and specified. The transition from financial to real options requires the transfer of information on financial markets to strategic decision making.

The world of options has their own unique terminology. It will help the reader to familiarize themselves with the language of options as briefly presented here. The price paid by the buyer of an option contract to the seller is called the premium or the option's price. An option to buy an asset is a "call" option while an option to sell an asset is a "put" option. The fixed price at which the buyer of an option can either buy or sell an asset is called the "strike" or "exercise" price. The right to buy or sell the asset exists up to a specific expiration date. European options can be exercised only on maturity dates of the option. They cannot be exercised before that day. The alternative is the American option which can be exercised any time up to and including the maturity date. Asian options have payoffs that depend on the average price of the underlying over the lifetime of the option. Anytime during the life of an option if its exercise generates a cash inflow for the buyer of the option then the option is said to be "in-the-money." Else, the option is out-of-the-money with the breakeven point being called "at-the-money."

Real options can provide management with operating flexibility and strategic adaptability in their capital investment opportunities. Figure 1 shows investment flexibility built into the operation of a start-up e-commerce firm.

The figure shows that evaluation of an e-commerce project has many built-in options. For example, a traditional firm such as Wal-Mart may not want to immediately jump into the construction of an elaborate Web presence. Instead of setting up a separate e-commerce division, they may initially want to contract the project out (lease) for a one- to two-year trial run. Contingent on the success of the project in the initial years, they may then want to make a sizeable investment in setting up an in-house e-commerce division. Management will invest the outlay I_1 (i.e., exercise its option to have a separate e-commerce division) only if the revenues from Web-based orders outweigh the costs of running an e-commerce operation. This may be dependent on technology in year 2 (which Wal-Mart cannot forecast today) and growth in Web-based commerce (fundamental change in buying habits of consumers). Just before the expiration of the two-year contract (lease), the investment opportunity's value will be max $(V - I_1, 0)$. The option to defer is thus analogous to an American call option on the gross present value of the completed

Figure 1: Timeline of a project with built-in flexibility

1   2   3   4   5   6   7   8....................t=T

BUILDING STAGE ⟶   OPERATING CASH FLOWS ⟶

| Option to Defer | Option to Abandon | Contract | Option to Expand | Switch Use or Abandon |

e-commerce divisions expected operating cash flows, V, with an exercise price equal to the required outlay, I_1. This option is highly valuable because of high uncertainties and the length of the investment (Trigeorgis, 1998).

Similarly, later in the life of the project, market conditions may turn more favorable than expected. Technological advances may allow the shopping experience on the Web to be nearly as close as that in the physical Wal-Mart store (with less of the annoying maneuvers around the aisles). With new data on market conditions becoming available, management can then accelerate the rate or expand the scale of operation (by x%) by incurring a follow-on cost of I_E. This is then similar to a call option to acquire an additional part (x%) of the base scale project, paying an exercise price of I_E. The e-commerce opportunity for Wal-Mart is then viewed as a base-scale project plus a call-option on future investments, i.e., $V + \max(xV - I_E, 0)$.

THE BASICS OF OPTION VALUATION

Options are priced using the concepts of arbitrage. In an efficient market, two assets with identical future payoffs and risks will have the same price today. The key idea in pricing options is to construct a portfolio consisting of buying a particular number, N, of shares of the underlying asset (e.g., common stock) and borrowing against them an appropriate amount, $B, at the riskless rate. This portfolio if constructed carefully will then exactly replicate the future returns of the option in all possible future states. Since the option and this replicating portfolio provides the same future returns, they must then have the same current price so as to avoid any risk-free arbitrage profit opportunities.

The pricing of options involves the assumption of the following:

A1: There are no market frictions and markets are competitive.
A2: Market participants have no counter-party or default risk.
A3: Market participants prefer more wealth to less.
A4: There are no arbitrage opportunities.
A5: There is no interest rate uncertainty.

Suppose the price of the underlying stock is currently $100 (S=100). Next period, the stock can move up to $S^+ = 180$ (i.e., with a multiplicative up parameter of $u=1.8$) or down to $S^- = 60$ (i.e., with a multiplicative up parameter of $d=0.6$). The probability of the uptick, u, and the downtick, d, are q and $(1 - q)$ respectively.

C^+ and C^- are the values of the call option at the end of the period contingent on the stock moving up or down. Now construct a portfolio comprising of two things:

a. N shares of the stock at a price of S.
b. Financed by borrowing $B at the riskless rate of r.

The cost of constructing this portfolio is N S - B.

Thus, call option. (Buy N shares at S and borrow $B at r)

Or, $C \approx (N \times S - B)$ (1)

Figure 2: Stock price movement in a two-period world

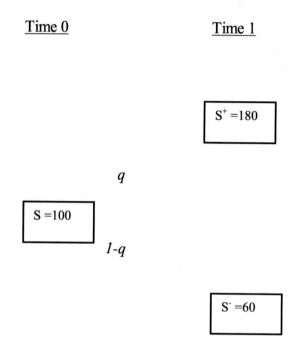

Time 0 Time 1

$S^+ = 180$

q

$S = 100$

$1-q$

$S^- = 60$

Assume a call option with a strike price (K) of $112 and a risk-free rate of 8%.

Figure 3: Price of a call option in a two-period world

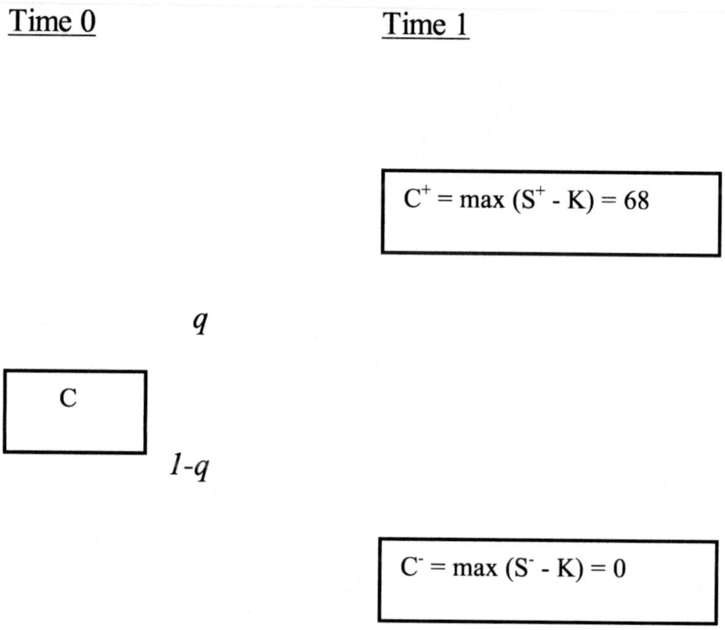

Time 0 Time 1

$C^+ = \max(S^+ - K) = 68$

q

C

$1-q$

$C^- = \max(S^- - K) = 0$

After, one period, the borrowed sum of B will have to be repaid with interest. Thus, the value of the portfolio over the next period will be:

If this portfolio offers the same return in each state at the end of the period as the option, then:

$$N*S^+ - (1 + r) B = C^+$$

and

$$N*S^- - (1 + r) B = C^-$$

Solving these equations for the two unknowns N and B, we get:

$$N = \frac{C^+ - C^-}{S^+ - S^-} = \frac{68 - 0}{180 - 60} = 0.56 \text{ shares} \qquad (2)$$

and

$$B = \frac{S^- C^+ - S^+ C^-}{(S^+ - S^-) \times (1 + r)} = \frac{60 \times 68 - 180 \times 0}{(180 - 60) \times (1 + 0.08)} = \$31 \quad (3)$$

The number of shares of the underlying asset needed to buy to replicate one option over the next period, N, is called the option's delta or the hedge ratio. In our example, we can replicate the return to the option by purchasing (N = 0.56) shares of the underlying stock at the current stock price of (S = 100) and borrowing ($B=31) at the riskless rate (r = 8%).

Finally, substituting the value of N and B into equation (1) we get:

$$C = \frac{p \, C^+ + (1 - p)C^-}{(1 + r)} = \frac{0.4 \times 68 + 0.6 \times 0}{1.08} = \$25 \qquad (4)$$

Figure 4: Value of replicating portfolio in a two-period world

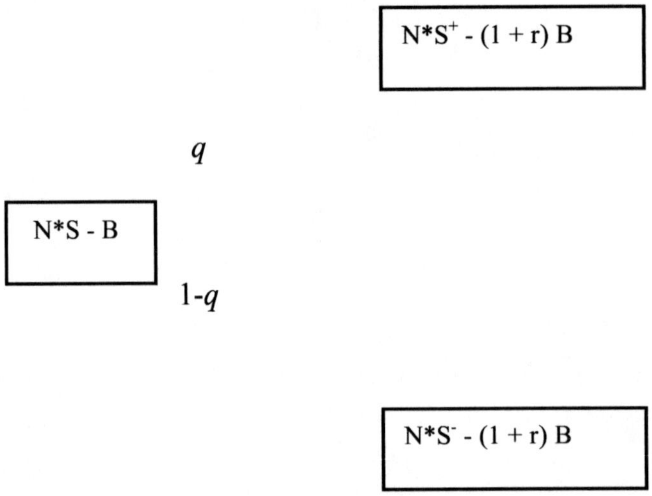

$$N*S^+ - (1 + r) B$$

q

$$N*S - B$$

$1-q$

$$N*S^- - (1 + r) B$$

where

$$p \equiv \frac{(1+r) \times S - S^-}{S^+ - S^-} = \frac{1.08 \times 100 - 60}{180 - 60} = 0.40 \qquad (5)$$

p is called the risk-neutral probability, i.e., the probability that will prevail in a risk-neutral world where investor's are indifferent to risk.

Cash Flows from Options

CALL OPTIONS

	Time 0	Time T
	Inception of Contract	Expiration of Contract

Action of Buyer:　　　BUY　　　　　　　　　　　　　　　EXERCISE
　　　　　　　　　　　　　　　　　　　　　　　　　　　　Or let option
　　　　　　　　　　　　　　　　　　　　　　　　　　　　EXPIRE

Cash Flow:　　　　　　<0　　　　　　　　Max $(S_T-K, 0) \geq 0$
At any time between 0 and T
Cash flow = 0 for European options
Cash flow $\geq$ 0 for American options

Action by seller:　　　SELL

Cash Flow:　　　　　　>0　　　　　　　　-Max $(S_T-K, 0) \leq 0$
At any time between 0 and T
Cash flow = 0 for European options
Cash flow $\leq$ 0 for American options

PUT OPTIONS

	Time 0	Time T
	Inception of Contract	Expiration of Contract

Action by Buyer:　　　　　　　　　　BUY　　　　　　　EXERCISE
　　　　　　　　　　　　　　　　　　　　　　　　　　　or let option
　　　　　　　　　　　　　　　　　　　　　　　　　　　EXPIRE

| Cash Flow: | <0 | Max $(K-S_T, 0) \geq 0$ |

At any time between 0 and T
Cash flow = 0 for European options
Cash flow $\geq$ 0 for American options

Action by Seller: SELL

| Cash Flow: | >0 | -Max $(K-S_T, 0) \leq 0$ |

At any time between 0 and T
Cash flow = 0 for European options
Cash flow $\leq$ for American options

Figure 5: Profit diagram for European call options at expiration

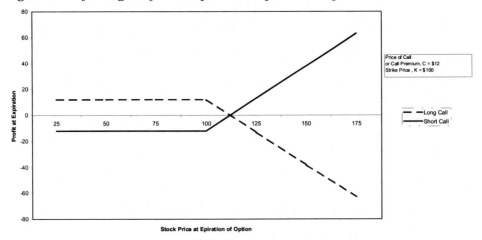

Figure 6: Profit diagram for European Put options at expiration

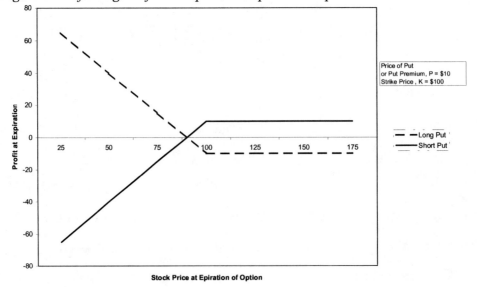

EXAMPLES OF USING REAL OPTIONS TO EVALUATE PROJECTS UNDER UNCERTAINTY

Suppose we wish to value an opportunity to invest $52 million in a project to build an e-commerce Web site and infrastructure. This project next year will generate an expected value of $90 million if the market remains bullish (or the economy keeps expanding) and an expected value of $30 million if the market becomes bearish (or the economy goes into a recession). The probability of next year being bullish or bearish is equal. Thus, using our concepts in the pricing options, we can denote the following variables:

$I_0 = \$52$

$V^+ = 90$ and $V^- = 30$

$u = 1.8$ and $d = 0.6$

$q = 0.5$

To determine the net present value (NPV) of this project, we need to estimate the project's opportunity cost of capital. There are two ways to determine the cost of capital (which is also the hurdle rate of return that the project must cross to be viable). If the risk of the project resembles the average risk of the firm, then the cost of capital for the project is the cost of capital for the firm. Cost of equity capital for the firm can be determined by solving the constant growth stock pricing equation:

$$k = (D_1 \div P_0) + g \qquad (6)$$

where, D_1 is the expected dividend next period, P_0 the current stock price and g the constant growth rate in dividends. For firms not paying any dividends, D_1 can be replaced by free cash flow to equity holders (FCFE).

If the project risk is not the same as that of the company's average project, the cost of capital is determined by a 'pure-play' method. In this method, we have to identify a stock that is traded on the financial markets and which has the same risk characteristics (i.e., perfectly or highly correlated) with the project under consideration. The cost of capital of the pure-play stock can then be determined using equation (6). Assume we have a $k = 20\%$. The risk-free interest rate, r, is 8%.

Applying DCF techniques, the NPV of the project is:

$$NPV = V_0 - I_0 \qquad (7)$$

and,

$$V_0 = E(C_1) \div (1 + k) = [q V^+ + (1 - q) V^-] \div [1 + k] \quad (8)$$

$V_0 = [0.5 \times 90 + 0.5 \times 30] \div [1 + 0.20] = \$50$

Thus, NPV = 52 - 50 = -$2

In the absence of managerial flexibility, the results from the NPV analysis using traditional DCF will lead us to reject the project. Trigeorgis (1998) notes that traditional DCF is unable to capture the value of the operating options, "because of their discretionary asymmetric nature and their dependence on future events that are uncertain at the time of the initial decision." Decision tree analysis (DTA) can offer some improvement over the DCF by properly taking into account the cash flows using conditional probabilities in each future state of nature. However, its main shortcoming is the determination of the appropriate discount rate or the cost of capital.

Contingent claim analysis can address the shortcomings of both DCF and DTA. Let V be the value of the project and the S the price of the twin security.

An open market transaction can be constructed that would follow a hedging strategy by putting together N shares of the twin security S partly financed by borrowing B at the riskless rate, r. If the portfolio is specified properly then,

$$N = (V^+ - V^-) / (S^+ - S^-)$$

and

$$B = [S^- V^+ - S^+ V^-] \div [(S^+ - S^-) (1 + r)]$$

Then the value of the project today, V is:

$$V = [p V^+ + (1 - p)V^-] \div [1 + r]$$

where,

$$p \circ [(1 + r) S - S^-] \div [S^+ - S^-]$$

Note, that the value of the investment opportunity does not explicitly involve the actual probabilities, but uses the risk-neutral probabilities, p. Using risk-neutral probabilities we can discount the future values at the risk-free rate, which is easily observed or determined.

Figure 7: Price path of twin security S

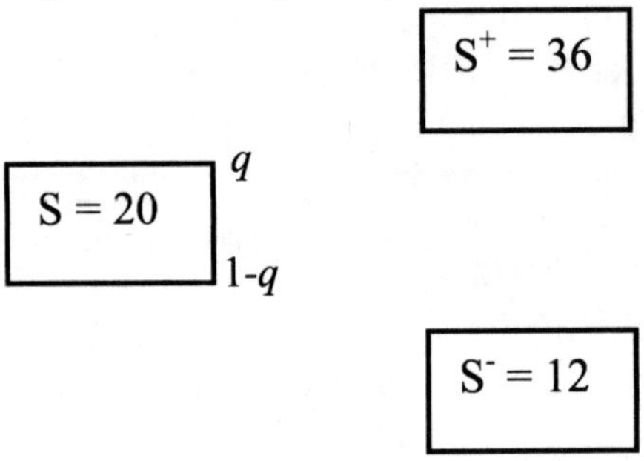

$$S^+ = 36$$

$$S = 20$$

q

$1-q$

$$S^- = 12$$

Figure 8: Value of project under different market conditions

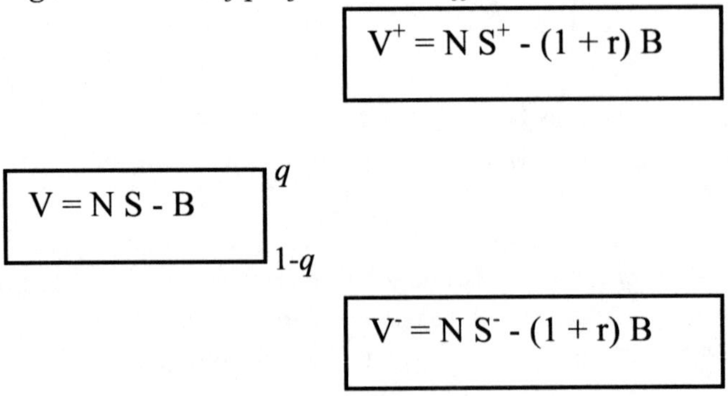

$$V^+ = N S^+ - (1 + r) B$$

$$V = N S - B$$

q

$1-q$

$$V^- = N S^- - (1 + r) B$$

So,

p = (1.08×20 - 12) / (36 - 12) = 0.4

And,

V = [0.4×90 + 0.6×30] ÷ 1.08 = 50

This is identical to the DCF V of:

V = [0.5×90 + 0.5×30] ÷ 1.20 = 50

Thus, in the absence of managerial flexibility, the real option and the discounted cash flow give the same result.

REAL OPTIONS TO EVALUATE PROJECTS UNDER UNCERTAINTY AND WITH MANAGERIAL FLEXIBILITY

We will continue to assume that the value of the project and its twin security traces a path as described below.

Option to Defer

Suppose the firm building this Web site has an option to postpone building this Web site for one year. What is the value of this option? Undertaking the project immediately was not feasible; as we saw in the previous section, it yielded a negative

Figure 9: Price path of twin security and project value

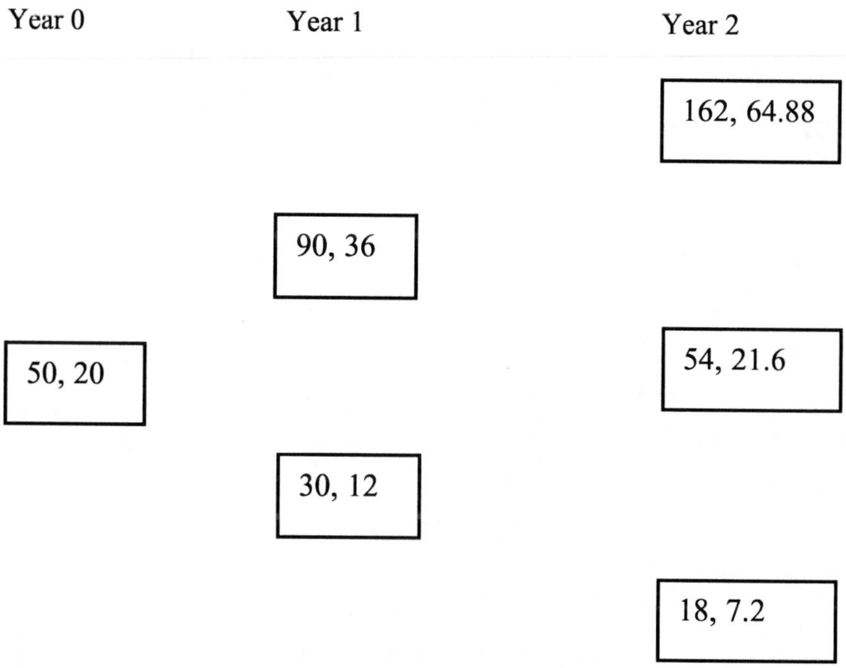

Year 0	Year 1	Year 2
		162, 64.88
	90, 36	
50, 20		54, 21.6
	30, 12	
		18, 7.2

NPV. The option to defer the project for a year gives the manager the right but not the obligation to make the investment next year. This option to wait is then equivalent to the manager holding a call option on the value of the project with the exercise price of I_1 which is the required investment next year.

$I_1 = I_0 (1 + r) = 52 (1.08) = \$56.16$

E is the value of the project to the shareholders. Thus the payoff structure will be as follows:

As in the previous section, the risk-neutral probability, p, remains 0.4. Thus the value of the option to defer is then:

$E_0 = [p \times E^+ + (1 - p) \times E^-] \div [1 + r] = [0.4 \times 33.84 + 0.6 \times 0] \div [1.08] = \$12.53$

Although he project had a negative NPV of $2 million if taken immediately, the investment should not be rejected because the opportunity to invest in the project within an year is actually worth $12.53 million. The net value of the option to defer is given as:

Option premium = Expanded NPV - Passive NPV = 12.53 - (-2) = 14.53

The main distinction between the option analysis and any analysis using decision trees is in the use of risk-neutral probabilities, p, and a risk-free discount factor, r. The use of these parameters is not just a matter of splitting hairs but addresses a fundamental conceptual weakness in both NPV and decision tree analysis. As we see in the option example, the option to defer produces an asymmetric payoff in the future. If in the future favorable investment opportunity exists, then the payoff for the project is $33.84 million. However, if the investment environment is unfavorable, the manager simply walks away with a payoff being simply 0. These asymmetric payoffs do not have the same risks. Option analysis thus does not use the true probability of these payoffs but transforms them to risk-neutral probabilities. Having done so, the relevant discount factor then has to be the risk-free rate and not the expected rate of return.

Option to Expand or Contract

Perhaps the more relevant flexibility that an e-commerce venture may have is the option to expand. Many e-commerce ventures have modest beginnings. The

Figure 10: Value of project

$$V^+ = 90, E^+ = \max (V^+ - I_1, 0) = \max (90 - 56.16, 0) = 33.84$$

$$V_0 = 50, E_0 = ?$$

$$V^- = 30, E^- = \max (V^- - I_1, 0) = \max (30 - 56.16, 0) = 0$$

modest initial investment is a result of both uncertainty about the success of the project and lack of sufficient initial capital. The most successful of e-commerce venture, Amazon.com, started with books as its only product. Based on its initial success, today Amazon.com offers products as diverse as electronics, toys, software to hardware, and new cars. Thus, as Amazon.com's product (online shopping) gained popularity, it saw the need of making follow-on investments that lead to the growth in production capacity. As Myers (1977) notes the initial investment by Amazon.com in 1995 can be thought of as an initial-scale project plus a call option on future growth opportunities.

Suppose in our example management was able to invest \$40 million in year 1 to expand production capacity and increase advertising. Thus, the option to invest $I1 = \$40$ million in year 1 allows the management to either keep the project scale the same as V or double it to 2V by making the new \$40 million investment. Thus,

$$E = \max (V, 2V - I_1) = V + \max (V - I_1, 0)$$

so,

$$E^+ = \max (V^+, 2V^+ - I_1) = \max(90, 180 - 40) = 140 \text{ (expand)}$$

and,

$$E^- = \max (V^-, 2V^- - I_1) = \max(30, 60 - 40) = 30 \text{ (maintain original scale)}$$

Management will exercise the option to expand only if market conditions are favorable (e.g., increased demand for online retailing). The value of the investment opportunity today then includes the value of the option in the future:

$$E_0 = ([p\,E^+ + (1 - p)\,E^-] \div [1 + r]) - I0 = ([0.4 \times 140 + 0.6 \times 30] \div 1.08) - 52 = 16.52$$

The value of the option to expand is $16.52 - (-2) = \$18.52$ million

Trigeorgis (1998) notes that the option to expand enables a firm to capitalize on future growth opportunities. A firm that undertakes a small negative NPV project or builds excess plant capacity or buys vacant development land, the firm is essentially buying a call option that it has the right but not the obligation to exercise at a future date. This call option will be exercised only if market conditions are in favor of the firm.

Option to Temporarily Shut Down

Traditional discounted cash flow analysis assumes that a project will generate sufficient cash flows each year of the project's life to warrant its on-going operation. Sometimes it may be necessary to temporarily shut the project down. This often happens when there is effectiveness concern for a product, when the firm may find it in its best interest to stop production (recall products) and conduct further safety studies before re-marketing the product. In such scenarios expected costs from litigation may be greater than cash revenues. Thus, the operation in each year is like a call option to acquire the year's cash flow revenue by paying as exercise price the expected cost of operating.

Assume cash revenues for the project to be 30% of project value. Thus, cash revenue flow, $C = 0.3V$. Thus, $C^+ = \$27$ million an $C^- = \$9$ million. Further assume that management pays a cost of $8 million to acquire cash revenues. However, a lack of product effectiveness may suddenly increase variable costs to $20 million in added costs of R&D, etc. Even with these high variable costs, the firm can continue to operate if the market remains good as revenues will exceed costs (27 > 20). However, if the market conditions get bad, then it may be better for the firm to shut-down the product line temporarily (9 < 20). The option not to operate allows management to acquire the project's value by paying the minimum variable costs (if the project does well and management continues to operate) or cash revenues (which would be sacrificed if the project does poorly and management shuts down operation).

$E = (V - FC) - min(VC, C)$, where FC = fixed costs and VC = variable costs

Thus,

$E^+ = (V^+ - FC) - min(VC, C^+) = (90 - 9.16) - min(20, 27) = 80.84 - 20 = 60.84$

$E^- = (V^- - FC) - min(VC, C^-) = (30 - 9.16) - min(20, 9) = 20.84 - 9 = 11.84$

$E_0 = ([p\,E^+ + (1 - p)\,E^-] \div [1 + r]) - I_0 = ([0.4 \times 60.84 + 0.6 \times 11.84] \div 1.08) - 25 = 4.11$

Thus, value of option to shut-down temporarily next year is $4.11 - (-2) = \$6.11$ million.

CONCLUSION

Real call options like financial options gives the buyer the right, but not the obligation to buy a security at a pre-specified price. The buyer of the call option is taking an optimistic view of the asset underlying the option. A capital investment in e-commerce gives the firm the right but not the obligation to make further real investments in the future. The factors that make this option valuable are uncertainty or volatility of the underlying technology and demand for such services.

Certain critical components of real options make them a powerful analytical tool today. First, they recognize the flexibility in today's capital investment. Second, they recognize the staged nature of the investment opportunity that are only made when additional information is revealed in the future. The traditional DCF analysis fails to recognize the staged nature of investments and views them as a series of investments whether they still make sense at a later date.

Trigeorgis (1998) notes that management should broaden its valuation horizon by considering the expanded or strategic NPV of the project. This strategic NPV captures the flexibility of operating strategies and can also accommodate more complex scenarios like interaction between several real options. The strategic NPV views the value of the project as the sum of its static NPV (coming from discounted cash flow analysis, which measures the present value of expected cash flows) and the value of the option premium that reflects managerial flexibility and strategic interactions. Adding this option analysis allows managers to develop projects that may have initial negative NPV (static) as long as the option premium exceeds the negative static NPV. Options analysis is particularly suited in an environment where uncertainty is high or the future payoffs are asymmetric, interest rates are rising and the project has a long-time horizon (making cash flow predictions difficult). While an increase in uncertainty, interest rates and time to maturity of the project all decrease the static NPV of the project, they all increase the option premium. Thus, the new decision rule to employ in evaluating projects should be to accept a project if option premium exceeds a negative static NPV.

REFERENCES

Amram, M. and Kulatilaka, N. (1999). *Real Options*. Boston, MA: Harvard Business School Press.

Myers, S. Finance theory and financial strategy. *Interfaces*, 14, 126-137.

Rosen, K. T. and Howard, A. L. (2000). R-retail: Gold rush or fool's gold. *California Management Review*.

Schiller, R. (2000). *Irrational Exuberance*. Princeton University Press.

Schwartz, E. and Moon, M. (2000). Rational pricing of Internet companies. *The Financial Analysts Journal*, May/June, 62-75.

Trigeorgis, L. (1993). Real options and interactions with financial flexibility. *Financial Management*, 22(3), 202-224.

Trigeorgis, L. (1998). *Real Options*. The MIT Press.

Section IV

Business Strategies

Chapter XII

A Concept for the Evaluation of E-Commerce-Ability

Ulrike Baumoel, Thomas Fugmann, Thomas Stiffel and Robert Winter
University of St. Gallen, Switzerland

INTRODUCTION

Although many corporations currently try to establish e-commerce as a new field of business and as many corporations are already in the middle of implementing it or have just finished doing so, only a few e-commerce concepts prove to be successful in the long run. The question "Why?" is indeed difficult to answer, especially if a systematic approach for the analysis is not available. We deduced from our current research that e-commerce can only be successful if the corporation is structured according to the requirements of its e-commerce activities. That is, it is most likely to fail if e-commerce is only realized basing on the Internet as a new distribution channel, without changing the internal view on customer processes and without restructuring certain elements such as internal processes and structures and inter-business networking.

However, corporations which want to implement successful e-commerce activities first of all need to have a framework for reflecting and analyzing their current status before measures can be defined to achieve e-commerce-ability.

The first step of such a systematic approach has to include not only a framework of dimensions which allows the reflection and analysis of patterns of e-commerce business models or roles, respectively, but also a set of parameters which represent measurable success. We therefore developed a concept consisting of two "pillars": first of all, a framework of four basic dimensions, which reflect the above-mentioned alignment necessities. Each of the dimensions is described by a set of characteristics which are used as a metric to render the creation and moreover the comparison of the patterns possible. Our hypothesis is that there are success patterns which depend on the specific roles existing in an e-commerce environment. The second pillar is an evaluation approach which allows the analysis of the corporation basing on value-driven quantitative and qualitative parameters reflecting economic success. The concept can be put to use by visualizing the pattern of the respective corporation to be analyzed, comparing it with the success pattern of the role, analyzing the status regarding the important value drivers, then identifying the gap and finally defining measures to close the gap.

But before we can start to develop the concept of e-commerce-ability, we have to take a closer look at the terms and models which represent a basis for this chapter: on the one hand we have to analyze whether the definitions of e-commerce to be found in literature are suitable for our purposes, and on the other hand we have to look at already existing e-commerce maturity models and decide whether they can be used for developing our e-commerce-ability concept.

DEFINITIONS OF E-COMMERCE

The understanding of e-commerce is widespread. A common definition is difficult to give because of many inconsistent approaches. But as e-commerce is the topic of the following investigation, it becomes necessary to discuss an appropriate definition.

Mostly definitions assume that e-commerce is enabled by the development and implementation of electronic media such as the Internet, whereby it is not uniform in how far "old" electronic media as telephone, telex, TV) are included.

The definition of e-commerce "doing business electronically" (European Commission, 1997) is too broad and interpretable, whereas the definition from GartnerGroup (1999)--"e-commerce is a dynamic set of technologies, applications and business processes that link corporations, consumers and communities"-- implicitly considers the often used transactional aspect. This definition is more explicitly given by Timmers (1998), who defines e-commerce as "any form of business transaction in which the parties interact electronically rather than by physical exchange or direct physical contact". Other approaches in this direction mostly differ in the degree of detail of the trade respectively transaction process or in the selection of specific processes such as procurement or distribution (Aldrich, 1999; Morasch et al., 2000). A further approach stresses the enhancements evoked by the enabling technologies in the form of more effective and efficient processes (cf., Baldwin et al., 2000).

Resuming this discussion Kalakota et al. (1997) can be cited: "depending on whom you ask, electronic commerce has different definitions," namely the perspectives communications, business process, service and online.

The definition used in this chapter focuses on the transactional approach and uses the definition of Kalakota et al. (1997) as a basis: "buying and selling over digital media," whereas buying can be left out: if the buying process is electronic the selling process is electronic as well. To be more precise: goods can also be services and the selling process can be either sale, commerce or distribution, as digital goods can be sold for free. So e-commerce is the trade (sales, commerce, distribution) of goods and services, i.e., products, by electronic means.

As a consequence e-commerce is mostly objectively observable activities of corporations. Implicitly it is also assumed that those activities have a deep impact on the structure of the corporation. This aspect, however, relates to the term "e-business."

Definitions of e-business are often close to e-commerce and moreover the definition space of e-business is complex and inconsistent. In this study e-business is interpreted as a superset of e-commerce and as a definition: e-business includes those business activities which (1) are a part of a value network, (2) address the customer process and (3) use information and communication technologies in an integrative way on the basis of the organizational and cultural rules of the network economy.

DIFFERENT APPROACHES AND FRAMEWORKS TO MEASURE E-COMMERCE-ABILITY

E-commerce-ability, the focus of this part of the chapter, describes the capability of a corporation to perform e-commerce successfully. Therefore two question should be answered: (1) how can e-commerce activities be categorized and (2) what are strategies to implement e-commerce activities? Numerous approaches give answers to those questions in different ways.

Many models reflect, explain, forecast factors and impacts on corporations but often with a special and narrow focus, what can be put down to different definitions of e-commerce. Schwartz (1998) for example claims essential principles to grow the business especially on the World Wide Web, as for example offer of experiences, compensation for personal data, high customer comfort, continual adaptation to the market or establishment of brands. Zerdick et al. (2000) and Kelly (1998), in contrast, are more general and describe 10 theses for the new economy, e.g., digitalization of the value chain, attainment of critical mass or competition and cooperation by value networks.

Approaches of that kind are numerous, but even though most of them seem to be valid, the transformation into business is difficult. Reasons are a missing methodology as well as the absence of a holistic view or framework in which the interconnection and most important dimensions are considered.

An approach given by the European Commission (1998) partly considers those aspects and distinguishes several levels of e-commerce activities in a continuum between easy and complex to implement into business respectively a continuum between standard and custom applications. Examples are electronic presences, national payment and international electronic distribution. The latter usually implies a high risk and high financial investments, whereas the others are mostly covered by standard and easy-to-realize applications. This model may give a clue for corporations on what they can do and which standard applications might exist, but a statement concerning their ability to do so or to know what to do can not be made.

A model which takes this into account is proposed by Canter (2000). A starting point is the need for agility in the information age because corporations have to react faster on their quickly changing environment. Bases of the framework are the capability maturity model (CMM) of the Carnegie Mellon University's Software Engineering Institute (cf., Paulk et al., 1993) and the decision cycle OODA (Observation-Orientation-Decision-Action). The five levels of the CMM are transformed into five levels with different characteristics of changeability and agility also known as the Change Proficiency Maturity Model (CPMM). This model can be used for business areas such as vision and strategy, innovation management or relationship management. The aim is to assist the OODA process supported by given tools to develop and reach a better maturity.

Even if the need for agility is accepted, the strong internal perspective which excludes external areas like external relationships or customer needs is the disadvantage of this model.

For the same reason approaches of Whitely (1998) and Grant (1999) cannot be used in this study.

Likewise the maturity of businesses is treated by Anghern (1997), but with an external focus on business activities on the Internet such as: information, communication, distribution and transaction. With those he distinguishes levels concerning the customization and sophistication. Additionally the author identifies a set of core competencies which are necessary to succeed within those levels. To summarize, this framework can be used for the "analysis of business-related Internet strategies, as well as a systematic approach to guide the strategic building process..." (cf., Anghern, 1997).

However, the neglect of internal matters also excludes this and the similar approach of Burgess et al. (1999). Indeed those implementations demonstrate that multidimensional models are more adequate for the complex e-commerce environment, but a holistic approach is missing.

Although PriceWaterhouseCoopers (PWC, 2000) and the similar Bain and Company (2000) present such an integrated approach, they both refer to e-business. The PriceWaterhouseCoopers approach consists of nine dimensions:
(1) E-business strategy
(2) Organization and competencies
(3) Business processes on the e-business value chain (advertising, ordering, delivery, billing debt collection, customer care)
(4) Web site performance (financially or otherwise)
(5) Taxation issues
(6) Legal and regulatory aspects
(7) Systems and technology used
(8) ICT and logistics processes
(9) E-business security

These dimensions are used on the one hand to evaluate the readiness of the corporation to develop and on the other hand to benchmark e-business performance.

Comparing those approaches with the proclaimed aim of the study, we believe only the latter approaches of PriceWaterhouseCoopers (PWC, 2000) and Bain and Company, respectively, to be appropriate. Nevertheless, they both have a too wide and complex scope for a quick and effective analysis of e-commerce activities.

Consequently a framework has to be developed which offers an integrative approach to the corporation and its capabilities as well as the coverage for most important success-defining factors.

DEDUCTION OF A CONCEPT FOR THE EVALUATION OF E-COMMERCE-ABILITY

The analysis concept for e-commerce-ability consists of two essential elements: first of all the framework for reflecting and comparing the patterns of e-commerce role profiles, and secondly a valuation approach for analyzing the economic success of the e-commerce activities. Both elements combined enable the evaluation of the e-commerce-ability of a corporation. Moreover, after analyzing the current status of the e-commerce activities, management can decide on further steps to be taken to render them e-commerce-able in a successful way.

The first pillar of the concept is a four-dimensional framework for creating patterns. This basic framework consists of four dimensions which represent characteristics we think to be important for a corporation of the net economy (also cf., Figure 2).

Degree of Orientation Towards Customer Needs

All ideas presented in this chapter are based on the strong belief that in the information age, every corporation has to align its activities with its customers' needs. Information and communication technology (ICT) has on the one hand been an enabler for the extensive gathering and processing of customer data. On the other hand, ICT made possible the adaptation of a corporation's range of services to customer needs. Therefore intensive consideration of customer needs seems to be an important means of differentiation. Often customers do not want to purchase a product or service, but rather intend to get a solution to a certain problem. This solution can be single goods and services or, more likely, bundles of goods and services. Successful e-commerce corporations offering those problem solutions therefore might be able to differentiate from their competitors (cf., Oesterle, 2000, pp. 45-47).

Another means of differentiation might be the ability of a corporation to provide highly customizable products and services to their customers, i.e., to a certain extent enabling them to modify product characteristics.

Therefore, we define the following categories for the measure "degree of orientation towards customer needs":

- *Standard products*: A corporation offers a range of products whose specifications are not modifiable.

- *Mass customization*: After intensively analyzing the customer needs, on the basis of standard products a set of customized products will be derived. Corporations offering those variations pursue the aim of making the product more attractive to groups of customers while at the same time limiting the costs of individualization.
- *Full coverage of needs*: This category is an extension of the previous one. A corporation does not only offer goods and services which are highly customizable as far as the individual customer needs are concerned, but also individual problem solutions consisting of a bundle of goods and services.

Degree of Systematic and Integral Use of ICT

Over the past 10 years, the role of information and communication technology has changed from a mere support function to a strategic tool for the generation of competitive advantages. We believe that e-commerce corporations need to pay special attention to the way of using ICT since they cannot–like in "normal" shopping marts–differentiate from their competitors by individualized face-to-face customer care. Instead they have to use electronic means for establishing the best possible customer relationship.

Venkatraman (1991) describes five levels of ICT-induced business reconfiguration:

(1) *Localized exploitation*: On this level corporations use ICT to support selected business functions. Thus they can realize efficiency gains in isolated functions, without any influence on daily operative business. However, localized exploitation does not lead to gains in effectiveness. If ICT is used only localized, i.e., without any strategic vision, a corporation's competitors can easily copy it. Therefore no long-term competitive advantages can be generated from its usage.

(2) *Internal integration*: This level is based on the localized exploitation of ICT. Internal integration enhances the benefits of localized exploitation by building an internal electronic infrastructure that enables the integration of tasks, processes as well as functions and therefore links all local ICT "islands." Internal integration aims at enhancing both efficiency (by reducing time and distance) and effectiveness (by improving information sharing between business processes). It has the potential to be an effective means of differentiation from a corporation's competitors, since it enables the creation of unique business processes.

According to Venkatraman (1991) those two levels form the basis for the purposeful deployment of ICT to 3) redesign business processes or 4) business networks and 5) redefinition of the business scope. Only by performing these activities, the potential of ICT can be fully exploited.

For the dimension "degree of systematic and integral use of ICT," this results in the following three measures:

Figure 1: Five levels of ICT-induced reconfiguration (cf. Venkatraman 1991, p.127)

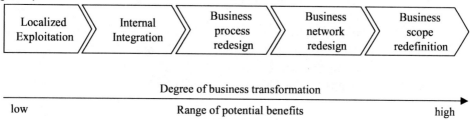

· *Support of internal or external business processes*: This degree corresponds to Venkatraman's level of internal integration. Moreover, integrated internal or external workflows become possible by integrating ICT solutions that support local business functions.

· *Support of internal and external business processes*: This degree enhances the first one by enlarging the extent of supporting business processes not only internally or externally, but both at the same time.

· *Support of internal and external as well as inter-organizational business processes*: ICT in this case is also used to support inter-business processes and thus enables the design of more efficient and effective processes throughout a business network.

Degree of the Alignment of the Business Towards Organizational and Cultural Rules of the Net Economy

Besides answering the question of the optimal degree of external coordination, a successful e-commerce corporation also has to think about how to align its internal organization towards organizational and cultural rules of the net economy. It has to review whether its organizational structure corresponds to the requirements resulting from the fast-changing environment.

Basically there are two extreme values within this dimension: on the one hand structures characterized by a high degree of organizational rules and hierarchy (e.g., matrix organization, divisional organization), and on the other hand very flexible organizational forms (e.g., project organization) where durable structures only exist during a certain project or task. The question whether the one or the other form of internal organization is more appropriate for a successful e-commerce corporation cannot be answered in general terms.

The fast-changing environment (technological innovations, new competitors, etc.) and an increased necessity to satisfy the ever-rising customer needs require the ability to flexibly make changes in the internal organization. However, there might be a critical size where corporations cannot exist anymore without a set of organizational rules (i.e., hierarchies).

Degree of External Coordination

This dimension has been added to our framework since we recognized that in the information age some general conditions have been changed which allow new efficient forms of interorganizational coordination. Our ideas are based on the relation established by Coase (1988) between the cost of using the price mechanism of a market and the existence of firms. The main reason for the existence of a firm is that "… the operation of a market costs something and that, by allowing some authority (an 'entrepreneur') to direct the resources, certain marketing costs are saved" (Coase, 1988, p. 40). Examples for those marketing (or transaction) costs are the costs of information procurement and processing or the costs of contracting.

The emergence of Internet technologies has resulted in a dramatic decrease of transaction costs. Examples are the costs of looking up business partners in electronic directories or the costs of exchanging data with them.

At the same time, Internet technologies also contributed to decreasing costs of intraorganizational activities, e.g., internal workflow management systems and document management systems dramatically reduced the processing time of certain business transactions and therefore increased the throughput.

Figure 2: Framework for creating patterns of roles in the e-commerce environment

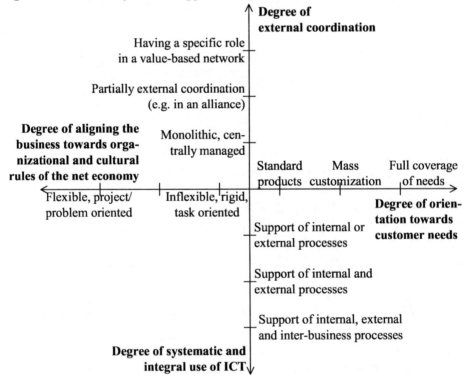

Depending on the individual corporation, the decrease in transaction costs may exceed the decrease in intraorganizational costs or vice versa. Therefore forms of external coordination via markets may become more efficient than the currently prevalent coordination within a firm.

Successful e-commerce corporations need to observe these trends, analyze their coordination of production and possibly adapt it to the new situation.

One possible form of adaptation might be to form alliances with certain corporations and to split the value chain into single steps, each of them to be provided by one corporation. An even more ambitious approach could be to participate in a value network, where each partner performs a dedicated role and is responsible for maintaining and driving both communication and cooperation concerning his "node" in the network.

ROLES IN THE E-COMMERCE ENVIRONMENT AND THEIR PATTERNS

There are basically two roles in the e-commerce environment which we included into our framework. This is first of all the role "service provider (SP)" who is specialized in the production of very specific goods or services that correlate to its core competencies. Secondly, there is the "service integrator (SI)" whose main goal is to fulfill a certain need of a customer which mostly consists of many different goods and services which must be combined to one solution. The SI integrates all the necessary products and sells this individual solution to the customer. Thus, the definition of these roles bases on different requirements.

The SP role requires very good logistics, i.e., deliver the product at the right time, in the right amount, in the right quality, to the right addressee. The addressees or customers, respectively, can be both different SIs needing the product for creating the individual customer solution and the end customer him- or herself, who only

Table 1: Characteristics of the SP regarding the dimensions of the e-commerce-ability framework

Dimension	Characteristic
Degree of orientation towards customer needs	The SP only produces standardized or mass customizable products due to reasons of efficiency, e.g. to be able to realize a very short "time to customer".
Degree of systematic and integral use of ICT	In this case, it is not necessary to realize the highest possible degree, because the external processes are fixed and do not request a fully flexible integration or coordination of constantly changing services, for example.
Degree of the alignment of the business towards organizational and cultural rules of the net economy	Due to reasons of efficiency and a short time to market, the organization should be task-oriented and have a hierarchical structure. This leads to standardized processes which seem to be helpful as far as the implementation of a short lead time of the core processes is concerned.
Degree of external coordination	Since the SP has a very specific and clearly defined role in a value-based network, the degree of external coordination is high, although with a limited set of partners.

expects a certain product, but not a specific solution or service. Since the performance of this role is very specific and mainly targets effectiveness and efficiency of the process, thus also focusing on economies of scale, for example, it shows a pattern with the following characteristics regarding the different dimensions (also cf., Figure 3):

The SI role, however, requires a maximum amount of flexibility as regards the creation of the performance needed. Therefore, effectiveness and efficiency, although of course still being important due to economic reasons, are not considered main targets. Much more important is the good and lasting customer relationship

Table 2: Characteristics of the SI regarding the dimensions of the e-commerce-ability framework

Dimension	Characteristic
Degree of orientation towards customer needs	The SI provides full coverage of any need the customer states.
Degree of systematic and integral use of ICT	The maximum degree of this dimension should be reached in order to establish the most efficient integration process possible.
Degree of aligning the business towards organizational and cultural rules of the net economy	Since each need is individual, the organization must be very flexible and problem-oriented. Creativity for problem solving is mandatory and is difficult to create in a rigid environment.
Degree of external coordination	The SI also has a very specific and clearly defined role in a value-based network, thus the degree of external coordination is very high.

Figure 3: Patterns of the roles of SI and SP in an e-commerce environment

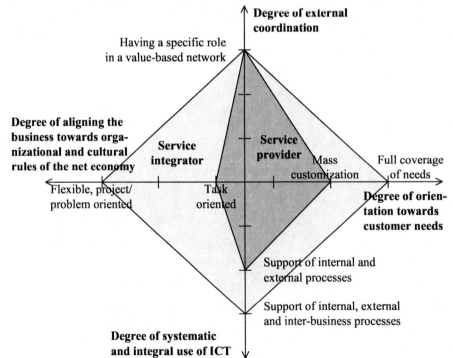

which is established by the ability to coordinate many different partners to establish a large "pool" of goods and services from which the most eligible ones can be chosen dynamically to create the best possible solution for the end customer. Taking this into account, we can deduce the following characteristics as regards the dimensions of the framework for the SI, also depicted in Figure 3:

Integrated into the framework, Figure 3 shows how the patterns evolve.

Having identified the patterns the different roles in an e-commerce environment should have, we now have to define the second part of being successful, i.e., we have to develop a concept for evaluating the economic success of e-commerce activities.

VALUE AS SECOND PILLAR OF EVALUATING THE SUCCESS OF E-COMMERCE ACTIVITIES

The success of a business model can be measured in many different ways. The most common way is to quantify it using financial figures such as the Return on Investment (ROI), Earnings before Interest and Taxes (EBIT), Cash Flow (CF). The shareholder value discussion focuses on long-term sustainability and thus uses ratios such as the Discounted Cash Flow (DCF) or Economic Value Added (EVA) (Stern et al., 2000). Business models of the net economy, however, have proven that the mere consideration of financial figures is not sufficient. Especially in the first stages of a start-up (i.e., the lowest point of the so-called "hockey stick," where the main financial figures take a dive), financial ratios are not sufficient for reflecting the real value of a corporation. Therefore, we think that although financial figures still play an important role, they have to be complemented by qualitative parameters. Moreover, we base on what the shareholder value approach for evaluating success. The term "value" implies that we drop the short-term perspective and analyze the medium- to long-term substance and sustainability of a corporation. Value is often defined using operating performance and long-term growth. Since this does not represent all perspectives of shareholder value, but only the financial ones, the important elements of creating shareholder value are depicted in Figure 4 (Copeland et al., 2000, p. 91).

The main reason for our decision to choose this approach is our definition of "successful" as the creation of value over a medium- to long-term period of time.

Applying the shareholder value approach for these kinds of business models, we base on Copeland, Koller and Murrin (cf., here and in the following Copeland et al., 2000) and thus choose the quantitative as well as the qualitative parameters from the value drivers discussed there. Value drivers are those factors which have the highest impact on value both as regards day-to-day business as well as investment decisions having a medium- to long-term horizon. Thus, value drivers are performance indicators that differ from corporation to corporation, but have to be fully understood on each management level to be able to control value.

Figure 4: Important elements of value creation

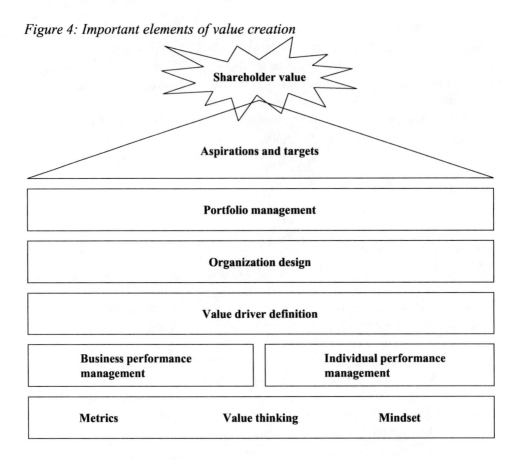

Copeland et al. suggest the drawing of a value tree for the representation of the value drivers chosen. We now adapt this for our purposes of valuating e-commerce activities of a corporation.

The e-commerce value tree is built by the following value drivers:

· Contacts over electronic channels with the "branches" types of information requested, customer segments attracted *and* time to reaction.

· Goods and services traded over electronic channels with the "branches" types of products traded, lead time of process and customer satisfaction.

· Traditional profit and loss tree with ROIC (Return on Invested Capital) and the "branches" revenue, costs and capital charges.

The value tree can be enlarged or modified according to the analysis needs of management. Moreover, key performance indicators (KPIs), which serve as metrics for operationalizing the value drivers, have to be defined (e.g., for the value driver "customer satisfaction" a KPI "# of returned products" and/or "% of returned feedback questionnaires below the evaluation <satisfied>" could be defined). There are a few more points which ought to be observed for successfully using the value

Figure 5: Value tree for valuing e-commerce activities

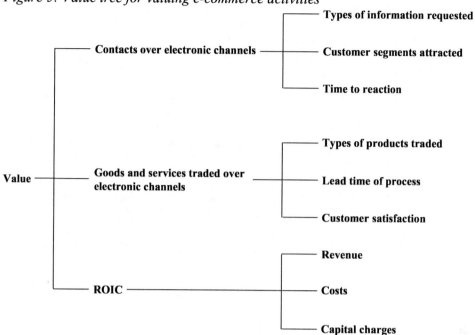

tree: firstly, it must be designed according to the specific analysis needs, the operative and strategic requirements and the environment of the corporation. Secondly, it must be appropriately cascaded down to each management level in order to ensure that its implications and the individual contributions to success become clear. Thirdly, it must be analyzed over several consecutive periods to be able to observe changes and decide on actions in case of unwanted deviations. Moreover, it must be regularly adapted in order to be able to take the current requirements of e-commerce and competition into account.

CONCLUSIONS

The above developed concept is a first step towards analyzing e-commerce activities in a broader context of qualitative and quantitative parameters. It is designed to support management decisions focusing on the medium- and long-term strategies regarding e-commerce activities, and moreover to enable the evaluation of the current status or rather position as far as e-commerce-ability, i.e., the ability to perform successful e-commerce, is concerned.

The next step must be the validation of the concept by applying it to e-commerce corporations and enhance it by developing a rule base for e-commerce success patterns regarding different business models within the role profiles.

REFERENCES

Aldrich, D. F. (1999). *Mastering the Digital Marketplace: Practical Strategies for Competitiveness in the New Economy*. New York: Wiley.

Angehrn, A. (1997). Designing mature Internet business strategies: The ICDT model. *European Management Journal*, 15, 361-369.

Bain and Company. (2000). *Bain and Company eQ–Test*. Available on the World Wide Web at: http://www.bain.de. Accessed October 15, 2000.

Baldwin, L. P. and Currie, W. L. (2000). Key issues in electronic commerce in today's global information infrastructure. *Cognition, Technology & Work*, 2(1), 27-34.

Burgess, L. and Cooper, J. (1999). A model for classification of business adoption of Internet commerce solutions. In Klein, S., Gricar, J. and Pucihar, A. (Eds.), *Global networked Organizations: 12th International Bled Electronic Commerce Conference*, 46-58.

Canter, J. (2000). *An agility-based ODDA model for the e-commerce/e-business corporation*. Available on the World Wide Web at: http://www.belisarius.com/canter.htm. Accessed October 15, 2000.

Coase, R. H. (1998). *The firm, the market, and the law*. Chicago: The University of Chicago Press.

Copeland, T., Koller, T. and Murrin, J. (2000). *Valuation-measuring and managing the value of corporations*. New York: Wiley.

European Commission. (1997). *A European Initiative in Electronic Commerce*. Available on the World Wide Web at: http://www.cordis.lu/esprit/src/ecomcom.htm. Accessed May 29, 1997.

European Commission. (1998). Electronic commerce-An introduction. Retrieved October 15, 2000 on the World Wide Web: http://www.ispo.cec.be/ecommerce/answers/introduction.html.

GartnerGroup. (1999). *Electronic Commerce Platforms and Applications* (Report No. R-07-1624). GartnerGroup RAS Services, January 13.

Grant, S. (2000). *E-Commerce for Small businesses*. Retrieved October 15, 2000 on the World Wide Web at: http://www.inst.co.uk/papers/small.html. Accessed October 15, 2000.

Kalakota, R. and Whinston, A. B. (1997). *Electronic Commerce: A Manager's Guide*. Reading, MA: Addison-Wesley.

Kelly, K. (1998). *New Rules for the New Economy*. New York: Viking.

Kranj, Sloenia: Moderna organizacija.

Morasch, K. and Welzel, P. (2000). Emergence of electronic markets: Implication of declining transport costs on firm profits and consumer surplus. In Bodendorf, F. and Grauer, M. (Eds.), *Verbundtagung Wirtschaftsinformatik 2000*. Aachen, Germany: Shaker.

Oesterle, H. (2000). Enterprise in the information age. In Oesterle, H., Fleisch, E. and Alt, R. (Eds.), *Business Networking*, 17-54. Berlin: Springer.

Paulk, M. C., Chrissis, M. B. and Weber, C. V. (1993). Capability maturity model, Version 1.1. *IEEE Software*, July, 10, 18-27.

PriceWaterhouseCoopers. (2000). *PriceWaterhouseCoopers E-Business: About PWC*. Available on the World Wide Web at: http://208.203.128.56/external/ ebib.nsf/docid 8149EB15B63E21508025691F004623AB?opendocument. Accessed October 15, 2000.

Schwartz, E. (1998). *Webonomics: Nine Essential Principles for Growing Your Business on the World Wide Web*. New York: Broadway Books.

Stern Stewart & Co. (2000). *Evanomics*. Available on the World Wide Web at: http:/ /www.evanomics.com. Accessed October 15, 2000.

Timmers, P. (1998). Business models for electronic markets. *Electronic Market*, 8(2), 3-8.

Venkatraman, N. (1991). ICT-induced business reconfiguration. In Morton, M. S. (Ed.), *The Corporation of the 1990s*. Oxford: Oxford University Press, 122-158.

Whiteley, D. (1998). EDI maturity: A business opportunity. In Romm, C. T. and Sudweeks, F. (Eds.). *Doing Business Electronically: A Global Perspective of Electronic Commerce*, 139-150. Berlin: Springer.

Zerdick, A., Picot, A., Schrape, K., Artope, A., Goldhammer, K., Lange, U. T., Vierkant, E., Lopez-Escobar, E. and Silverstone, R. (Eds.). (2000). *E-Conomics. The Economy of E-Commerce and the Internet*. Berlin: Springer.

Chapter XIII

Strategies for Bricks to Beat Clicks – How Established Businesses Can Incorporate the New Technologies

Martin Barnett and Janice M. Burn
Edith Cowan University, Australia

INTRODUCTION

This chapter looks at models for organizational development using the potential of virtual organization for established firms. For established businesses, particularly those in the consumer product area, much cash and knowledge is invested in the management of multiple physical outlets–bricks. The potential for the inexpensive and pervasive Internet technologies to reinvent the mail order shopping with a real-time interaction attraction has been widely touted and is under test. For books, music and perhaps even groceries, it is possible that the old measurement of value–"location, location, location" may be replaced with clicks of the mouse.

Any retailer of mass consumer goods must be looking over his shoulder for fear that a start-up enterprise, not needing to match him dollar for dollar, may be sneaking up to compete for the same number of customers. The phenomenon has been so sudden that strategies for encompassing and managing the integration of technological change and deciding on appropriate business forms have yet to be agreed. In this chapter the authors argue that there is a single best response to the opportunities and challenges presented by competition from start-up virtual organizations. Instead, organizations are invited to select a mix'n'match from a series of strategies, electing on the basis of individual strengths and industries. Six models of virtual organizations are proposed within a dynamic framework of change. In order to realize the flexibility promised by new technology, organizations must identify their long-term opportunities and match these with the appropriate model for structural alignment. The authors provide case descriptions of organizations and an analysis of their strategic positioning in relation to the virtual business models.

BACKGROUND

Established consumer business enterprises, particularly those with heavy sunk financial knowledge capital in brick-and-mortar retail outlets, are looking to formulate strategies to deal with the perceived threat of startup competition operating in virtual space. The lowering of cost barriers to entry into retail business over a wide geographical area that does, or is perceived to, result from the adoption of Internet technologies offers cause for concern.

After a discussion of current trends toward creating or moving toward virtual organizational forms, this chapter looks at business planning models for brick-and-mortar companies seeking to incorporate Internet advantages with existing assets. It challenges the notion that there is a static optimal model for virtual configuration as an answer to the opportunities and challenges presented by changes in the technology infrastructure for the 21st century.

The authors suggest that the basic concepts of organizational form as a response to the potential for virtual organizing are so poorly understood that there are likely to be far more real failures than virtual realities. The chapter attempts to redress some of these imbalances by providing clear working definitions of virtual organizations and models of virtuality, which can exist along a continuum within the electronic market. It is accepted that the value of different models for organization are likely to be constrained both by the extent of pre-existing linkages in the marketplace and the ease of their replacement with new ones, but also by the intensity of linkages which support the virtual model.

Six models of virtual organizations are proposed within a dynamic framework of change. In order to realize the flexibility promised by new technology, organizations must identify their long-term opportunities and match these with the appropriate model for structural alignment. The value of the adopted degree of virtuality which may result has then to be examined in relation to the structure/strategy alignment and to both the organization and its component alliances. In this way it is proposed that it is possible to identify factors which may inhibit or promote effective business value realization.

The authors provide case descriptions of organizations and an analysis of their strategic positioning in relation to the virtual business model. Detailed proposals are advanced to demonstrate the means by which these organizations can develop virtual organizing and management skills to allow them the flexibility demanded by such a dynamic environment.

We believe that this explication will allow for the clearer formulation and implementation of management strategies within ongoing business contexts. The illustration of the models within the continuum of virtual organizations is advanced as a tool with practical utility, and this it is believed is rendered immediately comprehensible by the examples adduced.

The chapter concludes by directing readers to further supporting evidence, and outlining means by which further research may be usefully integrated with management practice.

ISSUES AND CONTROVERSIES OVER THE VALUE OF BEING VIRTUAL

Management literature currently assumes that new organizational forms using communications technology to diminish the centrifugal pull of location will bring benefits arising from virtual rather than physical conjunction in space, time and (frequently) corporate identity. But there is very little empirical research to show that substituting "virtual" links for "real" links necessarily yields value. Indeed, there are so many fuzzy concepts related to virtuality that any broad statement made with regard to virtual organizations is likely to be false. It could be argued that there is a degree of virtuality in all organizations, currently controlled by the outcome of a (perhaps unmanaged) conflict between desire for control and adaptability. It is argued below that there is a continuum along which organizations can understand their position in the electronic marketplace according to their needs for flexibility and responsiveness as opposed to stability and sustained momentum.

While there may be general agreement that flexibility is a good thing, the extent to which virtuality offers flexibility and the accruing advantages thereof have yet to be measured. There is an assumption that an organization with minimal investment commitment to infrastructure will respond more rapidly to a changing marketplace. This, it is argued, could allow for speedy adaptation and hence global competitive advantage; but this ignores the very real power which large integrated organizations can bring to the market in terms of sustained innovation over the longer term (Chesbrough and Teece, 1996). Proponents of the virtual organization as automatically capable of rapid adaptive response also tend to underestimate the restraining power of the very links which currently define and constitute the organization. The transactional bonds, which define a virtual organization, may equally inhibit flexibility and change rather than nurture the concept of the opportunistic virtual organization (Goldman, Nagel and Preiss, 1995).

Discussion in the literature to date offers a profusion of concepts which fail to provide a unifying perspective and framework within which adaptive change models can be determined. These views are briefly summarized below and followed by a proposal for an integrated framework within which adaptive responses and a change model are identified.

One popular definition would suggest that organizations are virtual when producing work deliverables across different locations, at differing work cycles and across cultures (Gray and Igbaria, 1996; Palmer and Speier, 1998). Another suggests that the single common theme is temporality. Virtual organizations center on continual restructuring to capture the value of a short-term market opportunity and are then dissolved to make way for restructuring to a new virtual entity (Byrne, 1993; Katzy, 1998). Yet others suggest that virtual organizations are characterized by the intensity, symmetricality, reciprocity and multiplexity of the linkages in their networks (Powell, 1990; Grabowski and Roberts, 1996). Whatever the definition (and this chapter offers a resolution of some of the ambiguities), there is a consensus that the term "virtual" can be meaningfully applied to very dissimilar organizations (Hoffman, Novak, and Chatterjee, 1995; Gray and Igbaria, 1996; Goldman, Nagel and Preiss, 1995). It has been noted that different organizational structures arise in different circumstances (Palmer and Speier, 1998; Davidow and Malone, 1992, Miles and Snow, 1986). Such structures are normally inter-organizational and lie at the heart of any form of electronic commerce, yet the organizational and management processes which should be applied to ensure successful configuration have been greatly under-researched (Finnegan, Galliers and Powell, 1998; Swatman and Swatman, 1992).

It is further suggested that the relationship between tasks and structure and its effect on performance have not been studied at all in the context of virtual organizations (Ahuja and Carley, 1998). To resolve this we propose below a context for correctly understanding the impetus toward virtuality for organizations and a continuum along which clearly defined organizational forms emerge as effective adaptive responses to their environments.

THE CONTEXT FOR ORGANIZATIONAL CHANGE

Virtual organizations as a group are best understood as electronically networked organizations transcending conventional boundaries (Barner, 1996; Berger, 1996; Rogers 1996) with linkages both within (Davidow and Malone, 1992) and/or between organizations (Goldman, Nagel and Preiss, 1995). In its simplest form, however, virtuality exists where IT is used to enhance organizational activities while reducing the need for physical or formalized structure (Greiner and Metes, 1996). Degrees of virtuality then exist which will reflect:

- the virtual organizational culture (strategic positioning);
- the internal and external networks (in particular the intensity of linkages and the nature of the bonds which tie the stakeholders together);
- the market (IT dependency and resource infrastructure, product, customer).

Virtual Culture

We define culture as the degree to which members of a community have common shared values and beliefs (Schein, 1990). Together with Tushman and O'Reilly (1996), we suggest that organizational cultures that are embracing of new technology, highly decentralized and change oriented are more likely to seek out virtual forms and actively pursue these opportunities both inside and outside the organization. Virtual culture is hence a perception of the entire organization and its operations held by its stakeholder community.

This is operationalized in choices and actions that result in a feeling of unity with respect to value sharing (i.e., each client's expectations are satisfied in the product accessed), and time-space arrangement (i.e., each stakeholder shares the feeling of a continuous access to the organization and its products). The embodiment of this culture comes through the Virtual Strategic Perspective (VSP) that the organization adopts. Its value derives from the ability to operate with markedly diminished constraints of space and time, yielding unprecedented opportunities for expansion of reach with marked reduction of traditional transaction costs, becoming global if this is seen as advantageous.

Virtual Networks

Networks can be groups of organizations but also groups within organizations where the development and maintenance of communicative relationships is paramount to the successful evolution of a virtual entity. However, the need to both establish multiple alliances and at the same time retain a particular identity creates a constant tension between autonomy and interdependence, competition and cooperation (Nouwens and Bouwman, 1996). These relationships are often described as value-added partnerships based on horizontal, vertical or symbiotic relationships. These in turn relate to competitors, value chain collaborators and complementary providers of goods and services, all of whom combine to achieve competitive advantage over organizations outside these networks. The nature of these alliances, their strength and substitutability define the inherent advantageous virtual structure.

Virtual Markets

Markets differ from networks in that pricing mechanisms traditionally coordinate them. In this respect, the electronic market is no different, but it goes further in that "central to [the notion of] the electronic marketplace is the ability of any buyer or seller to interconnect with a network to offer wares or shop for goods and services. Hence, ubiquity is by definition a prerequisite" (Steinfield, Kraut and Plummer, 1995).

There are different risks associated with being a market maker and a market player, and different products also carry different risks. Criteria for successful electronic market development include products with low asset specificity, ease of description and a consumer willing to effect transactions by means of networks (Wigand and Benjamin, 1995). Necessarily, the defining characteristic of an electronic market is the availability of pervasive Information and Communication Technology (ICT) infrastructures available by the electronic market in which it operates and the extent to which its business environment consists of effectively deployed ICT. Figure 1 shows this set of relationships.

Figure 1: Virtual organizations and virtual cultures

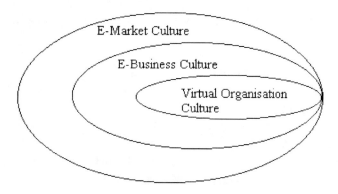

Despite the growth of online activity, many firms are nervous of the risks involved and fear a general deterioration of profit margins coupled with a relinquishment of market control as a consequence of market transparency and new forms of intermediation. Nevertheless, as existing organizations are challenged by new entrants using direct channels to undercut prices and increase market share, solutions have to be found that enable organizations to successfully operate within the electronic market. The authors suggest that there are six different models of virtuality commending themselves as efficient responses.

DERIVING STRATEGIC PLANNING MODELS

Many consumer retail organizations have based their electronic storefronts on traditional business models. Distribution systems need to be developed but require substantial investments. A likely scenario is that separate organizations will specialize in controlling each of the four main processes of the distribution: marketing, financing, ordering and transferring the purchases to the customers (Kallio, Saarinen, Tinnila and Tuunainen, 2000). It would appear difficult to combine traditional business methods with effective online methods and at the same time reduce costs and improve convenience for the customers. For this reason there is much interest in providing or describing new business and planning models to take advantage of improved technology (Hoffman, Novak and Chatterjee, 1995; Kallio, Saarinen, Tinnila and Tuunainen, 2000; Zimmerman, 2000). But the objectives of model makers varies, and a temptation exists to focus on a single strategic model and concentrate on the tactical implementation of subsets of this to the detriment of overall strategic creation (Hoffman, Novak and Chatterjee 1995; Lawrence, Corbill, Tidwell, Fisher and Lawrence, 1998).

Following Zimmerman (2000), we accept that the type of business model we seek for analysis and implementation at the strategic level should contain the following four levels:
·   an architecture for the service to meet business needs;

- a definition of the business community involved, together with an understanding of the respective roles of players within the model;
- an appreciation of expected benefits to be obtained by participating within the model; and
- a description of revenue sources.

Within this chapter the models we present for consideration are not analyzed to integrate the revenue stream perspective, although future research seeks to do so. We seek only to introduce the models and stimulate discussion and cooperation in this endeavour. The models below are currently descriptive as their prescriptive power has yet to be determined, but we offer them in the recognition that enterprises with varying resources, and/or placed differently within current supply chain relationships, will require different business trajectories. Until prescriptive power can be developed, these models are intended to serve as a convenient tool for description and analysis in conjunction with existing tools for model development, such as SWOT analysis and Balanced Business Scorecard.

RECOMMENDATIONS: FRAMING MODELS FOR EFFICIENT RESPONSE

Burn and Barnett (2000a) identify a minimal range of business models that can serve, singly or in combination, to fully describe strategic planning strategies emerging within the e-grocery trade as an exemplar of large-scale established brick-and-mortar retail operations. These, we suggest, can with advantage be taken as models for implementation; planned future research will identify any optimal development paths between them for concerns at different stages of development or with specific opportunities or threats to balance.

These models, taken from discussion and case examples with diagrams (Burn and Barnett, 2000b), are described thus: virtual faces, co-alliances, star alliances, value alliances, market alliances, virtual brokers and virtual spaces. The value of each of these forms lies in their being an appropriate response to the communication, channel and transaction needs within a given nexus of market forces and opportunities.

Virtual Face Model

Virtual faces are the cyberspace incarnations of an existing non-virtual organization, (often described as a "place" as opposed to "space" organization (Rayport and Sviokola, 1995). These commend themselves by creating additional value such as enabling users to carry out the same ICT-enabled transactions as they could otherwise do by using telephone or fax. Common examples include Fleurop selling flowers, and Travelocity selling air tickets. The interactivity of communications now available may provide an impetus for a shift in focus of activity. These services need not simply reflect and mirror the activities of the parent organization, but even extend them, as we see in the Web-based versions of television channels

Figure 2: Virtual face

and newspapers with constant news updates and archival searches. In addition they may extend the scope of activities by use of facilities such as electronic procurement, contract tendering or even electronic auctions or reach new markets by participating in an electronic mall with or without added enrichment such as a common payment mechanism.

Jane Brook Winery, a small family operated vineyard in Western Australia, provides an example of such a model. The company is a family run winery business established in 1972 and owned by two members of the management. The company cultivates a total acreage of 12.5 in addition to supplies from contract growers. Jane Brook produces a variety of Australian choice wine with main markets in Australia, Japan, Singapore, Malaysia and Taiwan. Its annual level is 10,000–15,000 cases. It established an online site in June 1995 focusing on marketing products and also providing corporate and industry information to its clients. The site also provided information about its key agents and sales outlets. A major emphasis in the site was to attract customers to visit the winery and to encourage cellar sales and enjoyment of dining and catering facilities. There is a total of five permanent staff of the company including three members of the Atkinson family. The company also employs approximately 15-20 part-time staff that perform a variety of tasks (e.g., cellar door wine tasting, wine sales and in-the-café activities).

In this model there is obviously a tight link between the virtual face and the parent organization. What is happening is simply that a fresh communications channel has been forged between the existing corporate structure and supply chain and the customer. This model is used by the majority of companies who offer Web pages, with varying degrees of interactivity, to complement rather than supplement other channels to market. In some cases organizations find that the different communication challenges require them to establish an entirely new management model independent from the parent group–this has been proposed in a number of electronic retailing situations where the traditional forms of supermarket management cannot be successfully maintained in an electronic market.

Co-Alliance Model

Co-alliance models are shared partnerships with each partner bringing approximately equal amounts of commitment to the virtual organization to form a consortium. The composition of the consortium may change to reflect market opportunities or to reflect the core competencies of each member (Preiss, Goldman and Nagel, 1996). Focus can be on specific functions such as collaborative design or engineering, or in providing virtual support with a virtual team of consultants. Links within the co-alliance are normally contractual for more permanent alliances or by mutual convenience on a project-by-project basis. There is not normally a high degree of substitutability within the life of that virtual creation. This organizational form is not unique to cyberspace, but its attractiveness as a virtual model is a consequence of the benefits flowing from low friction communications in real time and the ease with which such structures can be assembled and restructured. This form of cooperation is by no means a new response to business circumstances. The novelty lies in the speed and efficiency with which such alliances can usefully form, perform their tasks and reform owing to efficient communications, and hence the ease with which the other partners can treat the partners as a virtual (single) entity existing for a specified time.

Examples include real estate vendors who form a geographical alliance to cater for interstate relocations. Communications are direct between the specific state partnerships and may involve no other partner. These can evolve over time into much more complex structures such as those described below where other links may be formed along a value chain with legal services, shippers and decorators-all with different levels of intensity.

Star Alliance Model

The star alliance is a coordinated network of members comprising a core surrounded by satellite organizations. The core is typically a dominant player in the market on whom members rely for competency, expertise or leads to customers. Such an alliance is commonly based around similar industries or company types. While this form is a true network, typically the star or leader is identified with the virtual face (perhaps by brand ownership) and so the core organization is very difficult to replace whereas the satellites may have a far greater level of substitutability. Well-documented examples of this configuration are given by the Swiss watch industry and the Italian shoe industry.

Where the core controls communication channels, a quite hierarchical communication structure may emerge, as in the case of Recreational Equipment Inc.

Figure 3: Co-alliance model

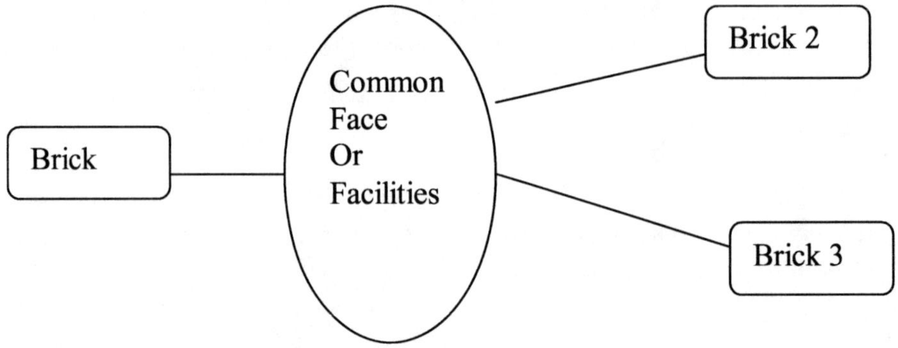

Recreational Equipment Inc. (REI) is an established outdoor gear and clothing cooperative mail-order business with 49 brick-and-mortar retail outlets across the USA. REI first considered the Internet as a channel for product information, in response to customer requests, in 1995. Now the biggest outdoor store on the Internet, REI.com is the company's virtual face which features more than 10,000 products for outdoor enthusiasts displayed in a 100-page catalogue. REI recently moved a step further by creating an online store offering special deals that has no brick-and-mortar counterparts. Having an online resource for product information has been a benefit not just for the online store, but for REI's physical stores as well. It has achieved this by creating virtual alliances, firstly by establishing firm and fast relationships with the printing company that continues to provide the paper brochures used by the physical stores, then by forming similar alliances by extranet technology between the online store and its suppliers. This vendor extranet will result in tighter integration for better supply chain management and stock planning– moving toward a star alliance model, or a value alliance in our terms. Business pressures will determine the balance between these and future extent of cooperation.

Value Alliance Model

Value alliance models bring together a range of products, services and facilities in one package and are based on the value or supply chain model. Participants may come together on a project-by-project basis, but generally the general contractor provides coordination. Where longer-term relationships have developed, the value alliance often adopts the form of value constellations where firms supply each of the companies in the value chain, and a complex and an enduring communications structure is embedded within the alliance. Substitutability has traditionally been a function of efficiency and transaction costs: searching for, evaluating and com- mencing operations with potential partners has been a costly and slow business procedure, relying as it does on information transfer, the establishment of trust and business rules across time zones, culture, currency and legal frameworks. These

Figure 4: Star alliance model

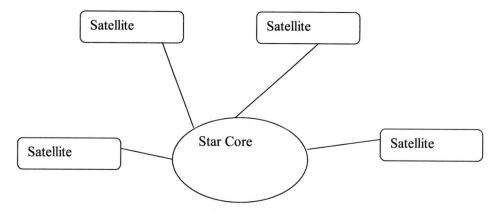

have determined the relative positioning of partners on the chain and the reciprocity of the relationship. This model is particularly suited to taking advantage of communications efficiencies not previously available and therefore changing components extremely rapidly in response to evanescent market forces and opportunities.

In the motor trade autobytel.com has demonstrated the viability of this model that puts customer in contact with a manufacturer and at the same time reinventing the dealer's mediation relationship to achieve price reduction to consumer through more efficient intermediation.

Market Alliance Model

Market alliances are organizations that exist primarily in cyberspace, depend on their member organizations for the provision of actual products and services, and operate in an electronic market. Normally they bring together a range of products, services and facilities in one package, each of which may be offered separately by individual organizations. In some cases the market is open and in others serves as an intermediary. These can also be described as virtual communities, but a virtual community can be an add-on such as exists in an e-mall rather than a cyberspace organization perceived as a virtual organization.

Amazon.com is a prime example of a market alliance model where substitutability of links is very high. Fast and responsive communication channels are essential to preserve such alliances, which could only have formed occasionally, and relied on duration to be cost-effective hitherto.

Many of the new business trading hubs that cut across industries exemplify this model in action.

Figure 5: Value alliance model

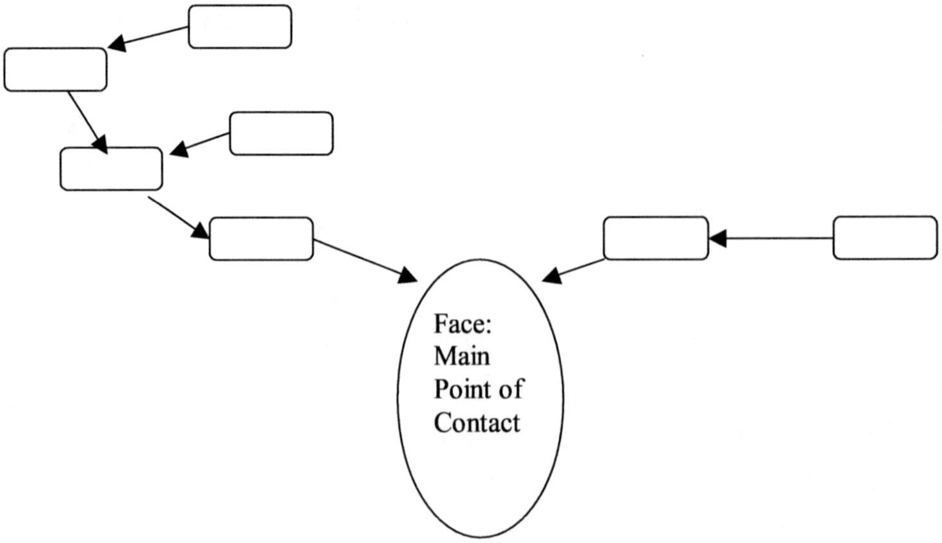

Face:
Main
Point of
Contact

Figure 6: Market alliance model

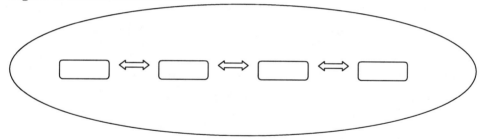

Virtual Broker Model

Virtual brokers are designers of dynamic networks (Miles and Snow, 1986). These seize upon their marketing or knowledge capital to make opportunities either as third-party value-added suppliers such as in the case of common Web marketing events (e-Xmas) or as information brokers providing a virtual structure around specific business information services (Timmers, 1998). This has the highest level of flexibility with purpose-built virtual organizations created to fill a window of opportunity and dissolved when that window is closed. New intermediaries using the Internet (such as e-Bay and the many auction enterprises) epitomize the growing trend to take fast and inexpensive communications across time and space for granted and to configure themselves for advantage accordingly. This provides an excellent model for (some) players in a crowded bricks environment–such as that offered by the estate agent or insurance broker to reinvent themselves as a value-adding intermediary.

The case of Sofcom illustrates how a firm may move to adopt this model as an effective response. Sofcom (www.sofcom.com) is a Melbourne company acting as an electronic intermediary, which provides, in addition to other online content publishing, a virtual shopping mall for about 60 virtual storefronts. Sofcom Shopping Mall advertises more than 4,835 products in about 60 stores. There are 10 categories of stores, including clothing, vehicles, business services, computers and electronics, gifts and collectables, home design, perfumery and jewelry and entertainment. Sofcom has an extensive online infrastructure to support its product lines and to manage the virtual stores of other businesses. All transactions at Sofcom pass through Sofcom's SSL secure server. The site offers an online **Store Builder™** facility for potential online storeowners. The facility takes potential storeowners step by step through the process of setting up a storefront at Sofcom and doing business online. There is a flat charge of 40AUD per month for stores available to the public and selling. Potential storeowners may develop and test run a store for free. Sofcom acts as virtual brokers (see below), and businesses using the facilities of the mall are embedded in a market alliance model.

The market may be described as an example of a virtual community, given this company's extensive linkages and the diversity of online firms involved with its

Figure 7: Virtual broker

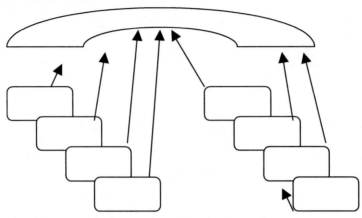

business. A detailed study of the various inter-firm relations would throw more light on the dynamics of the virtual community as an electronic marketspace. This should further facilitate understanding of the contributions of the online infrastructure to the competitive performance of participating businesses.

Virtual Alliance Framework

Each of these alliances embodies a set of tensions related to autonomy and interdependence. Virtual culture is the strategic hub around which virtual relationships are formed and virtual links implemented. In order to be flexible, links must be substitutable to allow the creation of new competencies, but links must be established and maintained if the organization is going to fully leverage community expertise. This presents a dichotomy. The degree to which virtuality can be implemented effectively relates to the strength of existing organizational links (virtual and non-virtual) and the relationship that these impose on the virtual structure. However, as essentially networked organizations they will be constrained by the extent to which they are able to redefine or extend their linkages. Where existing linkages are strong, e.g., co-located, shared culture, synchronicity of work and shared risk (reciprocity), these will reduce the perceived benefits from substitutable linkages and inhibit the development of further virtual linkages. Figure 8 provides a diagrammatic representation of these tensions and their interaction with the Virtual Alliance Framework (VAF).

These six models elucidated above are not exclusive but are intended to serve as a way of classifying the diversity of forms which an electronic business model may assume. Some of these are recognizable as an electronic re-implementation of traditional forms of doing business; as their attractiveness increased, the Internet reduces the transaction costs of implementation. Others are add-ons for added value, possibly through umbrella collaboration, and others go far beyond this through value chain integration or cyber communities. What these have in common is that they now exemplify innovative ways to add value to existing organizational forms

Figure 8: Virtual Alliance Framework (VAF)

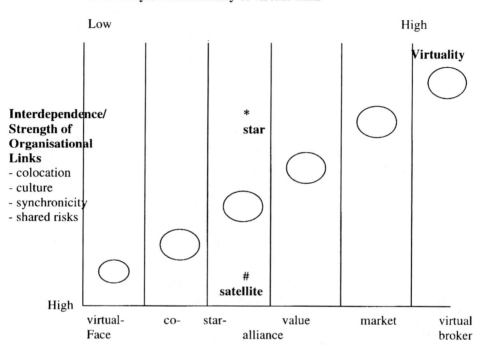

Autonomy/Substitutability of virtual links

and model pathways for growth through information and change management and a rich functionality.

OTHER ISSUES IN VIRTUAL ORGANIZATIONAL CHANGE

e-Market Ecosystem

As observed above, these forms of virtual organizations all operate within a dynamic environment where their ability to change will determine the extent to which they can survive in a competitive market. As we discussed earlier, organizational theorists point out that the ability of an organization to change is a function of internal and external factors (Miles and Snow, 1978). Primarily these include the organization's technology; structure and strategy; tasks and management processes; individual skills; roles and culture (Venkatraman, 1994); and the business in which the organization operates, together with and the degree of uncertainty in the environment (Donaldson, 1995). These factors also determine optimal organizational form for the virtual organization, but with different weighting.

Moore (1997) suggests that businesses are not just members of certain industries but parts of a complex ecosystem that incorporates bundles of different industries. The driving force is not pure competition but co-evolution. The system is seen as "an economic community supported by a foundation of interacting organizations and individuals. Over time they coevolve their capabilities and roles, and tend to align themselves with the direction set by one or more central companies" (p. 26). The ecosystems evolve through four distinct stages:

· Birth
· Expansion
· Authority
· Death

And at each of these stages, the system faces different leadership, cooperative and competitive challenges.

This ecosystem can be viewed as the all-embracing electronic market culture within which e-business maintains equilibrium.

Virtual Organizing

The organizational "virtual culture" is the degree to which the organization adopts virtual organizing and this in turn will affect the individual skills, tasks and roles throughout all levels of the organization. Henderson and Venkatraman (1996) identify three vectors of virtual organizing as:

· Virtual Encounters
· Virtual Sourcing
· Virtual Work

Virtual encounters refers to the extent to which one interacts with the market defined at three levels of greater virtual progression:

· Remote product/service experience
· Product/service customization
· Shaping customer solutions

Virtual sourcing refers to competency leveraging from:

· Efficient sourcing of standard components

Table 1: e-market ecosystem

EcoSystem Stage	Leadership Challenges	Cooperative Challenges	Competitive Challenges
Birth	Maximise customer delivered value	Find and Create new value in an efficient way	Protect your ideas
Expansion	Attract Critical Mass of Buyers	Work with Suppliers and Partners	Ensure market standard approach
Authority	Lead co-evolution	Provide compelling vision for the future	Maintain strong bargaining power
Renewal or Death	Innovate or Perish	Work with Innovators	Develop and Maintain High Barriers

- Efficient asset leverage in the business network
- Creation of new competencies through alliances

Virtual work refers to:
- Maximizing individual experience
- Harnessing organizational expertise
- Leveraging community expertise

where the third levels all relate to an organization with an "information-rich" product and the highest degree of use of ICT.

Virtual Organization Change Model

If we view this as the virtual culture of the organization, then this needs to be articulated through the strategic positioning of the organization and its structural alliances. It also needs to be supported by the knowledge management processes and the ICT. These relationships are depicted in the Dynamic Virtual Organization Change Model, as shown on the next page.

The degree to which virtuality can be applied in the organization will relate to the extent to which the VOCM factors are in alignment. When these are not aligned, then the organization will find itself dysfunctional in its exploitation of the virtual marketspace and so be unable to derive the maximum value benefits from its strategic position in the VAM framework.

Figure 9: Model of virtual organizing

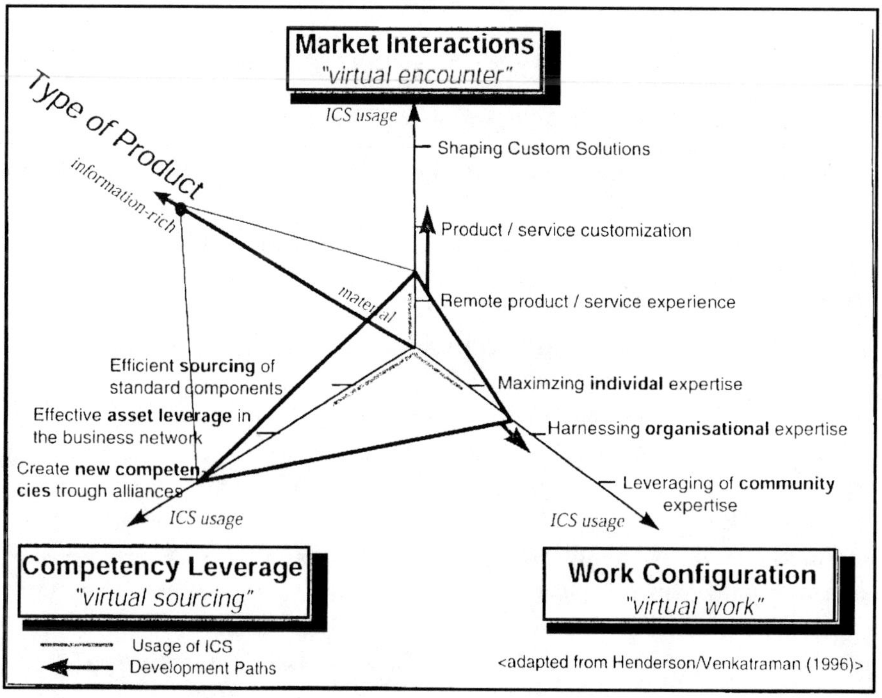

Figure 10: Virtual Organizational Change Model (VOCM)

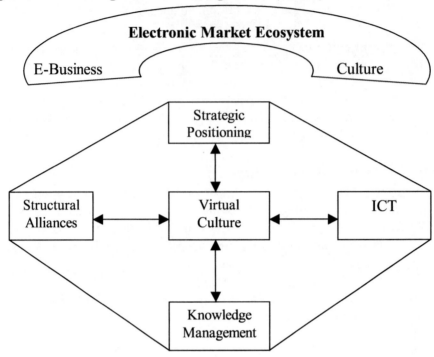

USING THE VIRTUAL VALUES FRAMEWORK TO MANAGE CHANGE

The VAF framework depicted in Figure 8 shows the opposing structural tensions which will pull the VAF in different directions and which may therefore force the organization into a less favourable strategic position. This framework shows the six models along a continuum relating the extent of substitutability of virtual linkages (virtual structure) to the extent of virtuality as embedded in the organization (virtual culture). This readily allows us to identify how to position the organization for effective value return.

Figure 11 illustrates the relative positioning of the development models introduced above. We contend that an organization needs to examine existing factors in order to evaluate effectiveness and identify vectors for change according to the virtual culture.

Change directions should be value led, but there is as yet little empirical research to identify how value is derived in a virtual organization. For virtual organizations performance measurements must cross organizational boundaries and take collaboration into account, but it is also necessary to measure value at the

Figure 11: VIrtual values vector

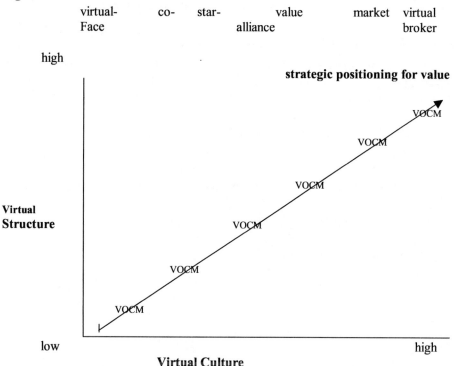

individual level since it is feasible that one could be effective without the other (Provan and Milward, 1995).

We note also an interesting difference of perception. Ahuja and Carley (1995) have completed one of the few empirical studies of the relationship between structure and performance in a virtual setting and conclude that perceived outcomes were seen as highly productive when tasks and structures were "in fit" but when measured objectively showed no correlation. This would suggest that future research cannot be based solely on quantitative measurement, but also cannot rely on anecdotal evidence or subjective "feel good" analysis. Research into virtual organizations must embrace reality at a number of different levels.

THE OUTLOOK FOR CHANGE

The virtual organization is recognized as a dynamic system (Timmers, 1998) and hence one where traditional hierarchical forms of management and control may not apply. Little however has been written about the new forms which management and control might take. In an organization where change is the only constant, there has to be a system that can capture the organizational core competencies and leverage these to provide strategic advantage. This may be a competitive advantage or a strategic advantage in collaboration with the competition. This implies that the virtual organization will have a far greater need than a traditional organization to manage communication channels and inter-organizational systems.

These six models are not exclusive but are intended to serve, singly or in combination, as an elegant set of models to describe forms which an electronic business model may assume. Some of these are essentially an electronic re-implementation of traditional forms of doing business; others are add-ons for added value possibly through umbrella collaboration and others go far beyond this through value chain integration or cyber communities.

What all of these have in common is that they seek innovative ways to harness efficient low-cost communications, change management and a rich functionality. Creating strategic advantage through virtuality is only feasible if the appropriate form is identified and the communications needs and opportunities are identified and accepted. Further these structures exist in a state of dynamic change and may evolve rapidly from one form to another (Miles and Snow, 1986). As this happens the communication channels will also change and a revised form of communications management is called for. The virtual organization that succeeds will be the learning organization where the storage and communication of knowledge is regarded as their greatest core asset. Communicating for advantage will become the primary mission in the virtual marketspace.

REFERENCES

Ahuja, M. K. and Carley, K. M. (1998). Network structure in virtual organizations. *Journal of Computer-Mediated Communication*, 3(4). Available on the World Wide Web: http://www.ascusc.org/jcmc/vol3/issue4/ahuja.html.

Barner, R. (1996). The new millenium workplace: Seven changes that will challenge managers and workers. *Futurist*, 30(2), 14-18.

Berger, M. (1996). Making the virtual office a reality. *Sales and Marketing Management*, SMT Supplement, June, 18-22.

Burn, J. and Barnett, M. (2000a). Virtual cabbages-Models for making kings in the e-grocery business. *Proceedings of the Asia Pacific Conference on Information Systems*, Hong Kong.

Burn, J., and Barnett, M. (2000b). Communicating for advantage in the virtual organization. *IEEE Transactions on Communication*, IEEE.

Byrne, J. (1993). The virtual corporation. *Business Week*, 36-41.

Chesbrough, H. W. and Teece, D. J. (1996). When is virtual virtuous?. *Harvard Business Review*, January-February, 65-73.

Davidow, W. H. and Malone, M. S. (1992). *The Virtual Corporation*, New York: Harper Business.

Donaldson, L. (1995). *American Anti-Management Theories of Organization*. Cambridge UK: Cambridge University Press.

Finnegan, P., Galliers, B. and Powell, P. (1998). Systems planning in an electronic commerce environment in Europe: Rethinking current approaches. *EM–Electronic Markets*, 8(2), 35-38.

Gray, P. and Igbaria, M. (1996). The virtual society. *ORMS Today*, December, 44-48.

Goldman, S. L., Nagel R. N. and Preiss, K. (1995). *Agile Competitors and Virtual Organizations: Strategies for Enriching the Customer*. New York: Van Nostrand Reinhold.

Grabowski, M. and Roberts, K. H. (1996). Human and organizational error in large-scale systems. *IEEE Transactions on Systems, Man and Cybernetics*, 26(1), 2-16.

Greiner, R. and Metes, G. (1996). *Going Virtual: Moving your Organization into the 21st Century*. Englewood Cliffs, NJ: Prentice Hall.

Henderson, J. C., Venkatraman, N. and Oldach, S. (1996). Aligning business and IT strategies. In Luftman, J. N. (Ed.), *Competing in the Information Age: Strategic Alignment in Practice*. Oxford University Press, Chapter 2, 21-42.

Hoffman, D.L., Novak, T.P. and Chatterjee, P. (1995). Commercial scenarios for the Web: Opportunities and challenges. *Journal of Computer-Mediated Communication*, 1(3). Available on the World Wide Web: http://www.ascusc.org/jcmc/vol1/issue3/hoffman.html.

Katzy, B. R. (1998). Design and implementation of virtual organizations. *HICSS*, Hawaii, 2, 242-331.

Kallio, J., Saarinen, T., Tinnila, M. and Tuunainen, V. K. (2000). Business models for electronic commerce-Analysis of grocery retailing industry. *Proceedings of the European Conference on Information Systems*, 1037-1044.

Lawrence, E., Corbill, B., Tidwell, A., Fisher J. and Lawrence J. (1998). *Internet Commerce-Digital Models for Business*. Jacaranda Wiley, Milton Qld.

Miles, R. E. and Snow, C. C. (1986). Organizations: New concepts for new forms. *California Management Review*, Spring, 28(3), 62-73.

Moore, J. F. (1997). *The Death of Competition: Leadership and Strategy in the Age of Business Ecosystems*. New York: Harper Business.

Nouwens, J. and Bouwman, H. (1995). Living apart together in electronic commerce: The use of information and communication technology to create network organizations. *Journal of Computer-Mediated Communication*, 1(3). Available on the World Wide Web at: http://www.ascusc.org/jcmc/vol1/issue3/nouwens.html.

OECD. (1996). Technology, productivity and job creation. *Analytical Report*, 2, OECD, Paris.

OECD. (1998). *Technology, Productivity and Job Creation: Best Policy Practices*, OECD, Paris.

OECD. (1998b). *The Economic and Social Impacts of Electronic Commerce*, OECD, Paris.

Palmer, J. W. and Speier, C. (1998). Teams: Virtualness and media choice. *Proceedings of HICSS*.

Powell, W. W. (1990). Neither market nor hierarchy: Network forms of organization. *Research in Organizational Behaviour*, 12, 295-336.

Preiss, K., Goldman, S. L. and Nagel, R. N. (1996). *Cooperate to Compete*. New York: Van Nostrand Reinhold.

Provan, K. and Milward, H. (1995). A preliminary theory of inter-organizational network effectiveness: A comparative study of four community mental health systems. *Administrative Science Quarterly*, 14, 91-114.

Rayport, J. F. and Sviokola, J. (1995). Exploiting the virtual value chain. *Harvard Business Review*, 73(6), 75-86.

Rogers, D. M. (1996). The challenge of fifth generation R & D. *Research Technology Management*, 39(4), 33-41.

Schein, E. (1990). Organizational culture. *American Psychologist*, 45(2), 109-119.

Steinfield, C., Kraut, R. and Plummer, A. (1995). The impact of electronic commerce on buyer-seller relationships. *Journal of Computer-Mediated Communication*, 1(3). Available on the World Wide Web: http://www.ascusc.org/jcmc/vol1/issue3/steinfld.html.

Swatman, P. M. C. and Swatman, P. A. (1992). EDI system integration: A definition and literature survey. *The Information Society*, 8, 165-205.

Timmers, P. (1998). Business models for electronic markets. *EM–Electronic Markets*, 8(2), 3-8.

Tushman, M. L. and O'Reilly, C. A. III. (1996). Ambidextrous organizations: Managing evolutionary and revolutionary change. *California Management Review*, 38(4), 8-29.

Venkatraman, N. (1994). IT-enabled business transformation: From automation to business scope redefinition. *Sloan Management Review*, Winter, 73-88.

Wigand, R. T. and Benjamin, R. I. (1995). Electronic commerce: Effects on electronic markets. *Journal of Computer-Mediated Communication*, 1(3). Available on the World Wide Web at:http://www.ascusc.org/jcmc/vol1/issue3/wigand.html.

Zimmerman, H. (2000). Understanding the digital economy: Challenges for new business models. *AMCIS*, 2, Long Beach, CA.

Chapter XIV

Cyber Shopping and Privacy

Jatinder N. D. Gupta and Sushil K. Sharma
Ball State University, USA

INTRODUCTION

As we enter a new millennium, we find cyber shopping has become the order of the day. Consumers find it easier to cyber shop than to take time from their schedules to visit malls. One can shop any time depending upon availability of time. Many working couples order the items as they leave from their workplaces and receive deliveries right when they reach home. Some people shop late at night and receive items the very next morning. Cyber shopping is exciting because: 1) one can shop directly from home or the workplace, and 2) the cost of items may be cheaper than the traditional buying. Considering these conveniences, many people prefer cyber shopping. Also, there are very many exciting sites such as E-auction etc. on the Net which otherwise are not available.

Some consumers consider cyber shopping as unsafe. They argue that: 1) giving credit card information on the net may bring problems if credit card information falls into the wrong hands; 2) the net does not provide the expected level of security; and 3) companies may record all their purchases, purchasing habits, etc., and may pass on or sell this information to other potential marketers who in turn may solicit the customer (Handerson, 1999).

The growing popularity of cyber shopping means information can be transmitted all around the globe with just one click of the mouse (Manes, 2000). However, it also means that some information that was thought to be private, such as medical records or financial data, is now out in the public domain for all to see and there are people who are actually hacking them all the time. Those hackers or companies know an individual's name, address, phone number, marital status, age and approximate income level. They know what publications people read, what catalogs they receive, what Web sites they visit and what products they buy both online and off. The ability of marketers to track customers' surfing and buying patterns can lead to abuses. Before the advent of cyber shopping, direct-mail marketers would at times collect information and threaten privacy, but they didn't have the breadth of information now available on the Internet (Lawton, 1998).

Today, when a customer goes online for rentals, credit card purchases, airline reservations and other such electronic transactions, s/he is required to complete a form which contains personal information that defines or represents his/her habits. This information is collected and can be passed to other marketing companies to market their product and services without their knowledge. Many believe that too much personal information is being collected when they go online (Caudill, 2000). Others are not willing to use credit card numbers to purchase items on the Internet. The strange contradiction is that people like to use the Internet for cyber shopping while at the same time they do not trust it. Millions of people are using the Internet everyday, for work, play, learning, business and for social interaction. As we depend on and enjoy it more, we are worried if and how others or organizations may be secretly watching us and collecting information for purposes that we are unaware. "Spamming," which is the practice of sending out unsolicited e-mail, is growing because it costs so little to send out millions of messages or advertisements electronically. Many prominent high-technology companies have already been caught attempting to quietly collect information about their customers via the Internet. DoubleClick, a popular supplier of online advertising services, and RealNetworks, the producer of the RealPlayer line of multimedia software, were subjects of a scandal when their millions of trusted users learned that their personal information was being collected without their consent (Kling, 1996; Gurak, 1997). Privacy can be defined as an individual's right to be left alone, free from interference or surveillance from other parties. Privacy requires security mechanism, policy and technology to provide control over information.

The way sites handle personal information is a concern to the general public. The general population is very cold to the idea of having personal information distributed without the knowledge of the individuals in question. It is an issue because of the risk of taking adverse actions based on inaccurate information, i.e., spam, phone call (Gillin, 2000a). Internet privacy is clearly controversial and can be confusing. As mentioned above there are companies who are keeping track of the Net users. Most of the time they do that with the help of a unique identifier called a cookie, usually a string of random-looking letters, that a Web server places on a computer's hard drive. Cookies enable Web sites to track usage patterns and deliver customized content to visitors.

At times, privacy issues are perceived as a part of security issues, therefore, let us differentiate them. **Security** refers to the integrity of the data storage, processing and transmitting system and includes concerns about the reliability of hardware and software, the protection against intrusion or infiltration by unauthorized users. **Privacy**, on the other hand, refers to controlling the dissemination and use of data, including information that is knowingly or unknowingly disclosed. Privacy could also be the by-product of the information technologies themselves (Cate, 1997).

Over the past decade, numerous surveys conducted around the world have found consistently high levels of concern about privacy. Many studies (Dorney, 1997; Allard, 1998; Harris and Westin, 1999) found that more than 80% of Net users are concerned about threats to their privacy while online. The Federal Trade Commission discovered (Privacy online: A report to Congress/Federal Trade Commission, United States, Federal Trade Commission, 1998) that many Web sites collect personal information and release the same without the users' knowledge and permission.

There are methods (Adam et al., 1996; Verton, 2000; Wen, 2001; McGuire, 2000; Feghhi, 1999) that make cyber shopping secure, although consumers may still have concerns about security aspects of cyber shopping. How can one keep information about his/her Internet browsing habits to oneself? It's a challenge in this era of technological advancements. In this chapter, we focus exclusively on privacy issues that arise in cyber shopping. In the recent past, many articles on privacy have appeared in journals. In this chapter, we review these publications on privacy.

PRIVACY CONCERNS

Privacy is currently front-page news and is the focus of much legislative activity. The privacy issue has been dominant since the passage of the Federal Privacy Act and similar state laws in the mid -70s and has created a legal battleground of conflicting expectations. On the one hand, employees assert that their privacy rights are being trampled upon by employers, while employers claim the need to protect business assets from employee abuse. The ability to shop online—anytime, anywhere—is drastically changing the way consumers shop and have added more dimensions to privacy. Privacy refers to controlling the dissemination and use of data, including information that is knowingly disclosed as well as data that are unintentionally revealed or a by-product of the information technologies themselves (Cate, 1997).

Cyber shopping is growing every year, and it is estimated that by 2010, 55% of retail sales will come from cyber shopping. While this may be great for consumers, it presents an enormous challenge for retailers and consumers. Further growth of the Internet will make the cyber-shopping experience much easier, faster and cheaper. This may reduce the cost of cyber shopping for consumers but at the same time may also benefit the companies by reducing the cost of gathering information about consumers to practically zero. Due to these low costs of data entry, computer processing, storage and communications, companies would be more encouraged to record every detail of their interactions with customers for later use and these details may be for sale. Loss of privacy is the price consumers pay for the convenience of shopping online. Web sites take personal information and use it themselves, sell it to other operations and sometimes have it stolen from them. Thus, privacy has become a key issue in the digital age because technological advances make it easier than ever for companies to obtain personal information and to monitor online activities, thus creating a major potential for abuse (Sykes, 1999). People are concerned about privacy, particularly on the Internet. The study conducted by Harris and Westin (1999) confirms this concern. Online privacy concerns focus on the protection of "customer identifiable" information, which an individual or other customer reasonably expects to be kept private. As the term suggests, "customer identifiable" information is information that can be associated with a specific individual or entity, including, for example, a customer's name, address, telephone number, e-mail address and information about online activities that are directly linked to them.

It is common practice and often a necessity for companies, governments or other organizations to collect customer-identifiable information in order to conduct business and offer services. For example, a telecommunications provider may collect customer-identifiable information, such as name, address, telephone number and a variety of other information in the course of billing and providing telephone service to a customer. Some activities on the Internet follow very familiar patterns. Consumers signing up for an Internet access service, for example, are usually asked to provide name, address, telephone number and credit card and other information that is typical when the consumer orders a product or service. Similarly, business Web sites may ask visitors to supply information about themselves, particularly when information, services or merchandise are requested, but often simply to be able to better target the company's services to the customer's interests and requirements (Blotzer, 2000). All instances cited above are examples of how consumers provide much information about themselves to companies that may misuse this information, thus creating concerns for privacy. Table 1 highlights the main privacy concerns surrounding cyber shopping and suggested remedies.

Spamming-Unsolicited Commercial E-Mail

When consumers receive many e-mails from unknown friends and organizations, this privacy intrusion is known as "spam" or receiving unsolicited commercial e-mail. Spamming is growing because it costs so little to send out millions of messages or advertisements electronically. Many prominent high-technology companies have already been caught attempting to quietly collect information about their customers and pass it to potential marketing companies who in turn send junk mail to market their products. Junk e-mail is becoming very pervasive, with one bulk e-mailer, Cyber Promotions, boasting that it sends 1.5 million messages a day (Smith, 1996). The users who receive junk mail can request the cyber shopping company from whom they have purchased to remove them from their e-mailing list and the company not to distribute the user's identity. E-mail service providers and browsers also offer a utility to block unwanted e-mail. One should use these utilities to protect oneself from an onslaught of undesired mail.

Unauthorized Access/Surveillance-Employee Monitoring

Some employers utilize workplace surveillance technology to ensure that they are getting the most out of their workers. Estimates indicate that employers

Table 1: Privacy concerns

Type of Concern	Description	Remedies
Spamming	Unsolicited commercial E-mail	Never respond to junk E-mail,
Unauthorised Access/Surveillance	Employers monitoring E-mail, computer and Internet use in the workplace	Review workplaces, ISP and Web site privacy policies
Collection of Information through Cookies	Cookies - Documenting consumers' buying habits etc. from their on-line interactions	Block cookies and manage their cookie files . Internet users can access free programs such as IDcide, AdSubtract, and Naviscope are free programs available at <http://www.pcworld.com/downloads > to help block cookies.
Selling Personal information by Information brokers	Desire to control the collection, compilation and transfer or sale of one's personal information to others	Opt out of profiling and market research services.
Intellectual Property Rights (IPR)	Copying, editing, morphing and otherwise manipulating information; S/W piracy - unlicensed distribution of copyright music	Use disclaimers to discourage, be prepared to file a law suit.
Privacy and Children's On-line Activities	Companies at times target children on-line for collecting information	Controlling children's access to on-line environment by their parents and educating them about on-line environment abuses.

eavesdrop on about 400 million telephone calls between employees and customers every year. It is particularly prevalent in the insurance, telecommunications and banking industries. Employer eavesdropping on electronic mail transfer is also widespread and currently not banned by federal wiretapping law (Kling, 1996). The key in this issue is the trade off between productivity versus employee comfort and morale. There isn't much doubt that monitoring will improve employee output, but at what cost? Workers may be under more stress and may generally be more edgy while at work. Employees may dread coming in to work, and absenteeism may be more frequent. It is more effective to have employees that want to be there and are comfortable working in their environments. The benefits of employee monitoring can be achieved by proper supervision from management. If the employer must secretively listen in on conversations or read employee e-mail, then he/she really doesn't know the worker too well and should get to know them better. On the other hand, one can also argue that reading employees' e-mail or eavesdropping on their telephone calls is not an invasion of worker privacy because, after all, they are being paid for working. Employers have the right to determine if the employee is not meeting expectations (Hubbart, 1998).

The issue of e-mail and e-mail monitoring has received a great deal of attention, both in the media and in legal writing, especially in the United States. Moreover, with increasing frequency, employers and employees alike are seeking answers to the question: may employers legally monitor employee e-mail and Internet use? A 1999 American Management Association (AMA) survey reveals that 67.3% of major U.S. firms monitor their employees by reviewing their e-mail, tracking their Internet usage, looking over their phone logs or even installing video cameras. And they often do this without letting their employees know. The computer, the telephone lines and the office space all belong to the company, and the company has a legal right to monitor its own property. Managers can use them as grounds to fire someone.

The forms of surveillance that employers use are diverse, generally inexpensive and are likely being used at the office. Several software can track the network server for keywords and if found can pass on the related material to the management. This kind of surveillance has become quite common in many companies. At times, management has taken harsh actions by firing the employee who was found to be spending a lot of time on e-mail and Internet use. All this monitoring may seem insidious, but in the opinion of legal experts, employers have a legitimate right to know about employees and the way employees spend their time in workplaces. This way, companies not only ensure productivity but also ensure that their trade secrets are not passed on to competitors.

Sending e-mail-Is it safe?

If employees know that their e-mails are monitored, then why do the employees use the e-mail facility of a company? Do the employees not understand that e-mails are not secure and network servers keep track of every bit of mail that employees send out or every Web page they view? There are two possible answers to these questions: one is that employees know these facts but still feel that employers may not take it seriously, and second is that the employee believes if they have passwords, it is secure. Whereas, the fact is that it is not only employers who can access this mail, but this mail is vulnerable to abuse by eavesdroppers because e-mail messages travel from the originating host computer to the destination and often pass through several relaying hosts. Administrators of any of these hosts can easily eavesdrop on the mail traffic.

How to protect e-mail invasion of privacy?

There are preventive measures which could be applied to avoid embarrassment or possibly even being fired for e-mail abuse:

1. It is better to have a personal account at home with an Internet service provider and direct all confidential messages to be sent to the home computer Internet account and not to the by workplace account.
2. E-mail should be selective and purposeful. It is not recommended to send any confidential or personal information.
3. E-mail accounts require proper management such as deleting old mail and sensitive mail, etc. One can also employ encryption technologies offered by e-mail service providers to avoid eavesdropping.
4. It is desirable that employees check the company e-mail policy before they start using e-mail.

Collection of Information Through Cookies

Many advertising and market research companies collect information from consumers through their online interactions. The companies can then create a database of preferences, habits and choices of consumers to be used to market their products and services. This is not a new phenomenon, but due to the breadth and speed of the Internet, it creates concerns for consumers.

How do these companies collect information?

As discussed earlier, companies often ask consumers to provide their personal details through online interaction. The more dominant method used by companies to collect information is to use "Cookies." Cookies are the most common privacy invader as they can store and even track down information about online travels and shopping without the user's knowledge (Bass, 2000). Cookies enable Web sites to track usage patterns and deliver customized content to visitors. Cookies are short pieces of data, usually a string of random-looking letters, that a Web server places on a computer's hard drive. They are planted on the consumer's computer by the Web sites which are visited or surfed. Cookies help to know the movements of consumers while surfing on the Web site. This information can be used by companies to figure out the buying habits and tastes of consumers, and at times can even be sold to third-party agencies for potential marketing.

Most consumers are blissfully unaware of the electronic footprint they leave when they surf Web sites. There are sites available such as www. privacy.net which help to know how cookies keep details of the consumers. Cookies keep information about computer's identity (referred to as the IP address), computer's configuration, the route from computer to the destination computer system, the last Web pages accessed and so on. Privacy campaigners fear that using cookies could lead to senders' identities being easily traceable.

While cookies don't give a Web site any personal information, such as an individual's name or address, they create a unique identity for the browser so that a site can recognize a person if he visits again using the same computer terminal. In some ways, cookies benefit Web surfers; without them, people would have to enter a user name and password over and over to see any personalized content on the Web. However, cookies actually act like hidden cameras or microphones capturing computer users' movements.

Cookies are meant to help consumers. Detailed marketing databases enable companies to better match their products and services to consumer demands. By performing statistical analysis of database information on consumers, the companies can target their products in a more focused manner and consumers can get their wish list items without spending the time searching for it.

How do advertising companies benefit from cookies?

When a browser sends a request to a server, it includes its IP address, the type of browser being used and the operating system of the computer. This information is usually logged in the server's log file. A cookie sent along with the request can add only that the same server originally sent information. Thus, there is no additional personal information explicitly sent to the server by allowing cookies. On multiple client sites being serviced by a single marketing site, cookies can be used to track browsing habits on all the client sites. The way this works is a marketing firm contracts with multiple client sites to display its advertising. The client sites simply put a tag on their Web pages to display the image containing the marketing firm's advertisement. The tag does not point to an image file on the client's machine but contains the URL of the marketing firm's advertisement server and includes the URL of the client's page.

The advertising firm sends a cookie along with the advertisement, and that cookie is sent back to the advertising firm the next time someone views any page containing one if its advertisements. If many Web sites support the same advertising firm, that firm will be able to track an individual's browsing habits from page to page within all the client sites. The firm will not be able to see what an individual does with the pages which he views; it will only know which pages are viewed, how often are viewed and the IP address of the computer. This information can be used to infer the things people are interested in and to target advertising to those people based on those inferences.

How to avoid cookies?

No files are destroyed or compromised by cookies. Cookies contain only text and cannot damage any computer. It is easy to block cookies. The new browsers have the capability to turn off the cookies and the computer can stop accepting any cookies. There are number of programs such as Webwasher, Cache and Cookiewasher which can remove footprints. These programs are available and can be easily downloaded from the Internet. Encryption and Decryption can also ensure personal privacy over the Net. In fact it is more desirable that companies make use of encryption method during their online interactions (Smith, 1996).

Blocking all cookies prevents some online services for cyber shopping. Also, preventing a browser from accepting cookies does not make the consumer anonymous, it just makes it more difficult to track usage. IDcide, AdSubtract and Naviscope are free programs available at www.pcworld.com/downloads that can help to block cookies. Users can also make their computer undetectable by using ZoneAlarm, a firewall free for personal use.

Selling Personal Information by Information Brokers

Many companies act as information brokers and collect information from various public record online databases and sell the information to various interested parties. At times, this is done for information entrepreneurialism (Kling, 1996) which refers to the dynamic attempts of organizations to take advantage of technology and principal social relationships to gain both organizational and competitive advantage. Computer-based information entrepreneurialism made significant strides in the early 1990s (Ackerman et al., 1996). Many companies consider personal data of customers to be a corporate asset that can be sold (Borrus, 2000; Lehman, 2000). Information broker companies use data-intensive techniques like profiling and data mining to aid in precision marketing. This has led organizations to sell information as a good or service much like how magazines can sell their mailing lists. The key issue here is, should these companies sell the personal information of consumers without their consent? Should the profits that information broker's companies earn be shared with the consumer because it is consumers' data? This may be serious concern for privacy because if this data is changed or gets into the wrong hands, it can lead to serious consequences for consumers. Another main problem, as stated by Jeffrey Rosen, legal affairs editor of the *New York Times* newspaper, is that information on individuals gained from computers creates a fractionalized image of the computer user. When agencies, companies and others make conclusions that are based on fragmentary information, society as a whole loses out, leading to potentially small-minded and dangerous results.

It has been observed that in an online environment, there is much unreliable information available. Researchers (Linowes, 1996) found that more than 70% of Net users always provide false information about themselves and hide their real identity. They see this as the convenient way to protect their privacy. While it may be a convenient way to protect privacy, it may allow an information broker to divulge wrong information about them that can create problems. That is why even today many data miners do not fully trust the Internet as a good resource of information because they feel that the information divulged is not accurate.

Knowing all these online privacy concerns of consumers, it is expected that companies will move toward self-regulation and mutual cooperation (Wazeka, 2000). Many companies have taken initiatives toward this, but the Enonymous.com survey, released in April 2000, revealed that among the 1,000 busiest Web sites, 63% post some sort of policy, but many do not provide a great deal of protection (Lehman, 2000). In May 2000, the Federal Trade Commission (FTC) recommended to Congress that it extend new powers to control the way companies collect and use personal information through the Internet because most of the Web sites are not implementing self-regulatory measures and are defying core privacy principles. It is expected that the FTC will play an important role in auditing cyber shopping sites and will set the guidelines from time to time in the future (Gillin, 2000b).

Intellectual Property Rights (IPR)

IPR includes copying, editing, morphing software piracy, unlicensed distribution of copyright music and otherwise manipulating information. Everyday there are millions of people who download or copy information without acknowledging the authors. At times the same information is modified and sold under a different name. Software piracy is another menace and yet still prevalent. Net users are becoming aware that Web sites may be encroaching on their privacy by collecting information thus infringing upon IPR. Realizing that the subject of IPR and copyrights need to be protected, Internet privacy requires federal and state politicians to introduce new bills aimed at safeguarding consumers' personal information from aggressive advertisers and direct marketers (Cate, 1997). Although, there are existing laws aimed at providing Internet privacy, they are not enough. The recent case of Napster is a good example of IPR as a privacy concern. There are many such legal issues which are yet to be resolved (Adam et al., 1996).

Privacy and Children's Online Activities

As the culture of cyber shopping grows, it also attracts the attention of children. Children may be encouraged to use online environments for educational and entertainment resources and certainly, it can be an important and useful tool to help enrich and educate children. Most of the schools have introduced computers at early stages, and children are capable of using the Internet for personal use. In the last few years, computer literacy increased and more children are joining the cyber space world for their day-to-day activities. Interactive online communications provides tremendous opportunities for children (United States Congress Senate Committee on Commerce, 1998), but at the same time, it presents unique challenges for protecting the privacy of young children.

When children go online, companies may lure them to play a few games, solve a few puzzles and attract them with offers of free gifts, free trips or awards, etc., and as a result may collect personal information from them. Unlike adults, they may not be fully capable of understanding the consequences of giving out personal information online. Parents will not always have the knowledge, the ability or the opportunity to intervene in their children's choices about giving personal information. Therefore, companies at times target children online for collecting information and create a serious threat for privacy. One remedy for this concern could be controlling children's access to the online environment by their parents and educating the children about online environment abuses. Another way could be thought of whether Internet service providers themselves can give options to parents to restrict interactions with sites that may be in the business of collecting information.

REMEDIES AND FUTURE TRENDS

As long as consumers look for online environments for cyber shopping, the privacy concern up to a certain extent will remain unresolved. As consumers look for convenience, companies may exploit these situations to collect personal information.

Possible Remedies

There could be two methods to resolve the privacy concern. The first method would be for the companies to enforce a self-regulated privacy policy as suggested by the Federal Trade Commission. The second method could be to use encryption technology (Encryption-the process of hiding the meaning of a readable message [clear text] in an incomprehensible text [cipher text]) for any cyber shopping interactions. Using a secure browser that complies with industry standards, such as Secure Sockets Layer (SSL) or Secure Hypertext Transfer Protocol (S-HTTP), would ensure that data cannot be read by undesired persons even if it is accessed. The standards such as SSL and Secure Electronic Transactions (SET) provide enough measures to protect the consumers' data from unauthorized access.

SSL and SET are the technology used to make cyber shopping transactions secure. For the cyber shopping experience, it is recommended to use a secure server. A secured server will use Secure Sockets Layer (SSL) technology to provide a safe way to transmit sensitive information, such as credit card numbers, online banking, e-mail messages, surveys and other personal information. Only authorized people or organizations can access consumers' data once the transactions are carried over the secure channel. It has been reported by some experts that if consumers use Secure Sockets Layer for online transactions, it would take $100,000 worth of computer equipment 100,000,000,000,000,000,000 years (10 to the 19 power of years), when a 128-bit key is used to decrypt the transaction information. Even when only an 80-bit key were used, it is estimated that it would take $100,000 worth of computer equipment 70,000 years to break the code used to encrypt credit card data.

Most up-to-date Web browsers have a small picture of a key or padlock indicating an SSL port. On a secure site, the key or padlock is usually located in the lower left corner of the browser. Secure sites are always listed as https:// at the beginning of the address of the Web page, instead of the more common, insecure http://. Using a secure channel would help to make sure that the information stays private.

Future Trends: The Clipper Chip

To make sure that every piece of information which goes out of consumers' computers or networks is secure, it would be desirable to implement encryption standards right at machine level. The clipper chip is an encryption device that could be used at every computer to provide a means to scramble communications. It is envisaged that in the near future all computers, hand-held devices such as personal digital assistants and even telephone sets would have clipper chips embedded in them to provide a secure communication channel. Any data sent by computers or any home call made by a telephone with a clipper chip, will go encrypted and the device on the other side having a similar clipper chip would decrypt the message. The chip would employ "escrowed encryption" meaning that a third-party (Denning, 1996), in this case the government, would hold the encryption keys. There are concerns expressed by a few groups that the clipper chip would keep record of every transaction and the government could take advantage of the information for tax raids to catch sensitive information. These fears are real to a certain extent, but the advantages to consumers outweigh the fear of loss. This technology cannot be easily cracked, as it is not software based but rather a physical piece of hardware (Rapalus, 1997). One of the concerns that may arise out of the clipper chip is the cost to consumers when purchasing cellular phones and other telecommunication devices and services. Still, the U.S. Department of Justice and the Federal Bureau of Investigation are making amendments to existing laws to take advantage of this new technology in the future.

CONCLUSION AND FUTURE DIRECTIONS

The growing popularity of cyber shopping means information can be beamed around the globe with just one click. However, it also means that some information that we believe to be private, such as medical records or financial data, is now in the public domain for all to see. Each time someone visits a Web site to get information or make a purchase, the site operator, as well as other third parties, can surreptitiously collect many types of information about that person. With more consumers buying books and music online and more new media companies, the power to track what people read and listen to will be in the hands of a few very large firms. These firms keep track of people while leaving a cookie in their system. Most of the companies have been doing this for years and they have developed intensive databases of the people surfing the Net. Employers are keeping an eye on their employees while reading their mail, and check which sites they click during official working hours. Later on, they may use them to fire a person. Even the Internet service providers keep track of the sites visited by their customers.

As cyber shopping grows, organizations may attempt to gather new and more revealing consumer data. Organizations like banks, credit card associations, direct mail marketers and other organizations started mining personal data for profit long before the Net burst into prominence. However, public concern about privacy protection today tends to focus on the Internet or online environments. Since we are interested in having more interactions with the online environment, maybe we need to question how much one is prepared to accommodate for the sake of convenience. It will also be worthwhile to research issues through empirical studies to determine if privacy concerns will have a direct impact on the number of cyber shopping transactions. Although many studies indicate that cyber shoppers list privacy as their concern for online shopping, further research is needed on whether the privacy concerns have a strong influence to convert cyber shoppers to traditional shoppers.

The question remains whether is it legal to track the personal behaviour of other people? Do these companies have a legal right to keep track of their customers and consumers? These issues will be debated for many years to come. Many are so controversial because they are "catch-22" situations. Gains are made on one front but losses occur on the other. Maybe even more government regulation is required to help clean up our information environment.

REFERENCES

Ackerman, M. S., Allen, J. P. and Kling, R. (1996). Information entrepreneurialism In Kling, R. (Ed.), *Computerization and Controversy*, 2nd ed. San Diego: Academic Press.

Adam, N. R., Dogramaci, O., Gangopadhyay, A., and Yesha, Y. (1999). *Electronic Commerce-Technical, Business and Legal Issues*. Prentice Hall.

Allard N. W. (1998). Privacy online: Washington report. *Hastings Communications and Entertainment Law Journal*, 20, 511-540.

American Management Association Report. (1999).

Bass, S. (2000). Fight for your online privacy, *PC World*. November 18(11), 45.

Blotzer, M. (2000). Privacy in the digital age. *Occupational Hazards*, July, 62(7), 29-31.

Borrus,-A. (2000). Online privacy: Congress has no time to waste, *Business Week*, September 18, (3699), 54.

Cate, F. H. (1997). *Privacy in the Information Age*. Washington, DC: Brookings Institution Press.

Caudill, E. M. and Murphy, P. E. (2000).Consumer online privacy: Legal and ethical issues. *Journal of Public Policy and Marketing*, Spring, 19(1), 7-19.

Denning, D. E. (1996). Clipper chip will reinforce privacy, In *Computerization and Controversy*, 2nd Ed, edited by Rob Kling. San Diego, CA: Academic Press.

Dorney, M. S. (1997). Privacy and the Internet. *Hastings Communications and Entertainment Law Journal*, 19, 635-660.

Electronic Communication Privacy Policy Disclosures. (2000). Government Publication.

Evans, J. (2000). Paranoids, unite!, *The Computer Paper*, 44. www.canadacomputers.com/v3/story/1.1017.3302.00html.

Feghhi J. (1999). Digital certificates: Applied Internet security, Reading, MA: Addision-Wesley.

Gillin, D. (2000a). How privacy affects us all: Friction between the researcher's need for information and a respondent's privacy grows. *Marketing Research*, Summer, 12(2), 40-41.

Gillin, D. (2000b). The Federal Trade Commission and Internet privacy. *Marketing Research*, 12(3), 39-41.

Gurak, L. J. (1997). *Persuasion and Privacy in Cyberspace–The Online Protests Over Lotus Marketplace and the Clipper Chip*. New Haven, CT: Yale University.

Handerson, H. (1999). *Privacy in the Information Age*. New York: Facts on File.

Harris, L. and Westin, A. F. (1999). *Harris-Equifax Consumer Privacy Survey*. Atlanta, GA: Equifax Inc.

Hubbart, W. S. (1998). The new battle over workplace privacy. *Business-Insurance*, April, 32(15), 18.

Kling R. (Ed.). (1996). Information technologies, and the continuing vulnerability of privacy. In *Computerization and Controversy*, 2nd ed. San Diego, CA: Academic Press.

Lawton G. (1998). The Internet challenge to privacy, *Computer*, June, 16-18.

Lehman, DeW. (2000). Privacy policies missing at 77% of Web sites. *Computerworld*, April, 34(16), 103.

Linowes, D. F. (1996). Your personal information has gone public. In Kling, R. (Ed.), *Computerization and Controversy*, 2nd ed. San Diego, CA: Academic Press.

Manes, S. (2000). Private lives? Not ours! *PC World*, June, 18(6), 312.

McGuire, B. L. and Roser, S. N. (2000). What your business should know about Internet security. *Strategic Finance Magazine,* 82(5), 50-4.

Privacy Online: A Report to Congress/federal Trade Commission, (1998). United States, Federal Trade Commission.

Rapalus, P. (1997). Security measures for protecting confidential information on the Internet and intranets. *Employment Relations Today*, Autumn, (24), 49-58.

Smith, H. J. (1994). *Managing Privacy*, Carolina Press.

Smith, W. (1996). How to get rid of all your junk e-mail. *Money*, July, (25), 21.

Sykes C. J. (1999). *The End of Privacy*. New York: St. Martin's Press.

United State Congress Senate Committee on Commerce, Science and Transportation. (1998). *Subcommittee on Communication*, Children's Online Privacy Protection Act of 1998.

Verton, D. (2000). How companies can enhance Web security, *Computerworld,* November, 34(46), 141.

Wazeka, R. (2000). Internet privacy. *Success*, September, 47(4), 64-65.

Wen, H. J. and Tarn, J. M. (2001). The impact of the next-generation Internet protocol on e-commerce security. *Information Strategy,* 17(2), 22-28.

ONLINE RESOURCES

Beyond Concern; Understanding Online Privacy Concerns. Available on the World Wide Web at: http://www.research.att.com/resources/trs/TRs/99/99.4/99.4.3/report.htm.

Canada Newswire, Privacy Code in Canada. Available on the World Wide Web at: http://www.newswire.ca/releases/September1998/18/c4437.html.

Consumer World. Available on the World Wide Web at: http://www.consumerworld.org.

Electronic Privacy Information Center. Available on the World Wide Web at: http://www.epic.org/.

Federal Trade Commission. Available on the World Wide Web at: http://www.ftc.gov.

Fraud on the Internet. Available on the World Wide Web at: http://www.emich.edu/public/coe/nice/fraudr1.html.

Georgetown Internet Privacy Policy Study. Available on the World Wide Web at: http://www.msb.edu/faculty/culnanm/gippshome.html.

Internet Privacy Coalition. Available on the World Wide Web at: http://www.privacy.org.

Keeping Secrets on the Internet. Available on the World Wide Web at: http://www.cme.org/priv698.html.

Securities and exchange Commission. Available on the World Wide Web at: http://www.sec.gov/consumer/cyberfr.htm.

Student Internet Privacy Guidelines. Available on the World Wide Web at: http://www.4j.lane.edu/4jnet/privacyguide.html and http://www.anu.edu.au/people/Roger.Clarke/DV/Surveys.html.

Tips for Online Privacy for Kids and Consumers. Available on the World Wide Web at: http://www.privacyalliance.org/join/background.shtml.

World Intellectual Property Organization. (WIPO). Available on the World Wide Web at: http://www.wipo.org.

About the Authors

Aryya Gangopadhyay is an Assistant Professor of Information Systems at the University of Maryland Baltimore County (USA). He has a BTech from the Indian Institute of Technology, MS in Computer Science from New Jersey Institute of Technology, and a PhD in Computer Information Systems from Rutgers University. His research interests include electronic commerce, multimedia databases, data warehousing and mining, geographic information systems, and database security. He has authored and co-authored two books, many book chapters, numerous papers in journals such as *IEEE Computer, IEEE Transactions on Knowledge and Data Engineering, Journal of Management Information Systems, Journal of Global Information Management, Electronic Markets-The International Journal of Electronic Commerce & Business Media, Decision Support Systems, AI in Engineering* and *Topics in Health Information Management*, as well as presented papers in many national and international conferences. He can be reached at gangopad@umbc.edu.

***

Parvez Ahmed teaches finance at Penn State Harrisburg. Prior to joining PSU, he taught at the University of North Carolina at Charlotte where he served as the Faculty Advisor for the Student Managed Investment Fund. He has focused his research in the areas of international finance and investments. His research includes articles on asset pricing, business cycle investing, derivatives and currency markets. His work has appeared in *Journal of Portfolio Management, Journal of Alternative Investments, Journal of Banking and Finance, Applied Economic Letters, Global Business and Finance Review, International Review of Economics, Managerial Finance* and *Financial Review*.

Leila Alem is a Senior Research Scientist at CSIRO Mathematical and Information Sciences. Her research spans a variety of HCI/cognitive psychology /AI research issues, as focused through investigations into systems that support human learning. Her specific interests lie in the areas of learner-centered design, models of skill development, dynamic and individualized instructional planning, and learner and student modeling. She is currently exploring the area of online negotiation agents systems in e-commerce, specifically exploring means for supporting the formation of coalition among those agents. She has published in several international conferences and journals, and has an active participation in the international research community (member of conference program committees, initiator of workshops and reviewer of PhD and master's thesis).

Kemal Altinkemer is a Guest Editor and Associate Editor of *Telecommunication Systems, Journal of Information Technology and Management*. His research interests are in design and analysis of LAN and WAN, infrastructure development such as ATM, distribution of priorities by using pricing as a tool, bandwidth packing problem, time restricted priority routing, infrastructure for e-commerce and pricing of information goods, bidding with intelligent software agents and strategy from *Brickandmortar* to *Clickandmortar* business model. He has published in *Operations Research, Operations Research Letters, Management Science, INFORMS Journal of Computing, Transportation Science, EJOR, Computers and OR, Annals of Operations Research* and various conference proceedings.

Akhilesh Bajaj is Assistant Professor of Information Systems Management at the H. John Heinz III School of Public Policy and Management at Carnegie Mellon University. He received a BTech in Chemical Engineering from the Indian Institute of Technology, Bombay, an MBA from Cornell University and a PhD in MIS (minor in Computer Science) from the University of Arizona. Dr. Bajaj's research deals with the construction and testing of tools and methodologies that facilitate the construction of large organizational systems, as well as studying the decision models of the actual consumers of these information systems. He has published articles in several academic journals and conferences. He is on the editorial board of the *Journal of Database Management*. He teaches graduate courses on basic and advanced database systems, as well as enterprise wide systems.

Martin Barnett is a Research Associate and Lecturer at Edith Cowan University, Perth, Western Australia. Professor Barnett has worked on three continents as a researcher, writer and academic. His current main interests are computer-meditated communication and change management strategies for the integration of Internet tools in retailing. His publications include privately commissioned reports, magazine and journal articles, and referred journal and conference papers.

Ulrike Baumoel is a Program Manager of the post-graduate program Master of Business Engineering (MBE HSG) of the University of St. Gallen (HSG), Switzerland. She received her master's degree in Business Administration (1992) from the University of Dortmund, Germany. As a research assistant at the University of Dortmund from 1992 through 1998, she received her doctoral degree, with a dissertation on software target costing.

Janice M. Burn is Foundation Professor and Head of the School of Management Information Systems at Edith Cowan University in Perth, Western Australia and Director of the We-B research center-working for e-Business. In 2000 she assumed the role of World President of the Information Resources Management Association (IRMA). She has previously held senior academic posts in Hong Kong and the UK. Her research interests relate to information systems strategy and benefits evaluation in virtual organizations with a particular emphasis on cross-cultural challenges in an e-business environment. She is recognized as an international researcher with more than 150 referred publications in journals and international conferences. She is on the editorial board of five prestigious IS journals and participates in a number of joint research projects with international collaboration and funding.

Rajesh Chandrashekaran is Associate Professor of Marketing in the Silberman College of Business Administration at Fairleigh Dickinson University, New Jersey. He obtained his PhD in Marketing from Rutgers University, New Jersey. Dr. Chandrashekaran research interests include behavioral perspectives on pricing, consumer responses to comparative price advertising, consumer information processing as it pertains to numerical attribute and price information. His research has appeared in *Journal of Marketing Research, Pricing Theory and Practice: An International Journal* and *Journal of Business Research*. His research has also appeared in the proceedings of several national and regional conferences including *American Marketing Association* and *Association for Consumer Research*.

Subhasish Dasgupta is Assistant Professor of Information Systems in the Management Science Department, School of Business and Public Management at The George Washington University. He obtained a PhD from Baruch College, The City University of New York, and MBA and BS degrees from the University of Calcutta, India. Dr. Dasgupta's research interests include electronic commerce, information technology adoption and diffusion, group decision support systems and global information systems. His research has appeared in *Electronic Markets Journal, Logistics Information Management, Journal of Global Information Management*, and the *Simulation and Gaming Journal*. Dr. Dasgupta has also presented his work at several conferences.

Pat Finnegan lectures in electronic commerce at University College Cork, Ireland, and is the Director of the University's master's program in Electronic Business and Commerce. He holds a Bachelor of Commerce and a master's degree in Management Information Systems from University College Galway, Ireland. His PhD is from Warwick Business School, England, where he studied information systems strategy in business-to-business electronic commerce environments. His research has appeared in international journals and conferences.

Thomas Fugmann is a Research Assistant and PhD student at the Institute of Information Management, University of St. Gallen (HSG), Switzerland. He studied Business Administration at the Humboldt University, Berlin (D), with a major in Informaiton Systems Management. His current research focus is on electronic service markets.

Jatinder N. D. Gupta is currently Professor of Management, Information and Communication Sciences, and Industry and Technology at the Ball State University, Muncie, Indiana. He holds a PhD in Industrial Engineering (with specialization in Production Management and Information Systems) from Texas Tech University. Coauthor of a textbook in Operations Research, Dr. Gupta serves on the editorial boards of several national and international journals. Recipient of the Outstanding Faculty and Outstanding Researcher awards from Ball State University, he has published numerous papers in such journals as *Journal of Management Information Systems, International Journal of Information Management*, and *Mathematics of Operations Research*.

Richard Holowczak holds a BS in Computer Science from the College of New Jersey, an MS in Computer Science from the New Jersey Institute of Technology, and MBA and PhD degrees from Rutgers University. He is presently Assistant Professor of Computer Information Systems at Baruch College, CUNY. His research focuses on digital libraries, electronic commerce and networked information systems. He has published articles in *IEEE Computer Journal, Online Information Review* and *ACM Computing Surveys*.

His research has been supported by the Professional Staff Congress-CUNY, NASA and the National Science Foundation. He is a member of the IEEE Computer Society and the Association for Computing Machinery (ACM).

Zhihua Jiang is a System Developer for American Management Systems (www.ams.com). He has been working on multi-tier applications using advanced J2EE technology since 2000. He was a graduate student of the CSEE program at the University of Maryland Baltimore County from 1998 to 2000. During his graduate study, he worked with Dr. Anupam Joshi on a Web data mining project and was the one of the major contributors to the "Retriever" system. He did his undergraduate studies at Peking University in China.

Anupam Joshi is an Assistant Professor of Computer Science and Electrical Engineering at UMBC. Earlier, he was an Assistant Professor in the CECS Department at the University of Missouri, Columbia, and a Visiting Assistant Professor at Purdue. He obtained a BTech degree in Electrical Engineering from IIT Delhi in 1989, and a master's and PhD in Computer Science from Purdue University in 1991 and 1993, respectively. His research interests are in the broad area of networked computing and intelligent systems, with a particular emphasis on mobile computing. He has worked on the problem of creating intelligent agent-based middleware to support mobile access to networked computing and multimedia information resources. Presently, he is investigating data management and distributed computation issues for ad-hoc networks, as well as m-commerce. He is also interested in Web mining and personalization, content-based retrieval of video data from networked repositories and networked HPCC. He has published more than 50 technical papers, and has obtained research support from IBM, AetherSystems, AT&T, Intel, DoD and NSF (including a CAREER award). He is an Associate Editor for IEEE Trans. Fuzzy Systems. He has presented tutorials in conferences, served as guest editor for special issues for *IEEE Personal Communications, Communications of the ACM*, etc., and has served on several program committees, including those of MobiCom '98 and '99. He referees for several journals and conferences, and has served on NSF IIS, CCR and DUE panels. He is a member of ACM, IEEE and UPE.

John Kilmartin holds a Bachelor of Common Law, a Higher Diploma in Business and Financial Information Systems, and a master's in Managerial Accounting and Managerial Information Systems from University College Cork, Ireland. He is currently an IT consultant with Deloitte & Touche in Dublin, Ireland. Previously, he spent a brief spell in the Irish civil service, and worked for a short time as a Research Assistant in the Executive Systems Research Centre in UCC. He has also worked with Fidelity Investments, Boston, in the Operational Systems Development (OSD) section overseeing systems development project management.

Ryszard Kowalczyk is a Principal Research Scientist with CSIRO Mathematical and Information Sciences. His current research interests include fuzzy systems, constraint-based reasoning, evolutionary computation and intelligent multi-agent systems for intelligent automation, decision support and collaborative solutions in dynamic e-commerce. He has published in several international conferences and journals, and has been an organizer, program committee member, invited paper presenter at a number of national and international conferences. He has been a reviewer for *International Journal on Information Sciences, IEEE Transactions on Fuzzy Systems, IEEE Transactions on Systems, Man and Cybernetics*, and a technical review editor for Kluwer Academic Publisher Group.

Maria R. Lee is Acting Group Leader of the Artificial Intelligence in e-Business group at CSIRO Mathematical and Information Sciences. She leads the group conducting research and development in applying artificial intelligence technologies to electronic business applications. Her research interests include inter-agent communication, ontology and knowledge acquisition. She has published more than 30 scientific/technical peer reviewed papers in international/national conferences/journals and has been referee, panelist, program committee member and organizer at a number of international conferences. She has also lecturered and co-supervised students in Australian and Hong Kong universities.

Peter Rittgen is currently Senior Research Assistant at the Institute for Business Informatics of University Koblenz-Landau (Germany). He earned a Master of Science in Computer Science and Computational Linguistics from that university in 1989, and a PhD in Economics and Business Administration from Frankfurt University in 1997 for a dissertation on "Process Theory of Scheduling and Planning" in the area of information systems. His current research focuses on business process modeling in conjunction with object-oriented and enterprise modeling.

Sushil K. Sharma is currently Assistant Professor of Management at Ball State University, Muncie, Indiana. He received his PhD in Information Systems from Pune University, India, and has taught at the Indian Institute of Management, Lucknow, for 10 years before joining Ball State University. Dr

Sharma also taught information systems courses at the University of Waterloo, Canada. Dr. Sharma's research interests include database management systems, networking environments, electronic commerce (e-commerce) and corporate information systems.

Thomas Stiffel is a Research Assistant and PhD student at the Institute of Information Management, University of St. Gallen (HSG), Switzerland. He received his master's degree in Industrial Engineering and Management (1999) from University of Karsruhe, Germany. His research focus is on business model innovation and transformation in the new economy.

Bernhard Strauch, lic.oec.HSG, is a Research Assistant and doctoral student at the Institute of Information Management (Chair Professor Dr. Robert Winter), University of St. Gallen (HSG). He received his master's degree in Information Management (1998) from University of St. Gallen. His research interests include strategic aspects of data warehousing, and design and development of Web applications.

Ramesh Subramanian has been a Senior Software Engineer at the IBM-Advanced Internet Technology Lab in Southbury, Connecticut, since August 2000. Prior to joining IBM, Dr. Subramanian was an Associate Professor of MIS at the University of Alaska, Anchorage. His current research interests include digital asset management, e-commerce, XML, XSL, Web content management, software bots, peer-to-peer networking and resource sharing and Distance-teaching technologies. He can be reached at rsubraman@us.ibm.com.

Kerem Tomak is Assistant Professor in the MSIS Department of the McCombs School of Business, where he teaches digital economy and commerce. His primary research examines the economics of information systems, and recent projects have examined the arena of online auctions and online purchasing behavior. Dr. Tomak's research activities fall broadly into three areas: pricing and market segmentation in data networks, online auctions and software agents in network resource allocation, concentrating on topics such as application service providers, metamediaries and economic analysis of information goods. Dr. Tomak received his PhD from Purdue University. His major publications include "Economics of Software Renting" (with V. Choudhary and A. Chaturvedi), *Journal of Organizational Computing and Electronic Commerce* (1998); and "A Distributed Algorithm for Network Resource Allocation Using Software Agents" (with K. Altinkemer), *Information Technology and Management* (2001). He is also a member of INFORMS, IEEE, AEA and ACM.

Merrill Warkentin is Associate Professor of MIS in the College of Business and Industry at Mississippi State University. He has authored over 100 articles, chapters, and books. His research, primarily in eCommerce, virtual teams, expert systems, and system security, has appeared in such journals as *MIS Quarterly, Decision Sciences, Information Systems Journal, Journal of Knowledge Engineering & Technology, Journal of Electronic Commerce Research, Logistics Information Management, ACM Applied Computing Review, Expert Systems*, and *Journal of Computer Information Systems.* Professor Warkentin is a co-author of *Electronic Commerce: A Managerial Perspective (2e)* (Prentice Hall, 2002), and is on the editorial board of several journals. Dr. Warkentin has served as a consultant to numerous companies and organizations, and has been a featured speaker at over one hundred industry association meetings, executive development seminars, and academic conferences. He has been a Lecturer at the Army Logistics Management College and since 1996, he has served as National Distinguished Lecturer for the Association for Computing Machinery (ACM). Professor Warkentin holds BA, MA, and Ph.D. degrees from the University of Nebraska-Lincoln.

Robert Winter is Managing Director of the Institute of Information Management, University of St. Gallen (HSG), Switzerland, and Director of HSG's post-graduate Master of Business Engineering program. He received master's degrees in Business Administration (1984) and Business Education (1986) from Goethe University Frankfurt, Germany. As a research assistant with Goethe University from 1984 through 1994, he received Dr.rer.pol for his work in the field of multi-stage production planning (1989) and venia legendi for his work on formal semantics of conceptual information systems design (1994). His research interests include business engineering/information systems development, information systems architectures and information logistics (particularly data warehousing and enterprise application integration).

Minnie Yi-Miin Yen is Associate Professor of Management Information Systems in the Department of Computer Information and Office Systems, University of Alaska, Anchorage. She received her PhD in Management Information Systems from the University of Houston. Dr. Yen's work has appeared in *IEEE Transactions on Software Engineering, Journal of Database Management, International Journal of Management* and *Human Factors in Information Systems.* Her current research interests focus on human-computer interaction, client-server database systems, e-commerce and Web-based learning.

Index